League of American Wheelmen

Fifty Miles around New York

A Book of Maps and Descriptions of the best Roads, Streets, and Routes

League of American Wheelmen

Fifty Miles around New York
A Book of Maps and Descriptions of the best Roads, Streets, and Routes

ISBN/EAN: 9783337146511

Printed in Europe, USA, Canada, Australia, Japan

Cover: Foto ©Lupo / pixelio.de

More available books at **www.hansebooks.com**

FIFTY MILES AROUND NEW YORK

A BOOK OF MAPS AND DESCRIPTIONS OF THE
BEST ROADS, STREETS AND ROUTES

FOR

CYCLISTS AND HORSEMEN

PREPARED UNDER DIRECTION OF
THE LEAGUE OF AMERICAN WHEELMEN
(NEW YORK STATE DIVISION)

TWENTIETH THOUSAND
PRICE, TWO DOLLARS PER COPY

Please Read Carefully

To the Members of the New York Division:

We hope and intend to make these road-books the very best of all road-books, and have exerted our zeal and labor to make this first edition at least acceptable. The Editor realizes that it contains many imperfections, but it is put forth as a promising experiment to prove the value of this form of tour book, and to form a basis for subsequent work in which the errors and short-comings of the present edition may be avoided. The book has been compiled entirely from voluntary contributions from League members, many of whom reside at a considerable distance from portions of the routes covered by them, and the details of the mapping have been worked up from a mass of other data, the separate parts of which seem to contradict each other in some particulars.

We earnestly request that members will freely criticise this work in all its details, and inform the chairman, clearly and at length, of the errors and omissions which come to their notice, so that at the close of the riding season the committee may take up the work of revision with data that will make next year's road book a model in every respect.

We also request that all members having knowledge of good routes not included in this book (located within the territory covered by the index maps) will send accurate data of distances and description so that such routes may be included in future editions.

The present committee claims no credit for devising the method of mapping routes, it having been inaugurated by the Road Book Committee of 1896. The committee is indebted for much information to the following named gentlemen: COL. E. P. NORTH, Department of Public Works, New York City; N. P. LEWIS and GEO. W. TILLSON, Department of City Works, Brooklyn; HENRY P. MORRISON, County Engineer, Richmond County; T. HARRY HOLMES, F. ADEE HULST, FRANK P. SHARE and to the contributors whose names appear at the head of the map plates.

WALTER M. MESEROLE,
Editor and Chairman.

ROAD BOOK COMMITTEE OF 1897.

WALTER M. MESEROLE, *Chairman*, 189 Montague St., Bklyn.
J. J. EHRLICH, 688 Ellicott St., Buffalo.
O. H. HAUENSTEIN, 309 Elmwood Ave., Buffalo.
A. G. SHERRY, care Squire, Sherry & Galusha, Troy.
FRED. L. RODEWALD, 49 St. Marks Pl., New Brighton, S. I.
HOWARD WATSON, 371 Broadway, Albany.
PETER SCHUMACHER, JR., City Hall, Albany.

Engraving by wax process by
BORMAY & CO., 19 Beekman St., New York City.

INDEX TO PLACES.

IMPORTANT NOTE.—The places named in this index are only those shown on *route* maps. Many other places are named on the *index* maps in order to show their location as related to the several routes. These routes will be increased and extended in future editions as fast as contributed by members who are interested in the progress of the work.

	Route.
Ackerson Station, N. J.	47
Allendale, N. J.	39, 44
Amagansett	25
Amawalk	15
Amityville	23
Andalusia, Pa.	51
Anderson, N. J.	45
Annadale	51
Annandale, N. J.	44
Annsville	1
Aquebogue	24
Aqueduct	1
Arcola, N. J.	39, 49
Arden	39, 53
Ardsley	2
Armonk	13
Arrochar	51
Art Village	25
Arverne-by-the-Sea	34
Asbury Park, N. J.	46
Augusta, N. J.	47
Babylon	23
Baiting Hollow	33
Baldwin Place	15
Balmville	36
Bartow	7, 9
Baychester	7, 9
Bayport	23
Bayshore	23
Bayside	29, 30
Beaver Dam	35
Bedford	13
Bedford Park	3, 4, 6
Bedford Station	12
Bell Haven, Conn	22
Bellmore	23
Bellport	24
Berkeley Oval	1
Berkshire Valley, N. J.	47
Birmingham, N. J.	50
Black Rock, Conn	14
Bloomfield, N. J.	47
Bloomingdale, N. J.	49
Blooming Grove	38
Bloomsbury, N. J.	50
Blue Point	23
Bogota, N. J.	39
Bonhamtown, N. J.	51
Bound Brook, N. J.	44
Boyd's Corner	17
Branchville, Conn	14

	Route.
Branchville, N. J.	47
Brentwood	23
Brewsters	20, 21
Bridgehampton	25
Bridgeport, Conn.	14, 22
Bridgeville, N. J.	50
Bridgewater, Pa.	51
Brinkerhoff	18
Bristol, Pa.	51
Broadway, N. J.	45, 50
Broadway Station	30
Boardville, N. J.	48
Bronx Park	1, 5, 9
Bronxville	6, 10
Brookhaven	24
Brooklyn, Detail maps and	23, 26
Brookville	31
Browntown, N. J.	46
Budds Lake, N. J.	52
Burlington, N. J.	51
Bushkill, Pa	35
Butler, N. J.	49
Butzville, N. J.	50
Byram, N. J.	50
Caldwell, N. J.	47
Calverton	33
Camelot	1
Cannon, Conn	14
Canoe Place	25
Carlstadt, N. J.	42
Carmansville	1
Carmel	17, 21
Cedar Grove, N. J.	48
Cedarhurst	34
Center Bridge, N. J.	50
Centerport	31
Centerville, Westchester Co.	1
Centerville, Ulster Co.	35
Central Bridge	2
Central Park	1, 2, 7
Central Valley	39
Centre Moriches	24
Chappaqua	12
Charlottesburg, N. J.	49
Chatham, N. J.	45
Chester	38, 53
Chester, N. J.	45
City Island	9
Clarksville	40
Clarksville, N. J.	44
Clifton	51

	Route.
Clinton, N. J	44
Closter, N. J	42
Cold Spring, Putnam Co.	1, 19
Cold Spring, L. I	31
Coles Corners	20
Coles Mills	17
College Point	29
Commac	31
Concord	51
Congers	42
Coram	32
Cornell	15
Cornwall Station	38
Cos Cob, Conn	22
Craigville	38
Creedmoor	26, 29
Cresskill, N. J	42
Cross River	13
Croton	1
Croton Falls	12, 20
Croton Lake	15
Croton Point	1
Crugers	1
Crystal Run	35
Culvers Gap, N. J	47
Cutchogue	24
Danbury, Conn	21, 22
Danville, N. J	45
Darien, Conn	22
Davenport Corners	1
Deal Beach, N. J	46
Delaware, N. J	50
Delaw'e Water Gap, Pa.	35, 44, 50
Demarest, N. J	42
Denton	53
Denville, N. J	47
Didell	17
Dingmans, N. J	47
Dingmans, Pa	35, 47
Doansburg	20
Dobbs Ferry	2, 10
Dolsontown	53
Douglaston	30
Dover, N. J	47, 52
Dover Plains	20
Drakesville, N. J	52
Dunellen, N. J	44
Dunwoodie	8
Dutchess Junction	19
Dutch Hollow	49
East Chester	38
East Hampton	25
East Islip	23
East Long Branch, N. J	46
East Moriches	24
East Norwich	31
East Norwalk, Conn	22
Easton, Pa	45
East Patchogue	24
Eastport	24, 25
East Portchester, Conn	22
East Quogue	25

	Route.
East Rockaway	34
East Setauket	31
East View	1, 15
East Walden	35
Eddington, Pa	51
Edgemere	34
Elberon, N. J	46
Elizabeth, N. J	46
Elmsford	1, 11, 15
Eltingville	51
Elwood	31
Englewood, N. J	42
Erwinna, Pa	50
Experiment Mills, Pa	35
Fairfield, Conn	14
Fairhaven, N. J	46
Fairview, Bergen Co., N. J	49
Fairview, Monmouth Co., N. J.	46
Farmer Mills	17
Farmingdale	31
Far Rockaway	34
Fenhurst	34
Finchville	35
Finderne, N. J	44
Fire Place	25
First House	25
Fishkill Village	1, 18
Fishkill-on-the-Hudson	18, 19
Fishkill Plains	17, 18
Five Mile River, Conn	22
Flint	35
Floral Park	26
Flushing	29, 30
Fordham	5, 6
Fordham Heights	1, 2
Fort Lee, N. J	39
Fort Schuyler	7, 9
Fosters Meadow	23
Frankford, Pa	51
Franklin, N. J	47
Franklin Park, N. J	51
Franklinville	24
Freedom Plains	18
Freeport	23, 28
Frenchtown, N. J	50
Garden City	27
Garnerville	41
Garretson	51
Garrison	1
Georgetown, Conn	14
German Valley, N. J	45
Giffords	51
Glen Cove	30
Glen Gardner, N. J	44
Glenham	18
Glen Island	7
Glen Ridge Station, N. J	47
Glenville	11
Godeffroy	35
Goldens Bridge	12
Good Ground	25
Goshen	53

	Route.
Grand View	42
Grand City	51
Grant Avenue Station, N. J.	44
Grasmere	51
Gray Oaks	1, 2, 10
Great Neck	30
Great River	23
Greenlawn	31
Greenport	24, 25
Greenvale	31
Greenwich, Conn	22
Greenwich Point	28
Greenwood Lake	49
Greenwood Lake, N. J.	48, 49
Greycourt	38, 53
Groveville	18
Guaymard	35
Guttenburg Race Track, N. J.	42
Hackensack, N. J.	39, 49
Hackettstown, N. J.	45
Haledon, N. J.	49
Hammel's Station	34
Harbor Hill Observatory	31
Hardenburgh Corners, N. J.	46
Harrington Park, N. J.	42
Hartsdale	6
Hastings	3, 10
Hauppauge	31
Haverstraw	41, 42
Hawthorne, N. J.	49
Hempstead, L. I.	27, 23
Hempstead, Rockland Co.	41
Hewitt Station, N. J.	48
Hicksville	26
High Bridge	2
High Bridge, N. J.	44
Highland Landing	35, 36
Highland Mills	39
Highland Park, N. J.	51
Highland Village	35, 36
Highwood, N. J.	42
Hillburn	39
Hilton, N. J.	44
Hohokus, N. J.	39
Holland Station	34
Hollis	26
Holmesburg, Pa.	51
Hopatcong, N. J.	47, 52
Hopewell	17
Houghtonville, N. J.	46
Huguenot, Orange Co.	35
Huguenot, S. I.	51
Hughsonville	19
Huntington	31
Hurdtown, N. J.	47
Hyde Park	26, 27
Iona Island	41
Ireland Corners	35
Irvington	2
Irvington, N. J.	44
Iselin, N. J.	46
Islip	23

	Route
Jamaica	26, 29
Jamesport	24
Jefferson Valley	16
Jenkintown	35
Jericho	26
Jersey City, N. J.	42, 48
Junction, N. J.	44
Katonah	12
Kensico	12
Kent Cliff	17
Kenvil, N. J.	52
Keyport, N. J.	46
Kingsbridge	1, 2
Kingston, N. J.	51
Lafayette, N. J.	47
Lake Hopatcong, N. J.	52
Lake Mahopac	17
Lakeside, N. J.	49
Lake Success	26, 30
Lakeville	30
Lake Waccabuc	13
Lambertville, N. J.	50
Larchmont	7
Larchmont Manor	7
Lattingtown	36
Lawrence	34
Lawrenceville, N. J.	51
Lebanon, N. J.	44
Leonia, N. J.	39, 42
Lindenhurst	23
Little Falls, N. J.	48
Little Ferry, N. J.	49
Little Neck	30
Lloyd Station	35
Locust Valley	31
Long Branch, N. J.	46
Low Moor, N. J.	46
Lumberville, Pa.	50
Lynbrook	23, 27, 34
Madison, N. J.	45
Mahopac	15, 16
Mahwah, N. J.	39
Mamaroneck	7, 54
Manhasset	30
Manhasset Hills	30
Manhattanville	1
Manor	24
Manunka Chunk, N. J.	50
Mastic	24
Matawan, N. J.	46
Matteawan	18, 19
Mattituck	24, 33
Meads Corner	17
Mechanicstown	35
Mechanicsville, N. J.	46
Medford	32
Mendham, N. J.	45
Menlo Park, N. J.	46
Merrick	23
Merrits Corners	15
Mertons Station	15

	Route.		Route.
Sylvan Grove	42	Warwick	38
Syosset	26	Washington, N. J.	44, 45, 50
		Washington Bridge	1, 2, 3, 4, 5
Tallman	40	Washington Corners	18
Tappan	42	Washington's Crossing, N. J.	50
Tarrytown	2, 11	Washingtonville	38
Tenafly, N. J.	42	Waterloo, N. J.	52
Ten Mile River, N. J.	51	Water Mills	25
Terryville	32	Waverly, N. J.	46
Third House	25	Wayne, N. J.	48
Thomaston	30	Weehawken, N. J.	49
Three Mile Harbor	25	Westbury Station	26
Tilly Foster Mine	21	Westchester	7, 9
Titicus, Conn.	14	West Craigville Station	38
Titusville, N. J.	50	West End, N. J.	46
Tompkinsville	51	West Farms	9
Tottenville	51	West Hampton	25
Townsbury, N. J.	45	West Hampton Beach	25
Tremont	6	West Haverstraw	41
Trenton, N. J.	50, 51	West Milford, N. J.	49
Trenton Junction, N. J.	50	West New Rochelle	7, 8
Tri-States Rock	35	West Nyack	40
Tuckahoe	2, 6	Weston, Conn.	22
Tullytown, Pa.	51	Weston's Mills, N. J.	46
Turners	53	West Point	41
Tuttles Corner, N. J.	47	Westport, Conn.	14, 22
Tuxedo	39	West Somers	14
Tuxedo Park	39	West Sayville	23
		Wheatsheaf, N. J.	46
Uhlerstown, Pa.	50	White Plains	6, 11, 12, 54
Unionport	7	White House, N. J.	44
Unionville	12, 15	Whitestone	29
Upper Saddle River, N. J.	43	Whitson	15
		Willets Point	29
Vails Gate	38, 39	Williamsbridge	3, 6
Vails Gate Junction	38, 39	Wilton, Conn.	14, 22
Valhalla	12	Woodbridge, N. J.	46
Valley Stream	34	Woodbury Falls	39
Van Cortlandt Park	1, 2	Woodhaven	26
Van Wyck's Station	17	Woodlands	1
Verbank	18	Woodlawn	4, 9
Verona, N. J.	47, 48	Woodport, N. J.	47
Verplank's Point	1	Woodruff's Gap, N. J.	47
		Woodsburgh	34
Wading River	33	Woodstock	9
Wainscott	25	Woodville Landing	33
Walden	35	Wyoming, N. J.	44
Waldwick, N. J.	39		
Wallkill	37		
Wanaque, N. J.	48	Yonkers	1, 2, 8, 9
Wantagh	23	Yorktown	14
Wappingers Falls	1, 19	Yorktown Heights	15

FRAUDULENT "L. A. W. HOTELS."—It has come to be the practice for proprietors of various third-class hotels and road house groggeries, and occasionally for more pretentious hosts, to display, without authority, signs bearing the "L. A. W." initials or insignia. I am informed also that certain hotel proprietors holding official certificate of appointment are ignoring their contract requirements, and refuse to give L. A. W. members a lower rate than is charged to non-members. These proprietors of L. A. W. hotels have received large advertising from the L. A. W. and *have agreed in writing to give L. A. W. members from 10 to 30 per cent. lower rates than are charged to other wheelmen.* They further agree to forfeit $50 to our division for every violation of this contract. These two offenders, the fraud proprietor and the forgetful proprietor, are the men we are after. Please report them as fast as discovered to

ISAAC B. POTTER, Chief Consul,
Vanderbilt Building, New York, N. Y.

ROUTES WANTED.

Our road book committee is still at work, making new maps, adding new routes, correcting, revising and in a patient, painstaking way, doing everything possible to make these road-books the very best on earth. They are a committee of voluntary workers who at odd times have some trifles of personal business to attend to and so it may not be always possible for them to answer grumbling letters which come to them from L. A. W. members in lieu of salary. What they want is the help of every intelligent rider who will carefully prepare and contribute a new, pleasant or popular route, or who can send printed detail maps (drawn on large scale) showing the roads and streets in any of the towns within the territory covered by the index maps. Don't tell the chairman that this book is wrong and that you could have made a better one with your eyes shut. All this he knows, and you are just the man he's been looking for. Write him a friendly, encouraging letter, praising the good points of his faithful work, and send him carefully prepared sketch of at least one excellent route with notes of distances between all prominent points, crossroads and turns, and see to it that these distances are accurately slated from cyclometer measurements.

In no way can you spend a more pleasant and satisfactory day than by taking a stroll on your wheel in quest of new matter for the next edition. If you contribute a new and acceptable route it will bear your name on the printed map page when it appears. If the new route contains features which are specially famous or beautiful, or of historical note, write a description of these features, as tersely and gracefully as you can and send them to the chairman with your map sketch. In making a sketch map of the route *don't confuse your notes by attempting to get too much on one sheet.* Better use a dozen pages for a ten mile route if necessary, and have them all clear. It will be easier to make and vastly easier to understand. Finally, don't attempt to cover a route that has already been sent to the committee. If you have a good route in mind write a line to Mr. Meserole and ask him whether it is included among his notes. THAT is the sort of letter he delights to receive and will promptly answer.

Fraternally,

ISAAC B. POTTER,
Chief Consul.

ELECTION DAY IS COMING.

If you wish to know how the Senator and Members of Assembly who represent your district stand on the Good Roads Question, write a postal card inquiry to the Chief Consul. Get the wheelmen voters together in your town and let the "statesmen" know you are alive on election day. We may catch larks if ever the heavens fall but we'll never have good roads till we elect men to office who are broad and brainy enough to know that a good road is a good thing for everybody.

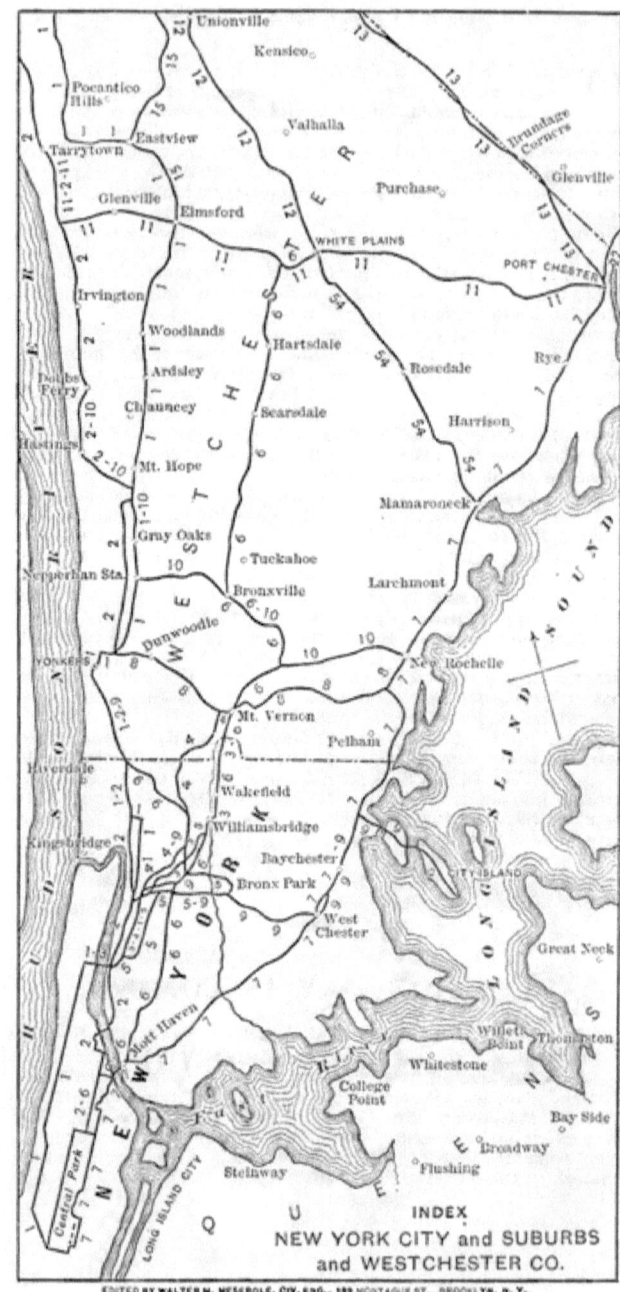

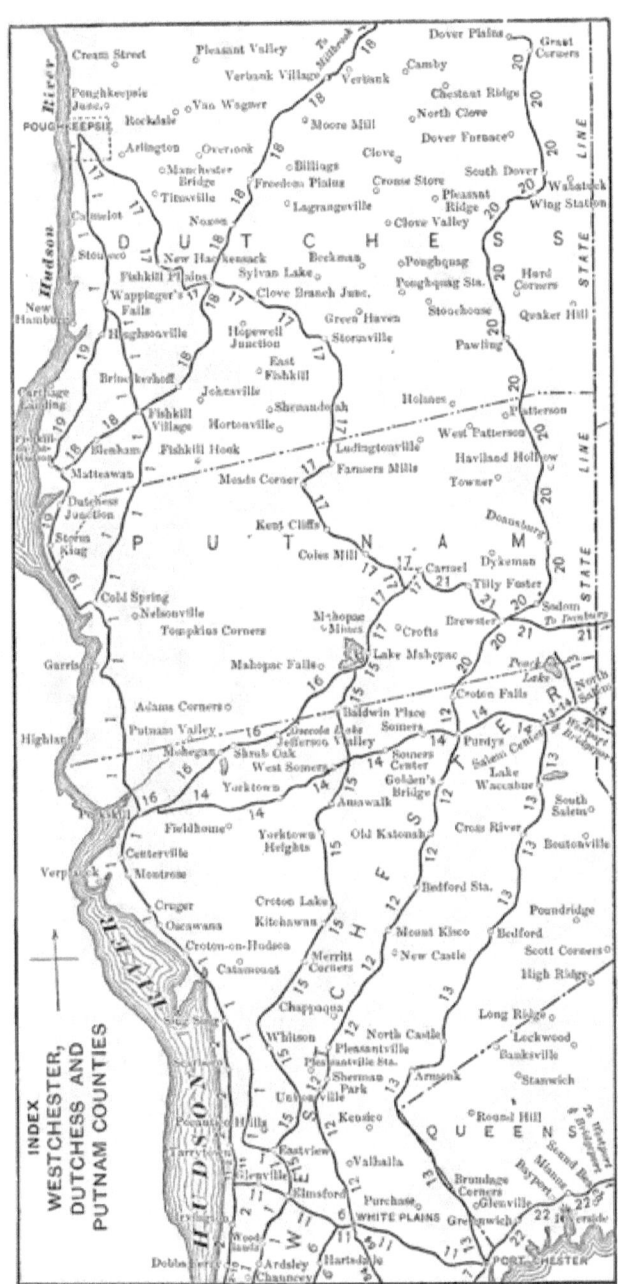

INDEX
WESTCHESTER, DUTCHESS AND PUTNAM COUNTIES

EDITED BY WALTER M. MESEPOLE, CIV. ENG., 188 MONTAGUE ST., BROOKLYN, N. Y.

COPYRIGHT, 1896, BY THE NEW YORK STATE DIVISON, L. A. W.

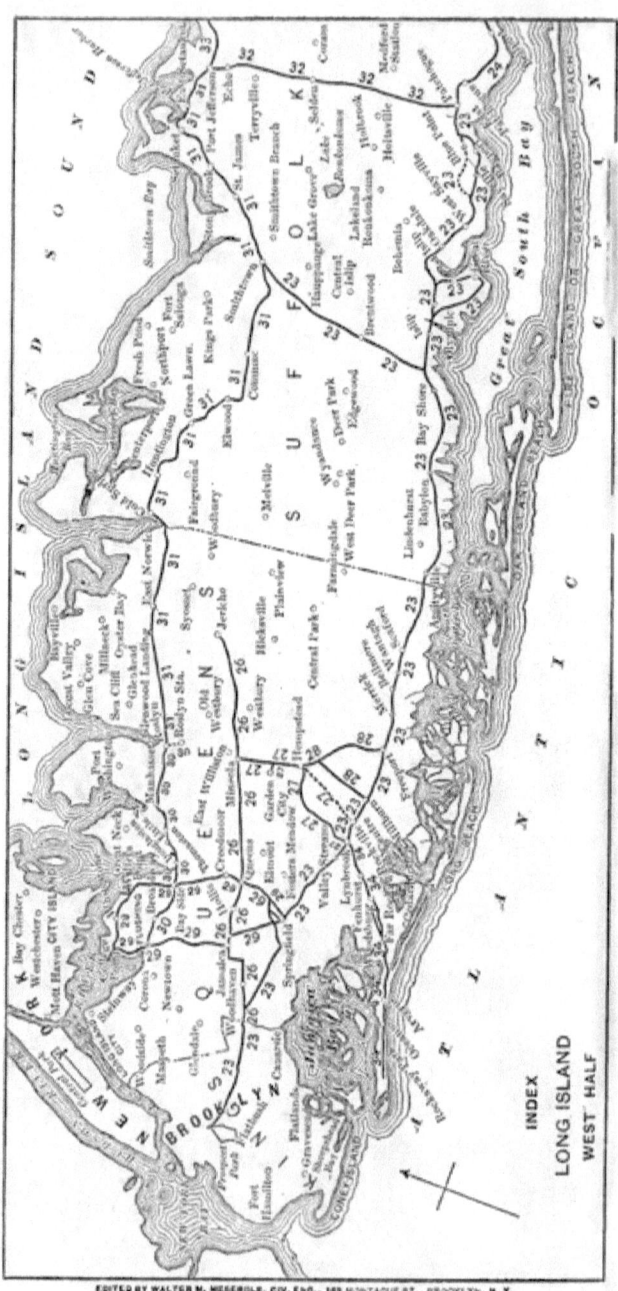

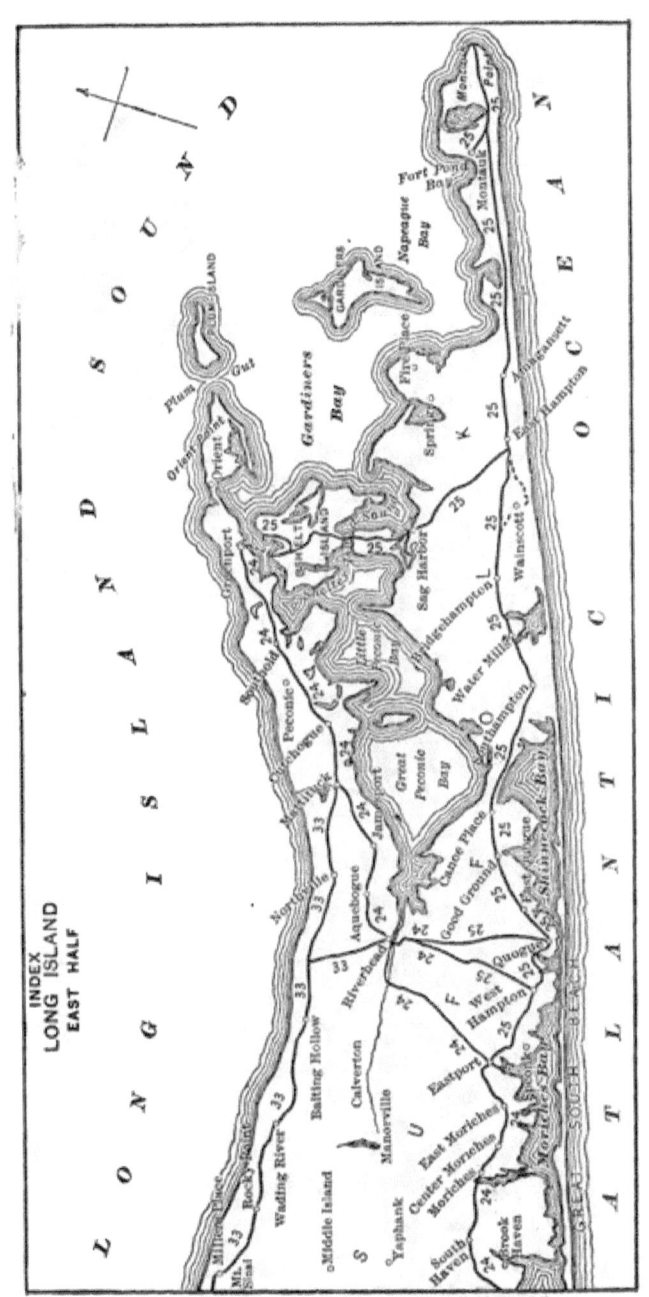

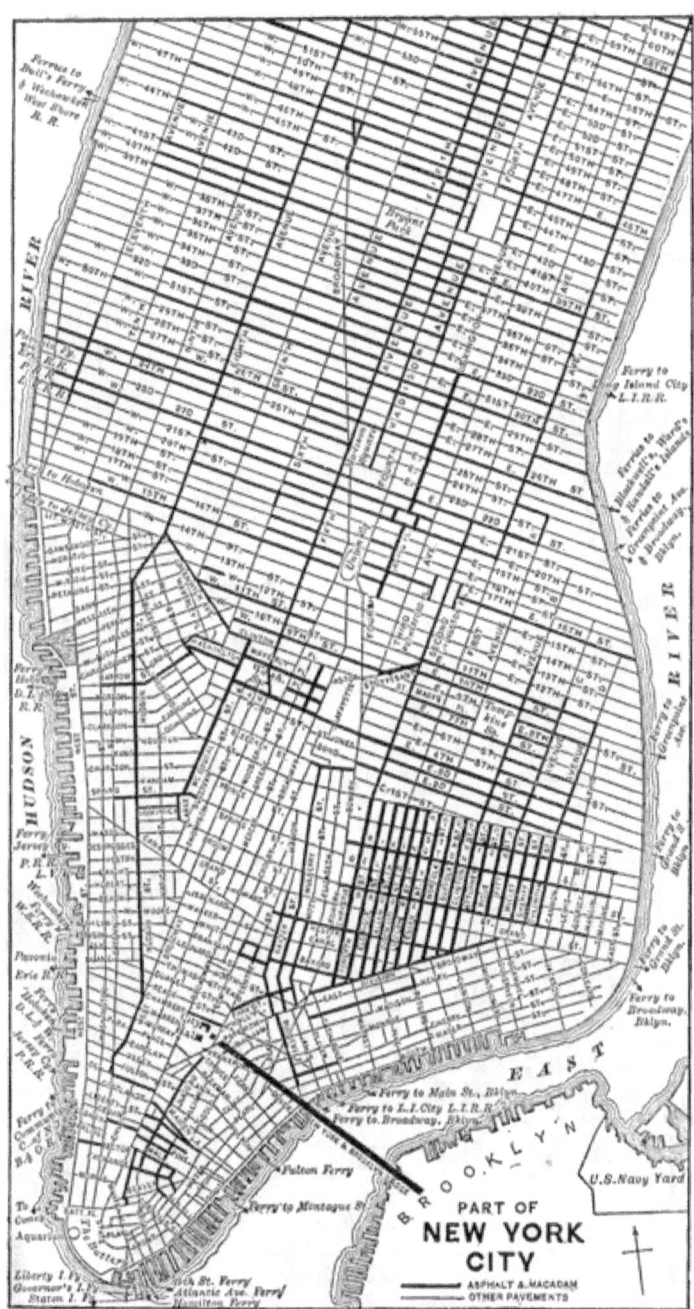

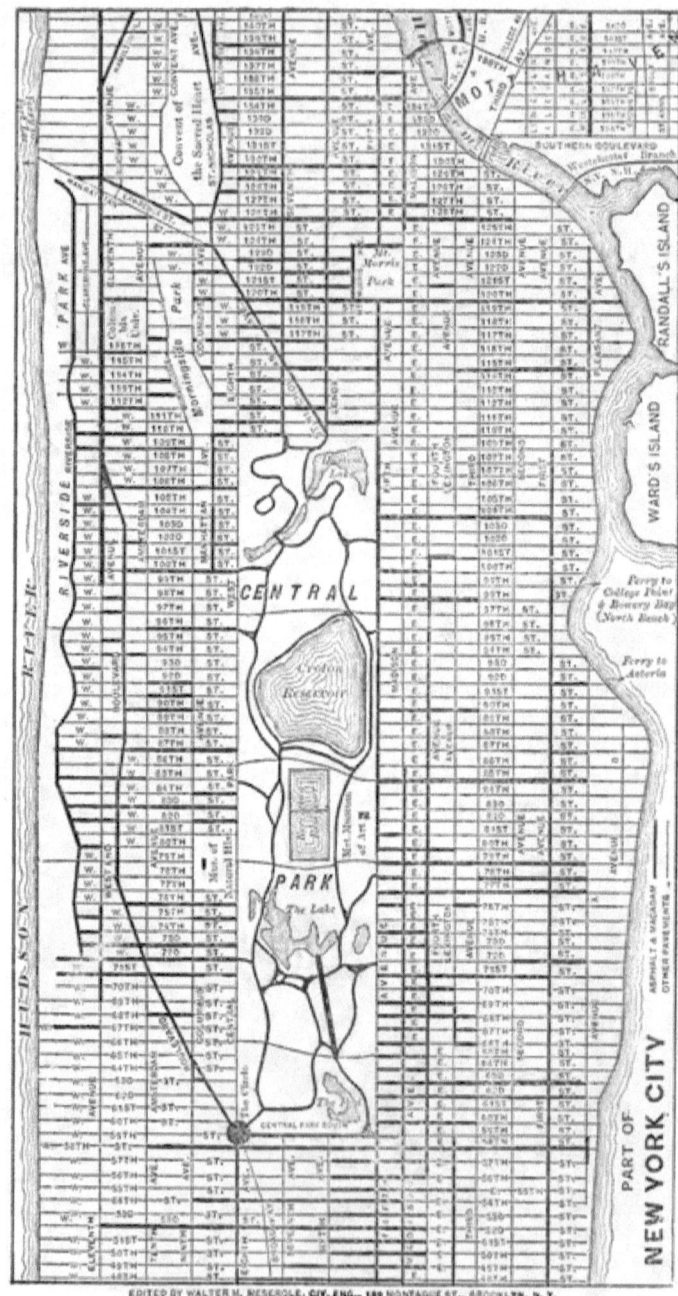

PART OF NEW YORK CITY

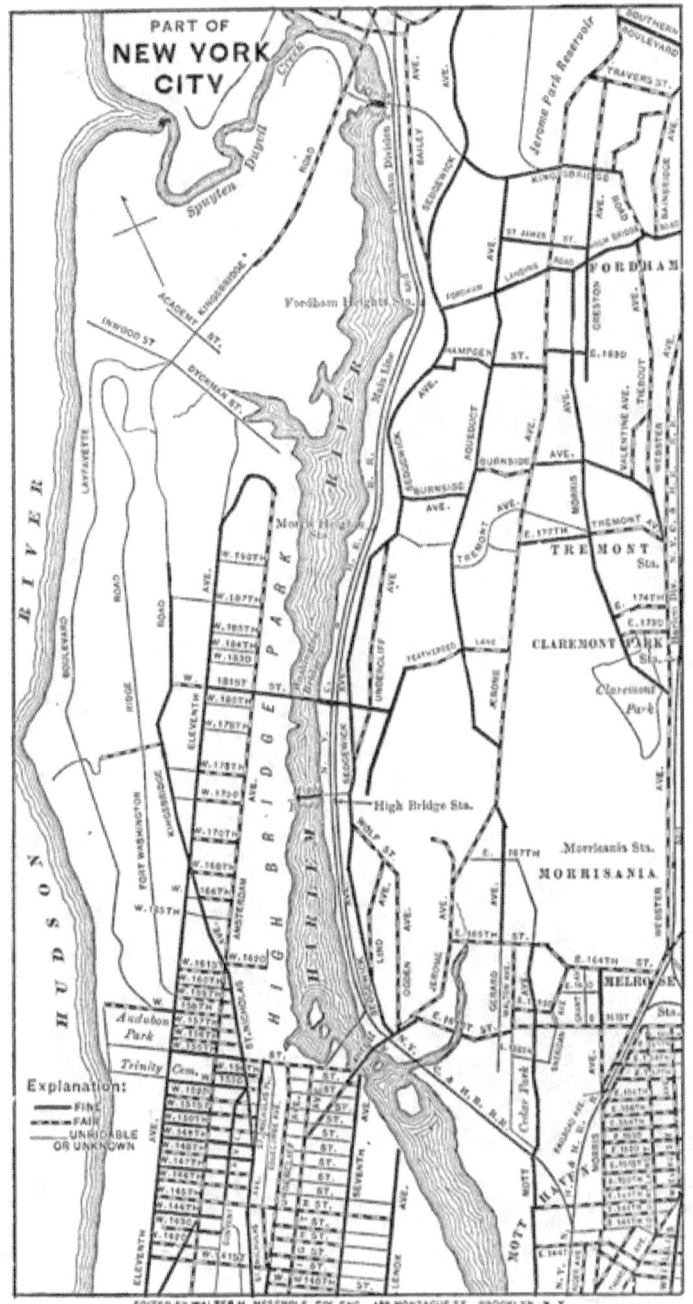

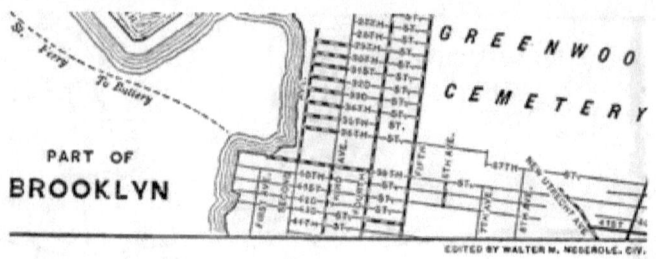

HEADQUARTERS
CENTURY WHEELMEN

VAN BUREN'S-BY-THE-SEA

BRIGHTON, L. I.

AT THE END OF THE FAMOUS CYCLE PATH

EVERY ATTENTION GIVEN TO CYCLISTS
CUISINE UNSURPASSED

CONVENIENT TO MANHATTAN BEACH, SHEEPSHEAD,
CONEY ISLAND AND BRIGHTON BEACH RACE TRACK

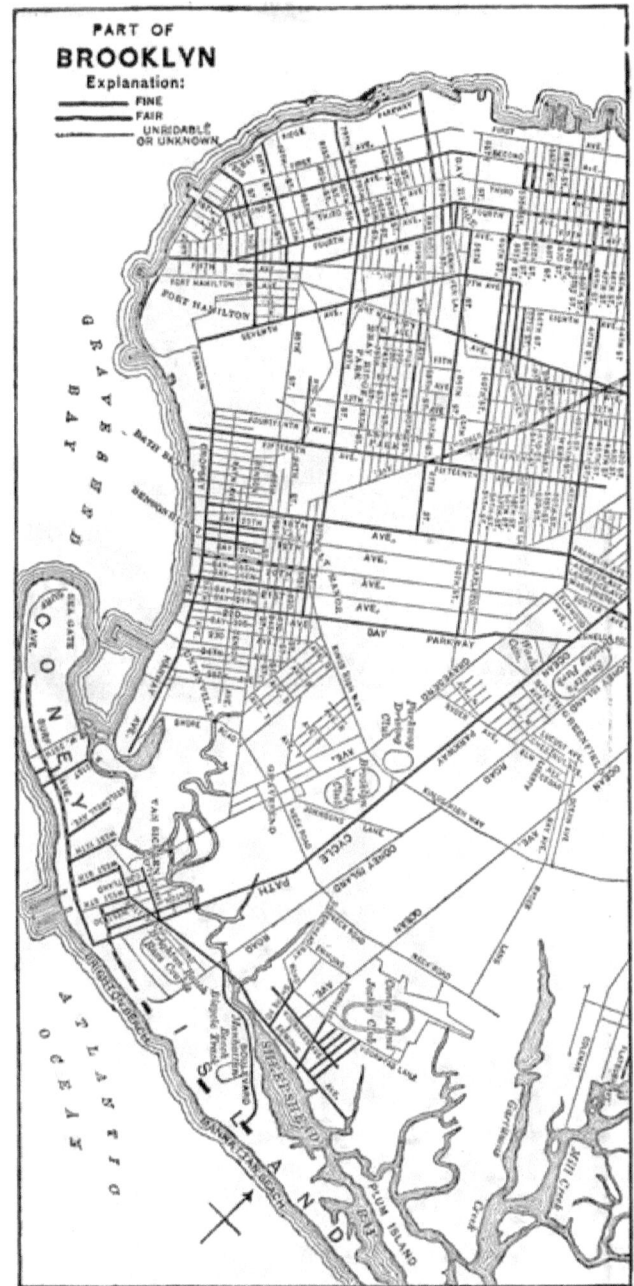

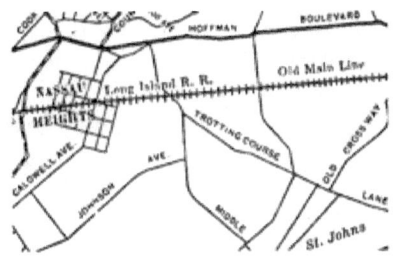

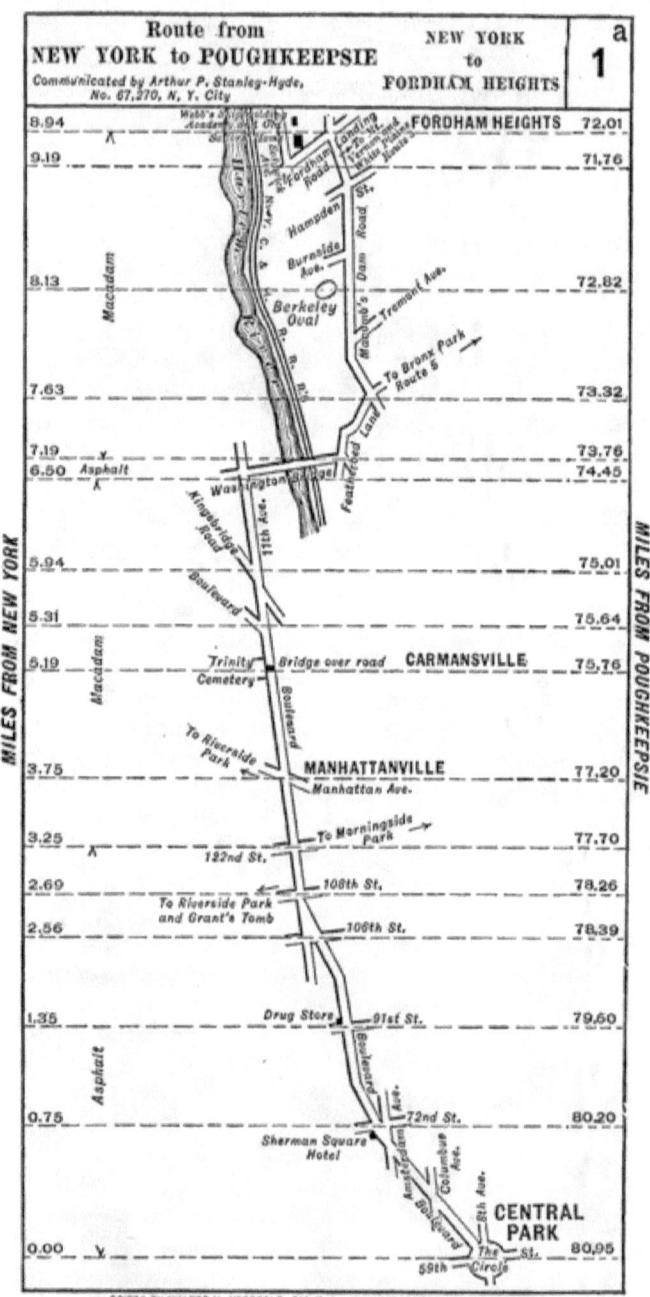

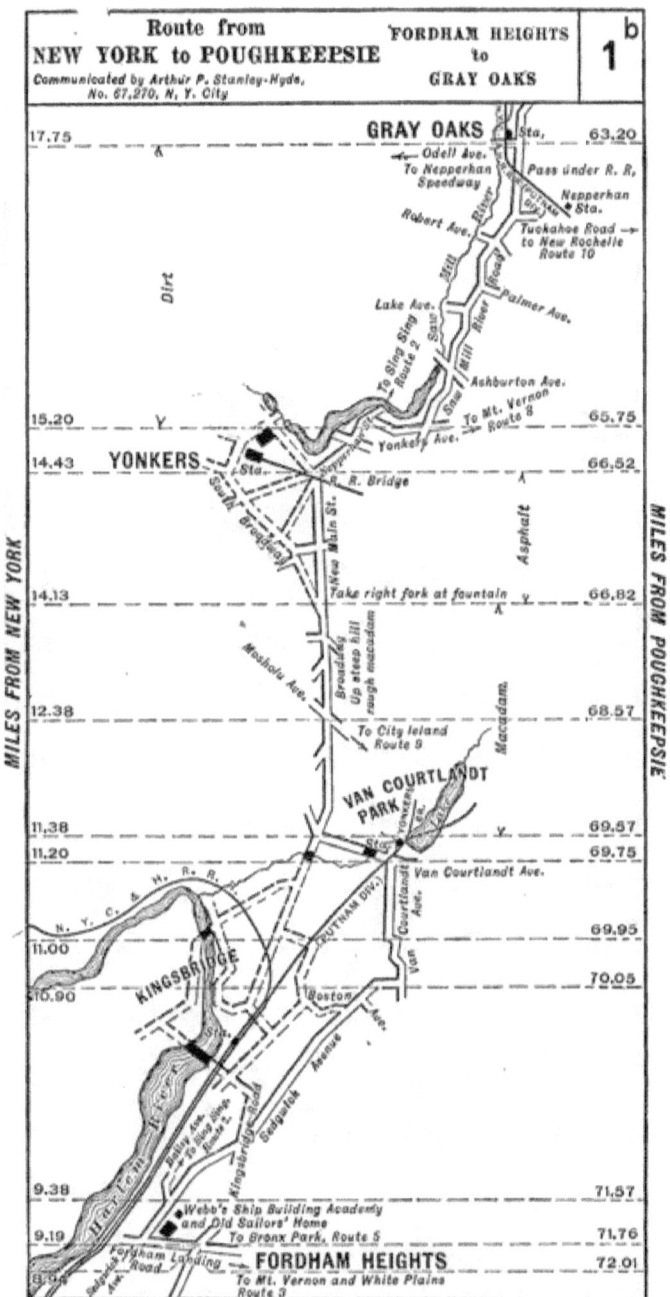

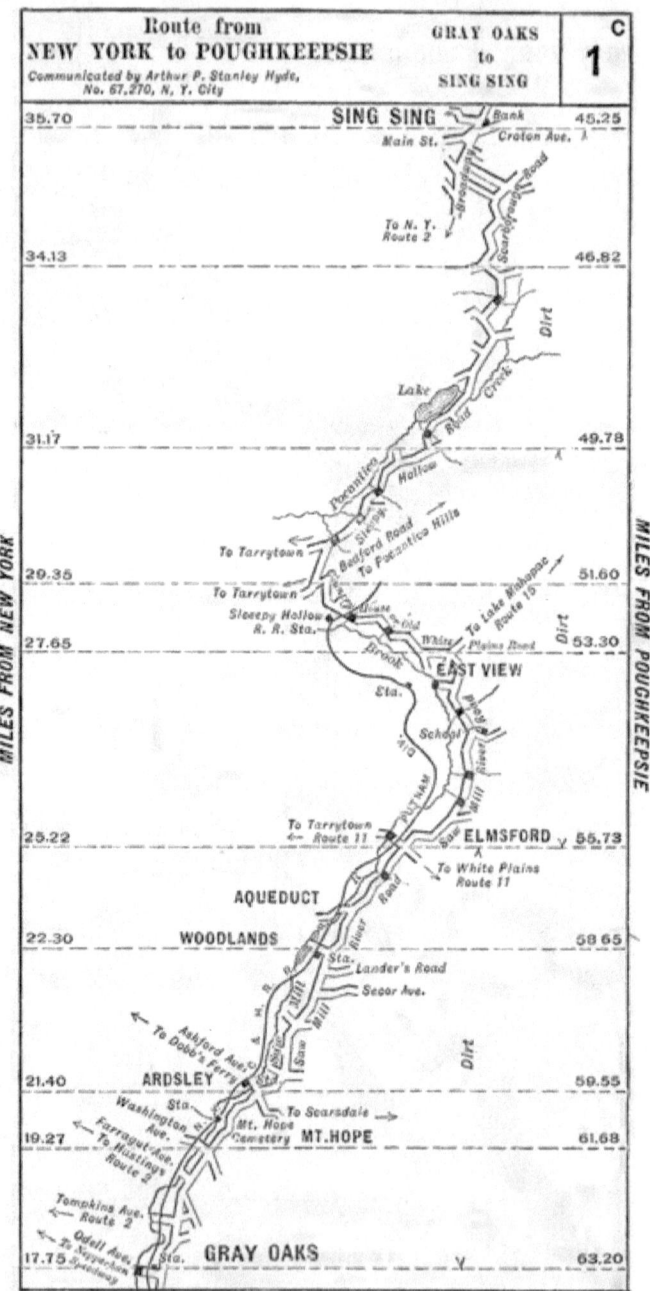

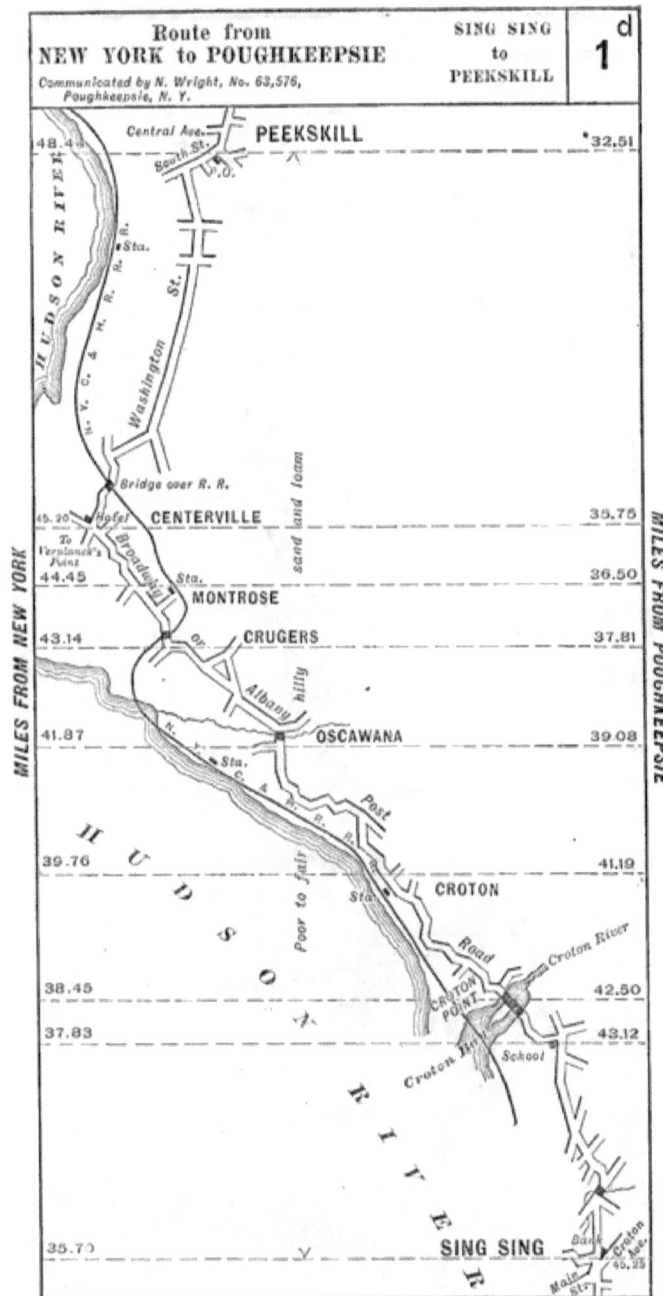

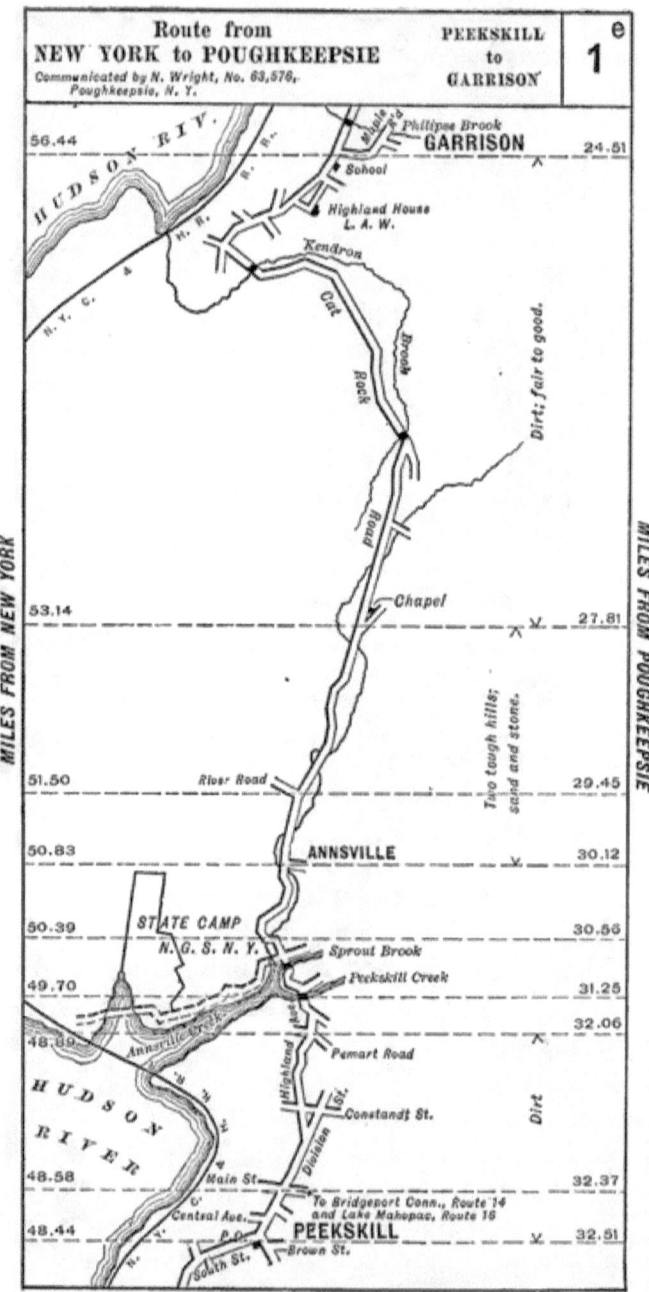

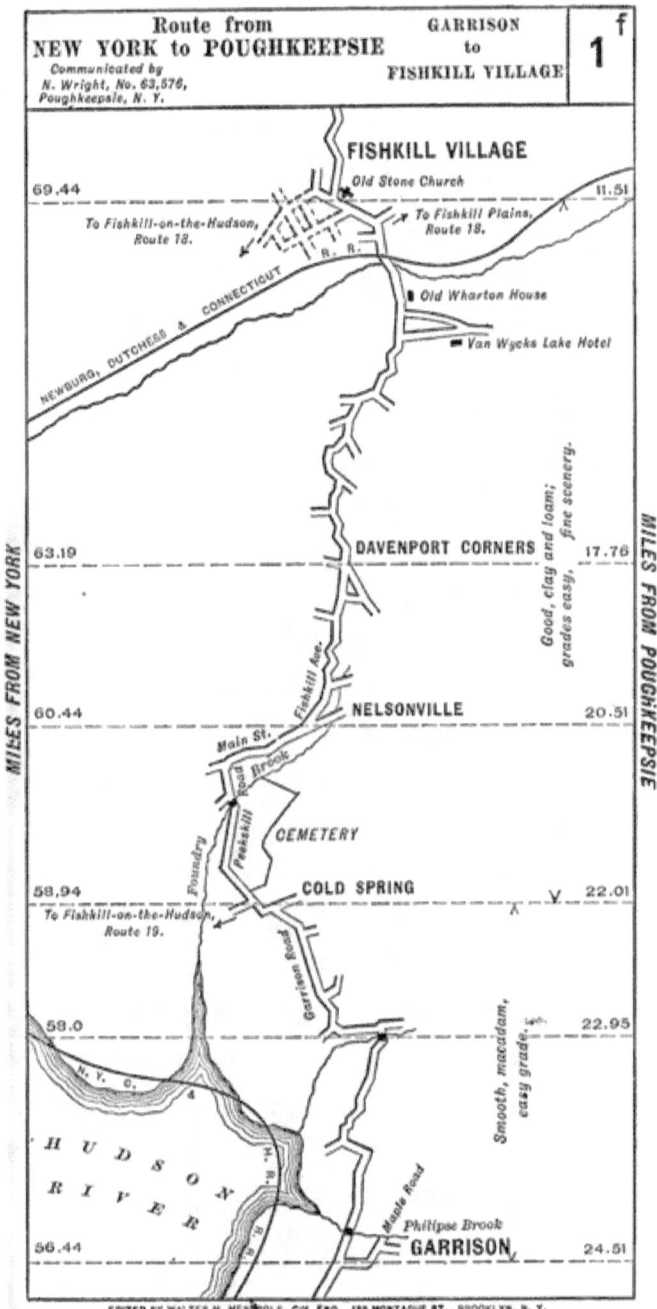

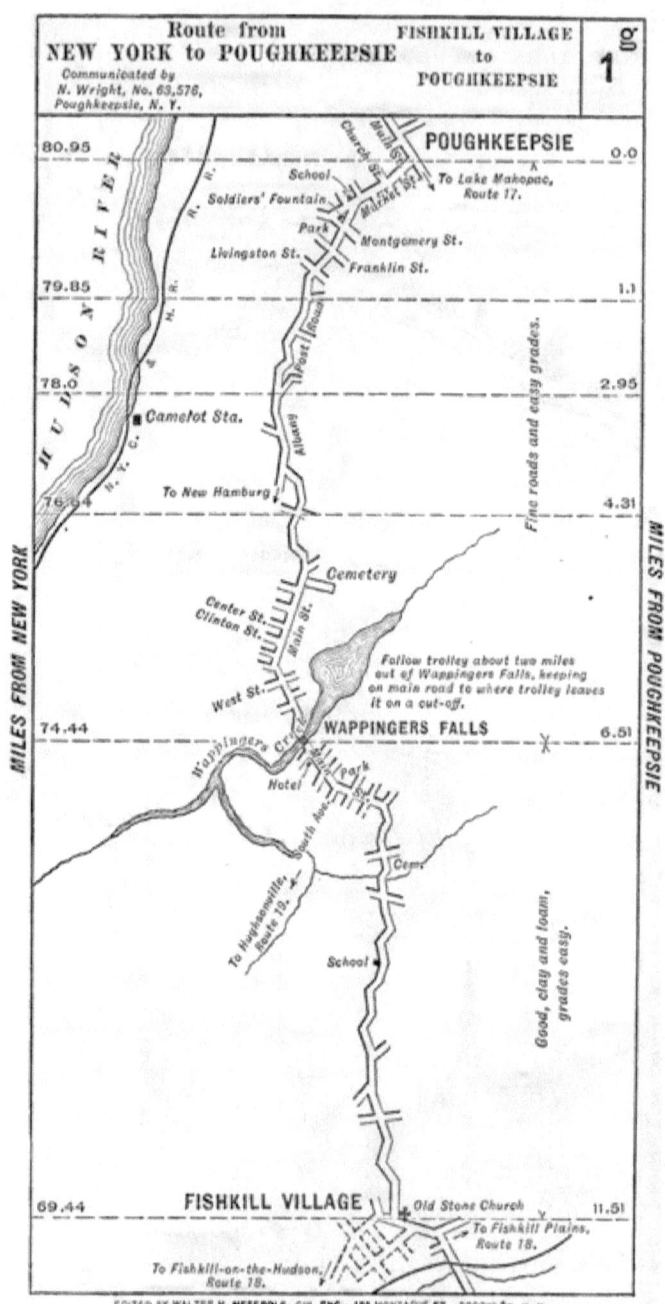

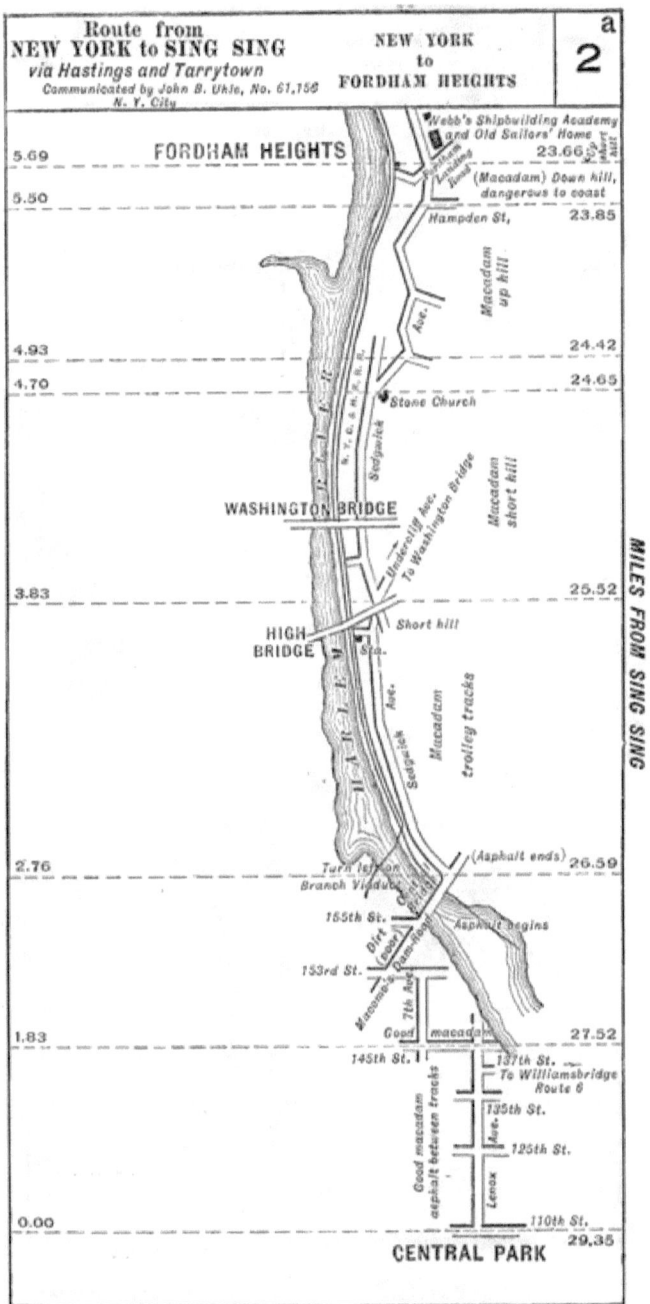

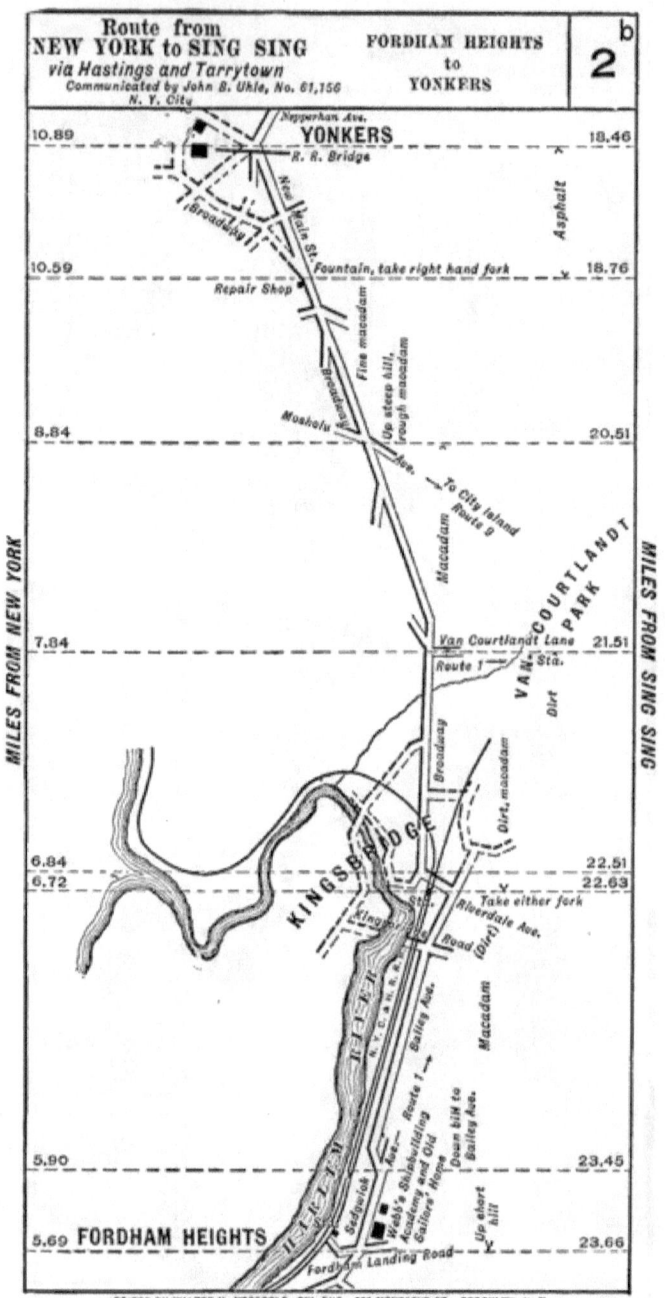

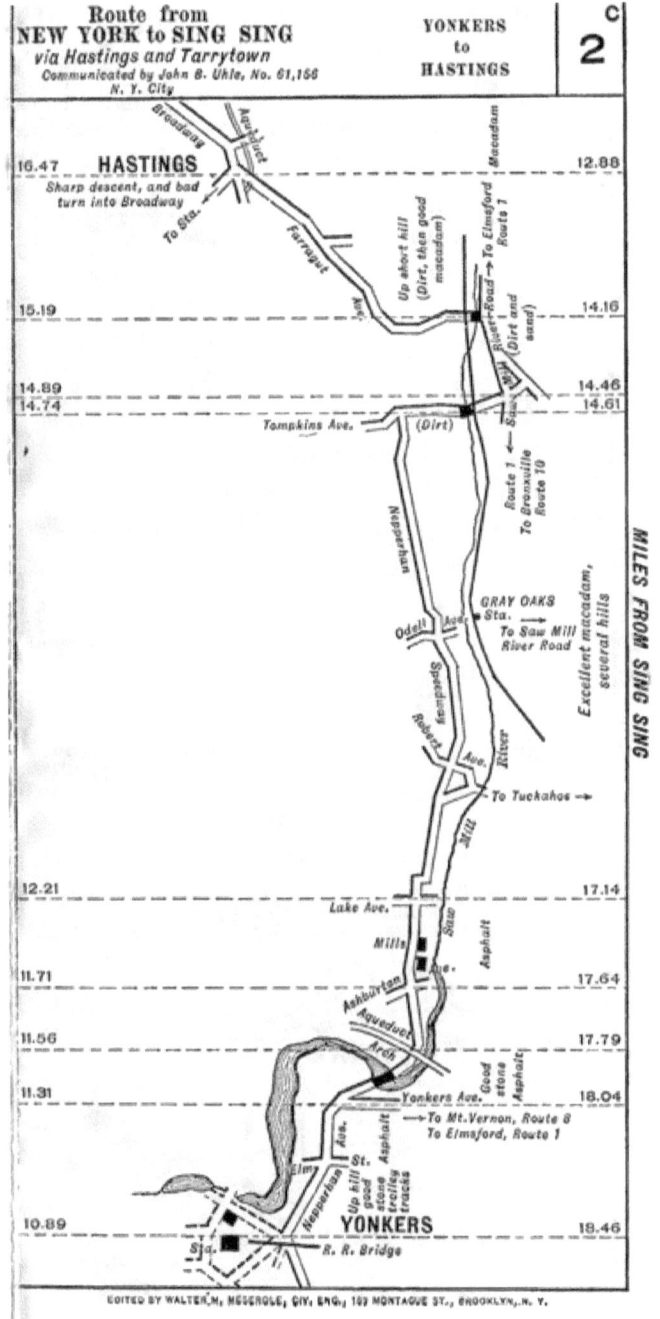

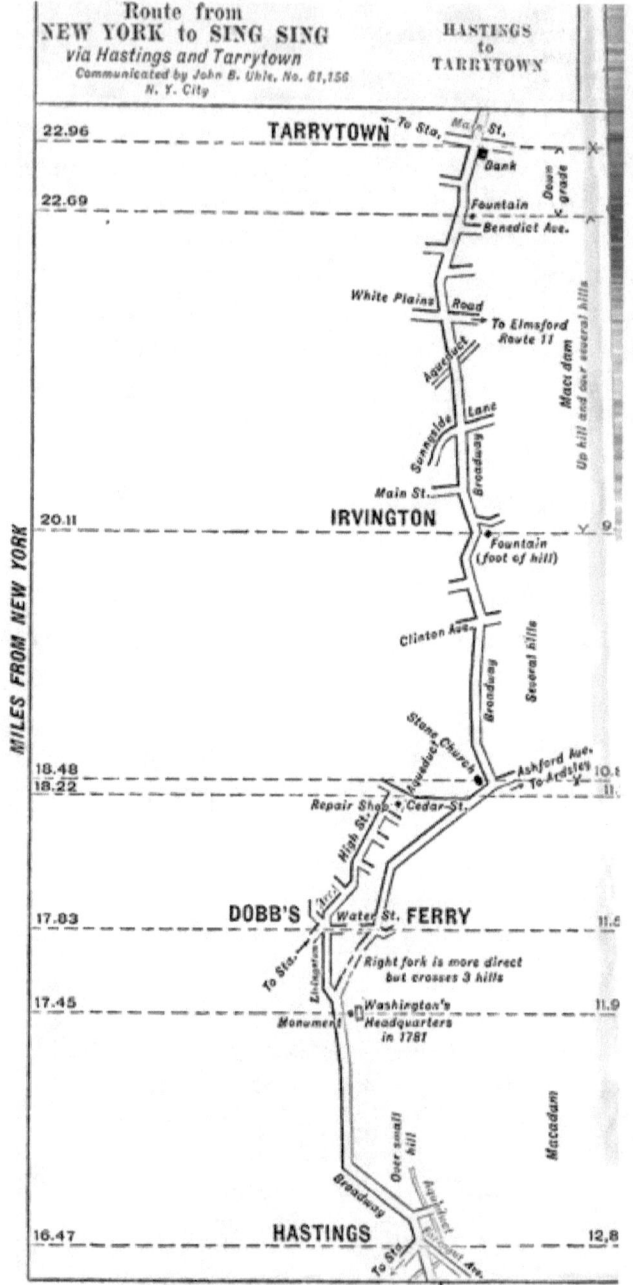

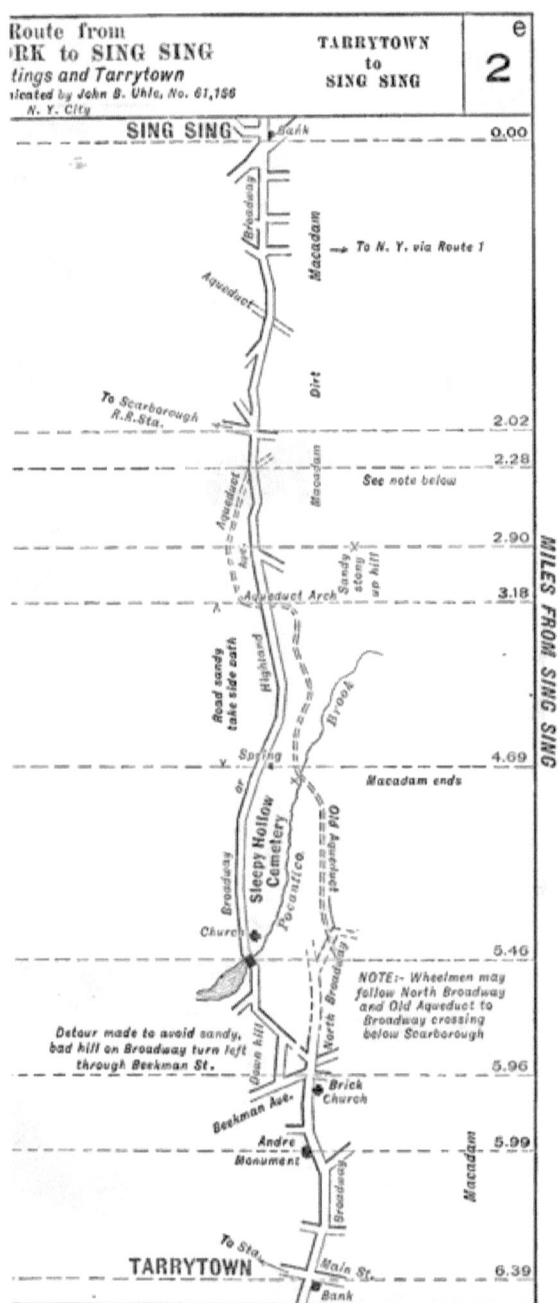

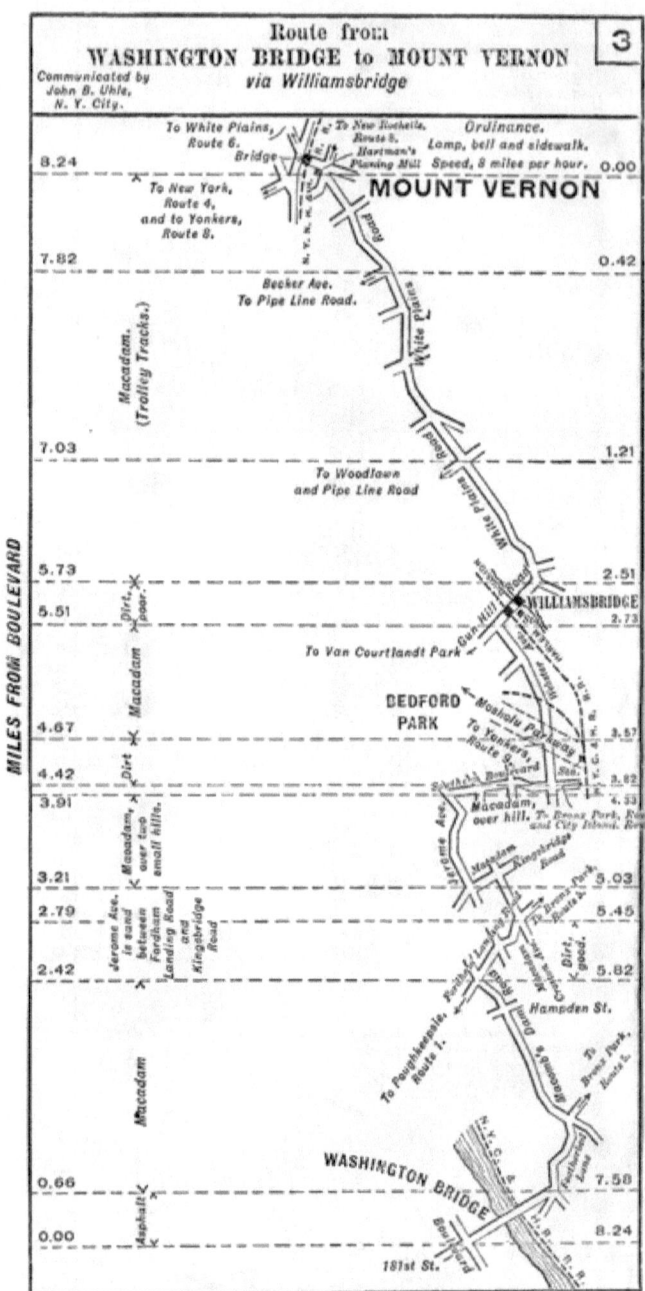

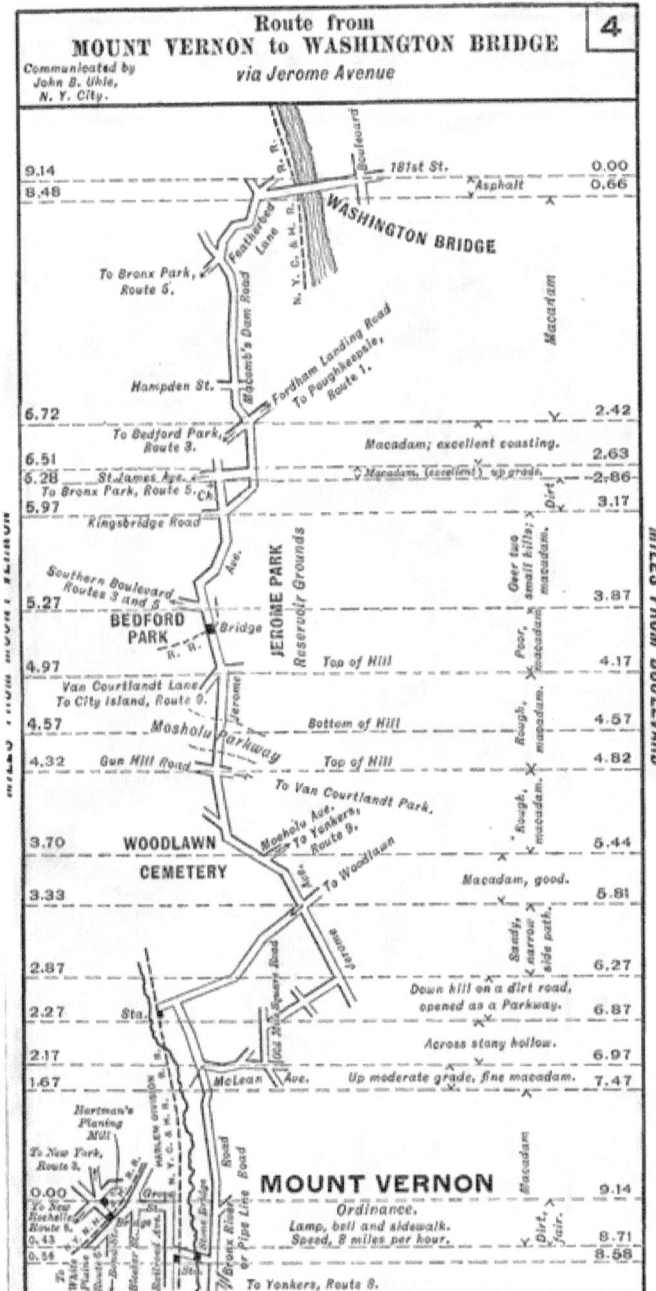

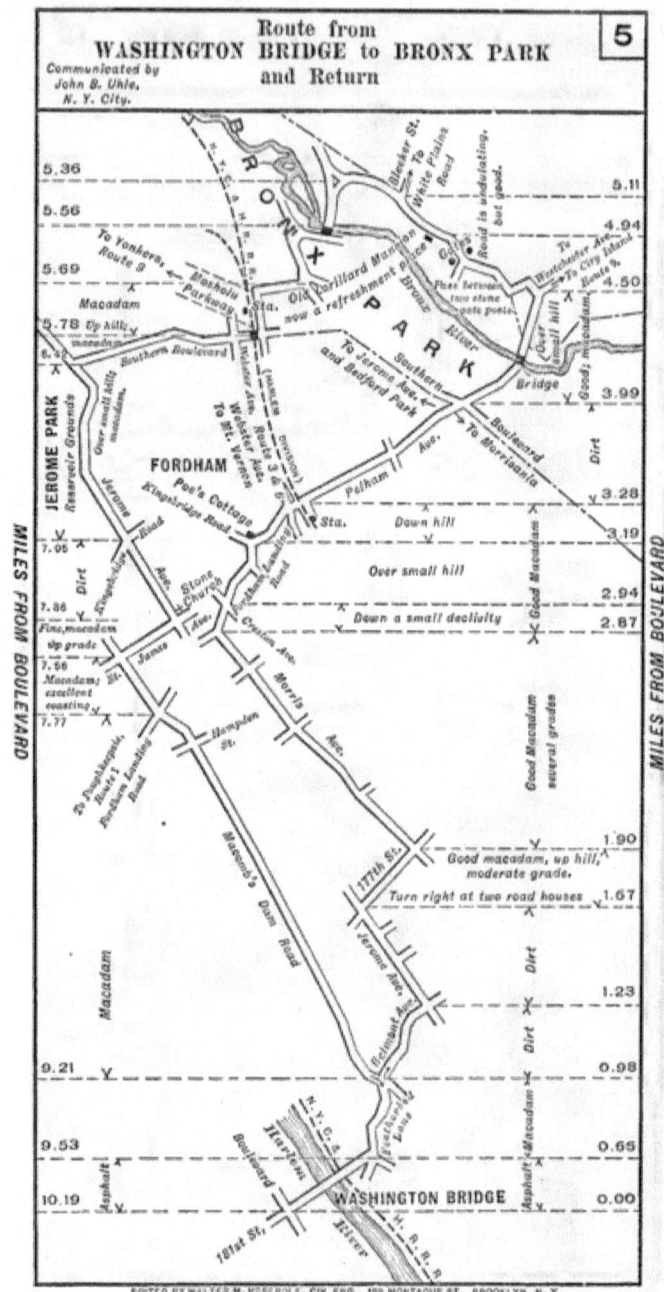

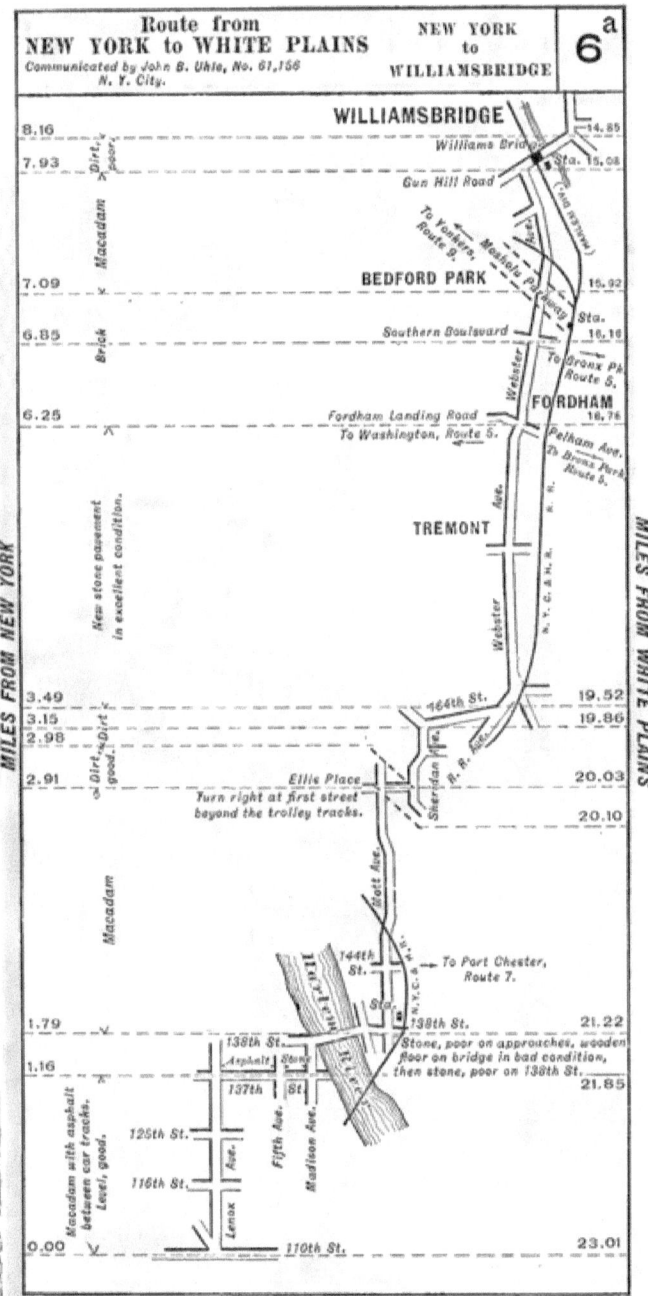

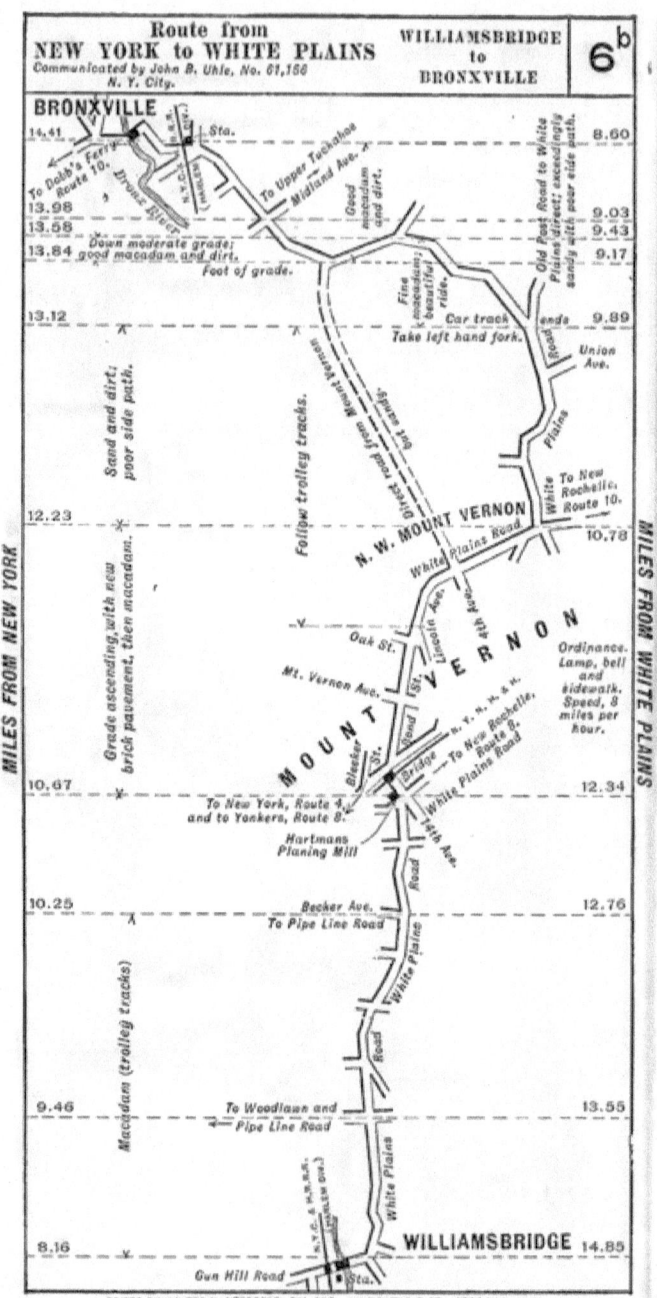

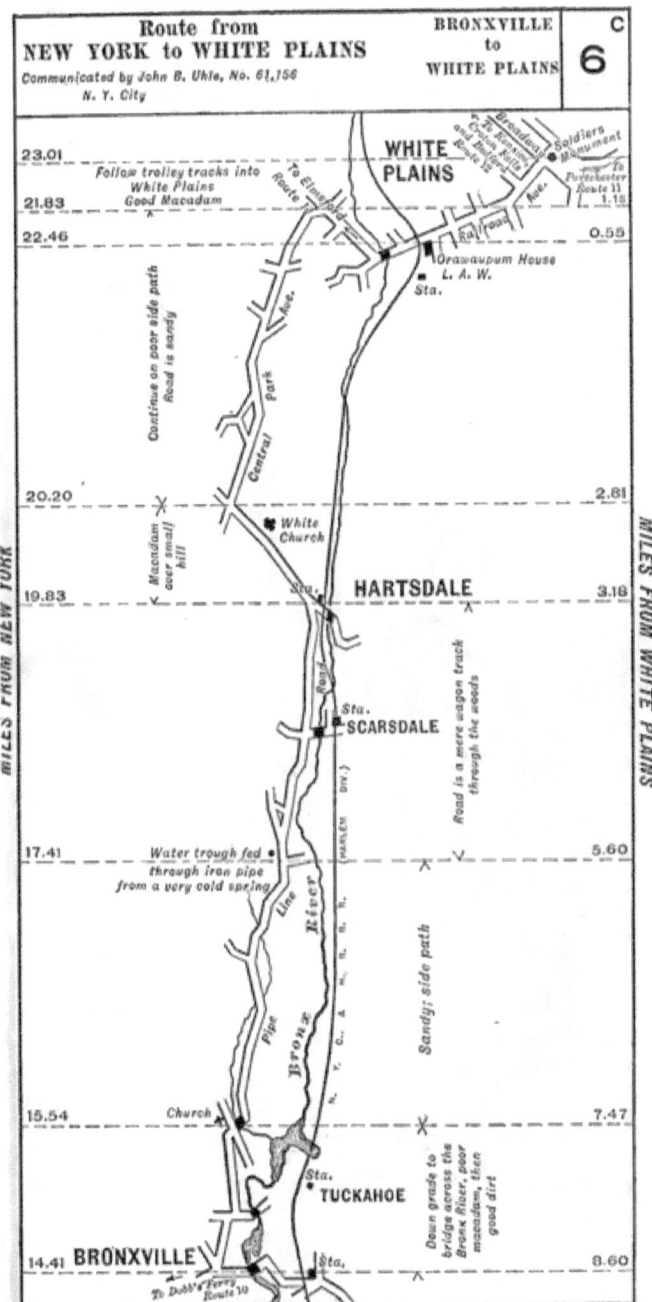

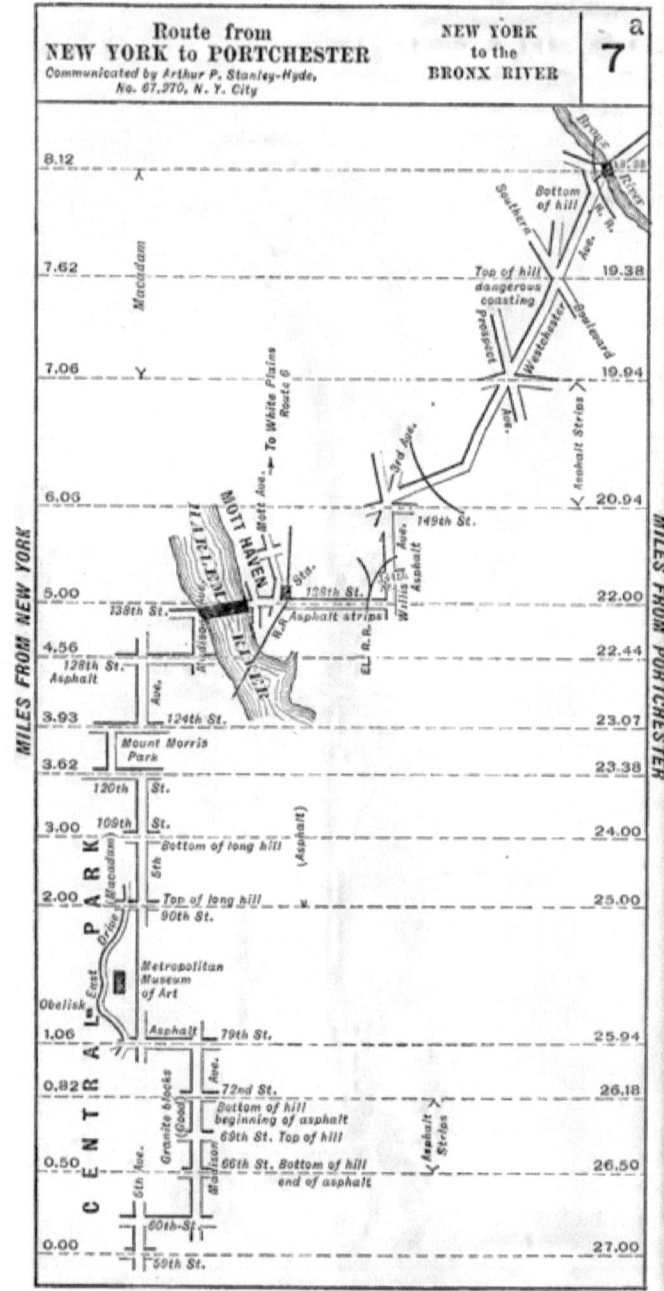

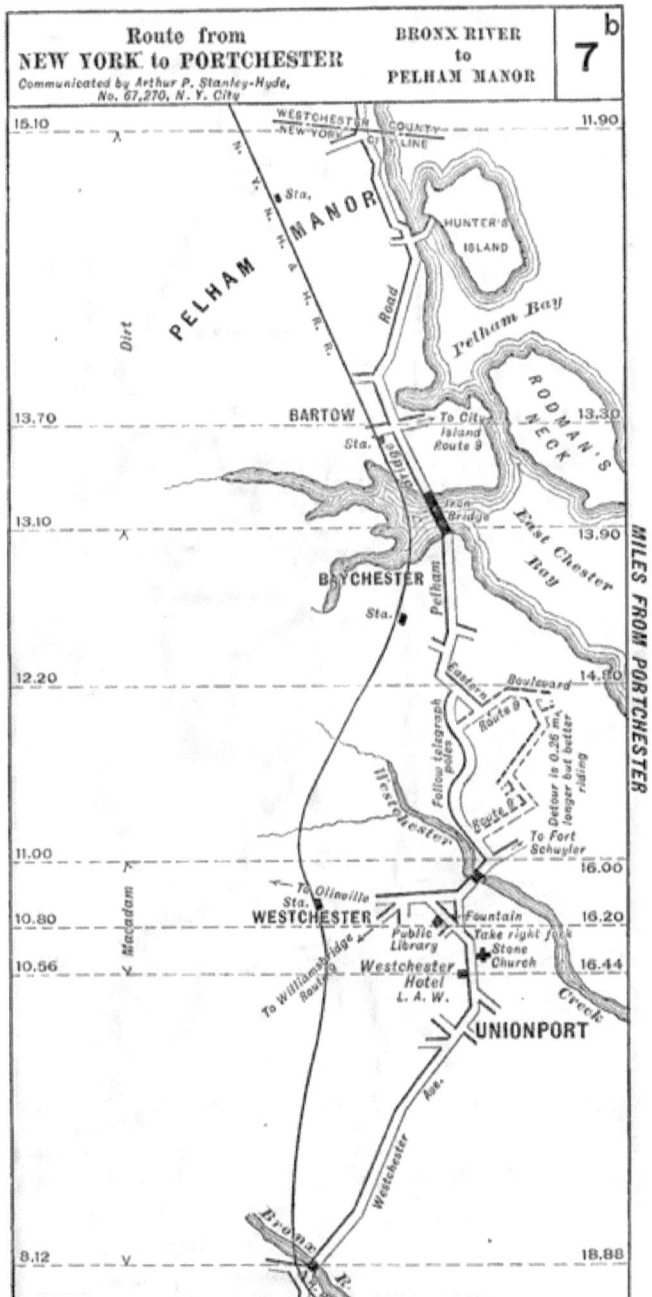

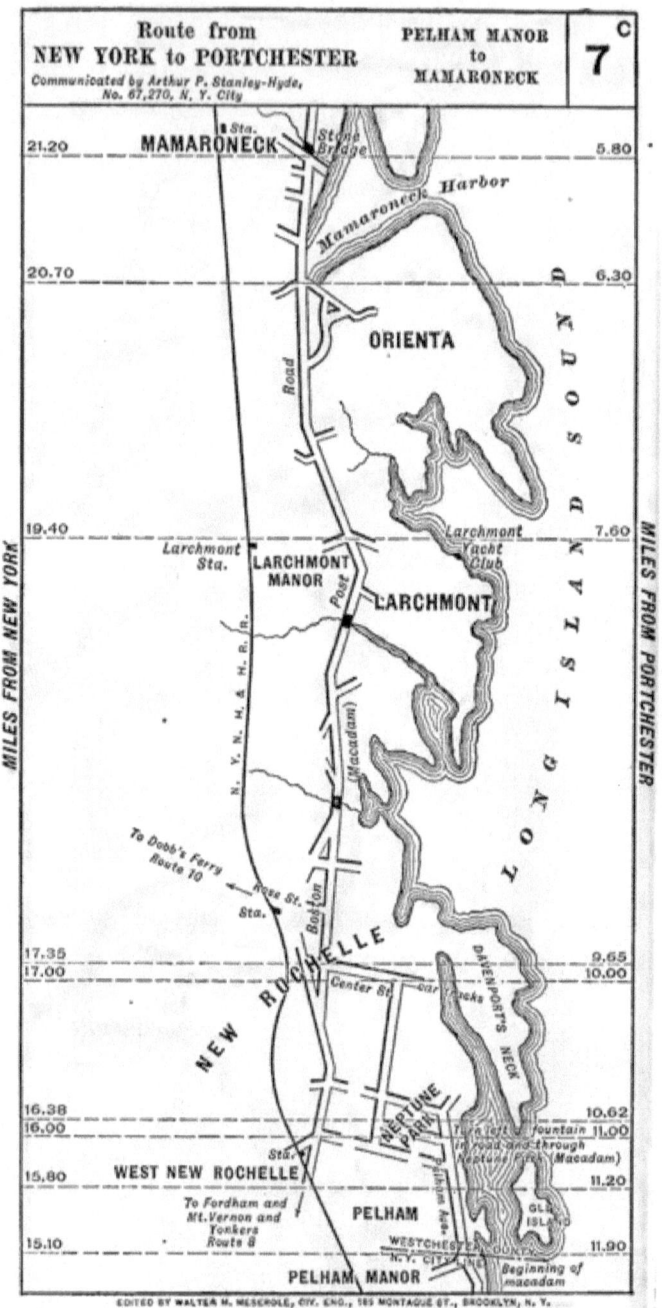

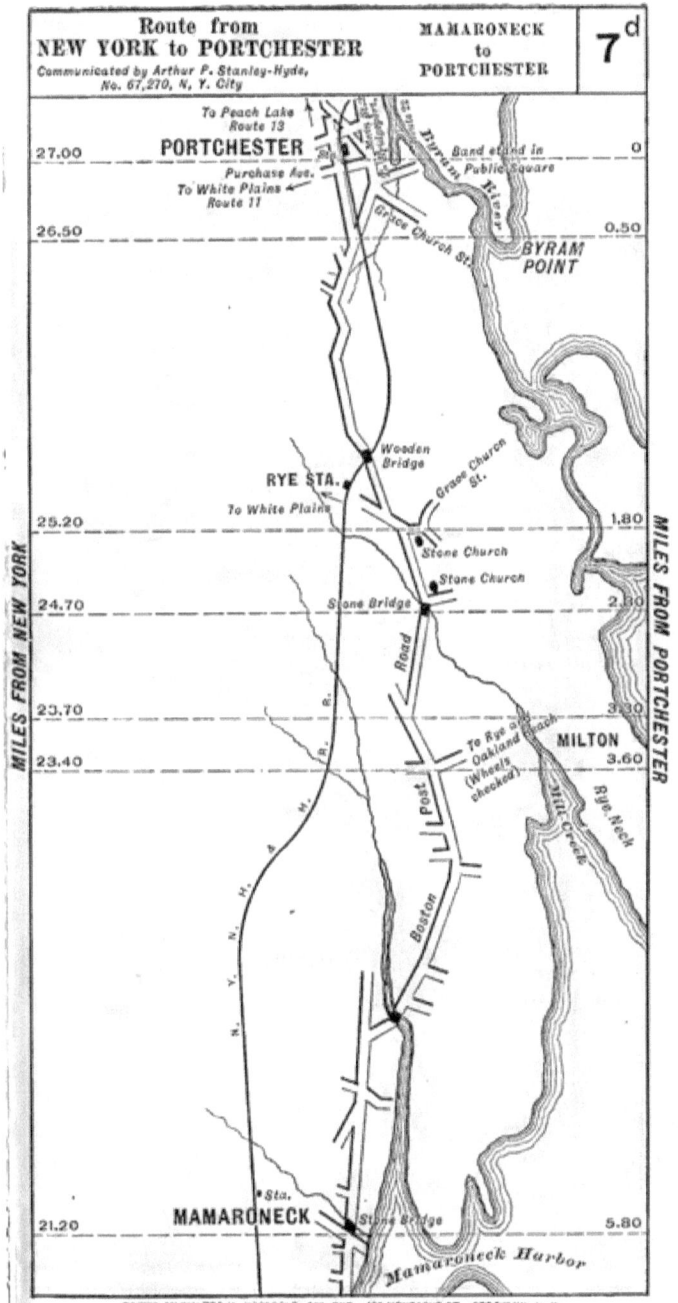

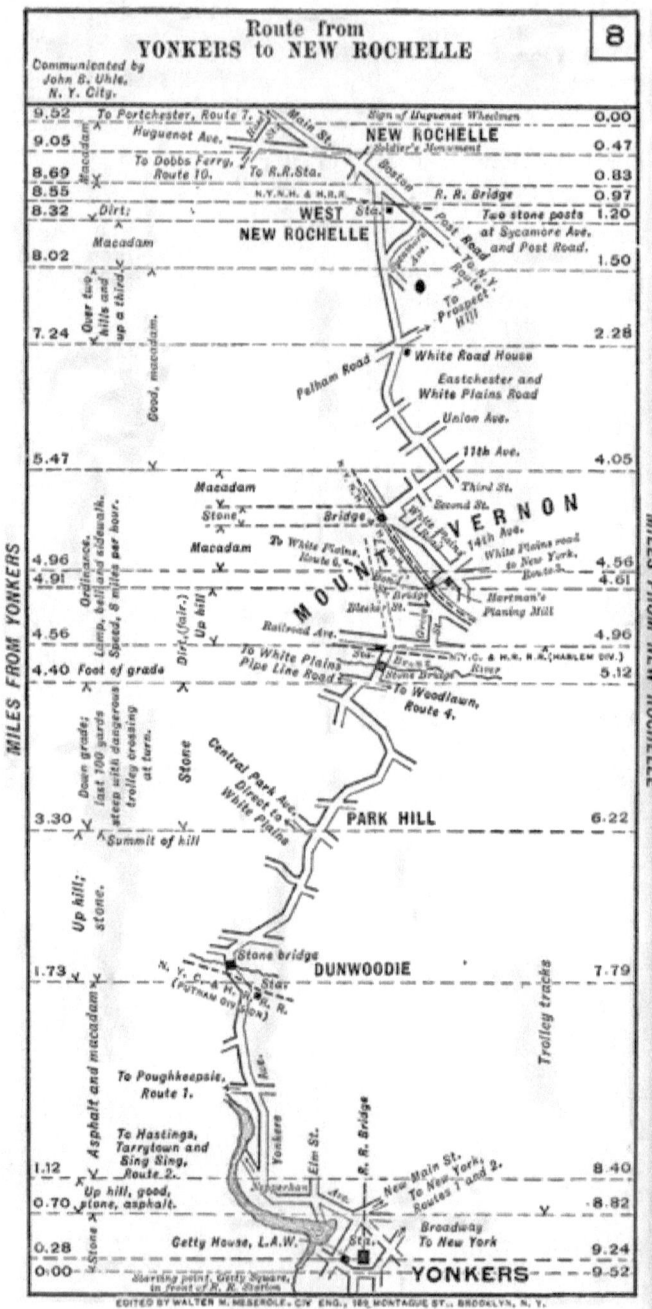

| | Route from YONKERS to CITY ISLAND | YONKERS to MORRIS PARK | 9a |

Communicated by John B. Uhle, No. 61,156, N. Y. City.

MILES FROM YONKERS / MILES FROM CITY ISLAND

Miles from Yonkers	Description	Miles from City Island
8.13	N.Y., N.H. & H. R.R. HARLEM RIVER BRANCH. Trolley tracks turn here to right to West Farms. Park Entrance	7.56
	Follow trolley tracks to front of Morris Park Race Course. Trolley turns here; do not turn but keep straight on. Good macadam.	
7.34	Trolley tracks come in on the left from Mt. Vernon.	8.38
7.24	Up small grade	8.46
7.06	Up grade. White Plains Road. Good Macadam	8.66
	Entrance to Bronx Park. Over small sharp grade.	
6.61	Good macadam. Route 5	9.11
	To Fordham, Route 5.	
	Good macadam, moderate hill.	
	BRONX PARK	
5.85	Bridge over R. R. Route 5	9.87
5.61	Dirt	10.11
	To Washington Bridge, Routes 3 and 5, and Williamsbridge, Route 6.	
	Excellent macadam for half the distance, then good dirt road.	
	To New York, Route 4.	
4.78	Bottom of hill. To Mt. Vernon and White Plains, Routes 3 and 5.	10.94
	Poor macadam.	
4.53	Top of hill.	11.19
	WOODLAWN CEMETERY	
	Gun Hill Road	
	Poor macadam.	
3.93	Y.	11.79
	Poor sandy road, no side path.	
	To Van Courtlandt Park	
3.52	Macadam ends. To Mt. Vernon, Route 4.	12.20
	To Woodlawn	
	Up moderate grade; excellent macadam.	
	Mosholu St.	
3.01		12.71
	Pass under R. R. bridge over small grade; excellent macadam.	
	To New York, Routes 1 and 2.	
	Mosholu Bridge	
2.15		13.57
	Down grade, rough macadam, narrow roadway.	
1.55		14.16
	Up grade, good macadam.	
1.12	Asphalt ends.	14.60
0.50	Asphalt begins.	15.22
	Fountain. Repair Shop	
	Over hill; good macadam.	
	R. R. Bridge	
0.00	YONKERS Sta.	15.72
	Route begins in Getty Square in front of railroad station and runs south. Routes 5 and 8. Getty House L.A.W.	

EDITED BY WALTER M. MESEROLE, CIV. ENG., 159 MONTAGUE ST., BROOKLYN, N. Y.

COPYRIGHT, 1898, BY THE NEW YORK STATE DIVISION, L. A. W.

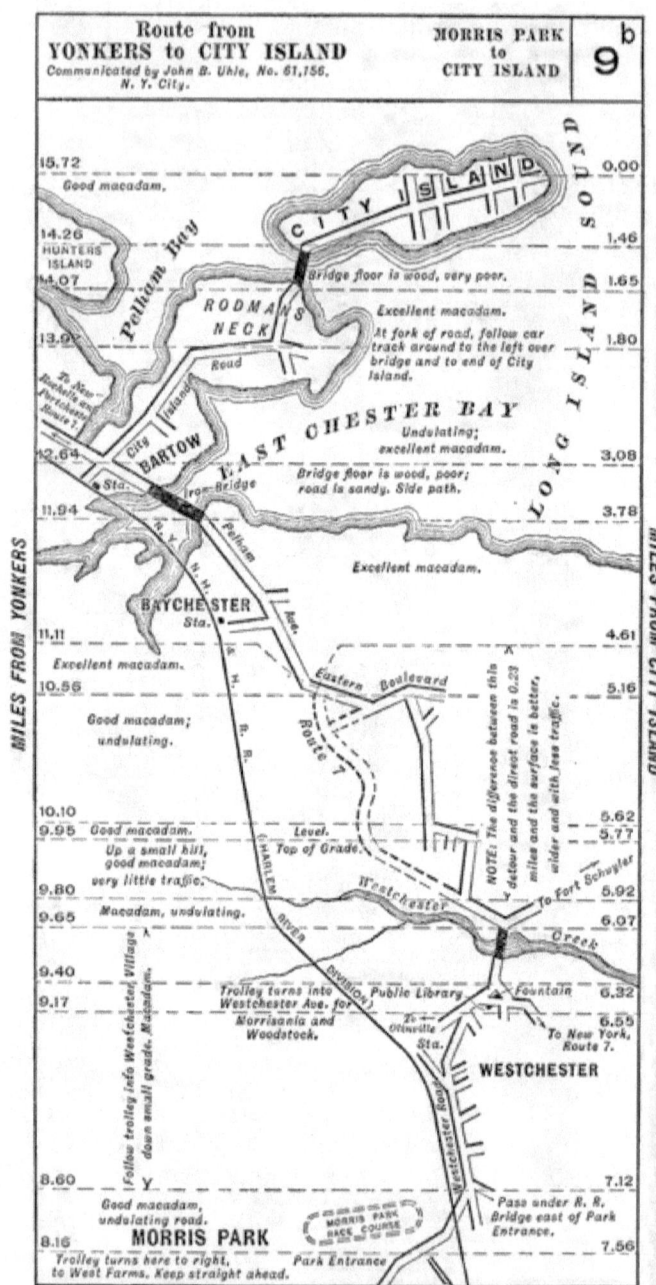

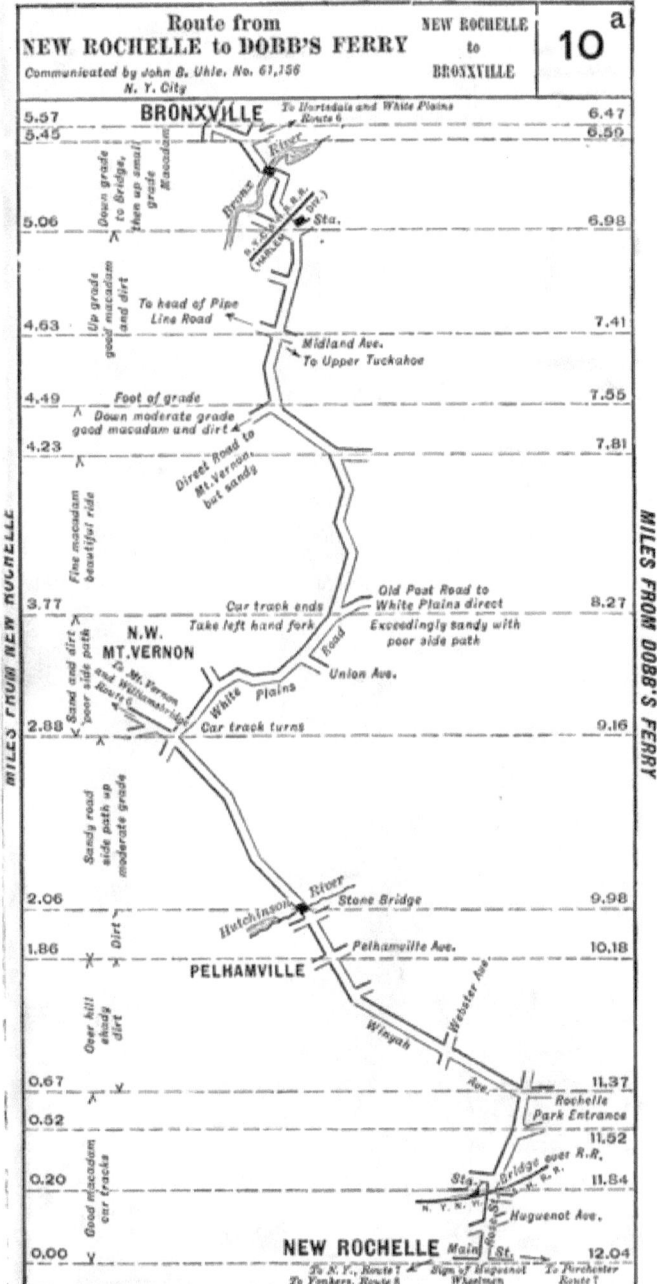

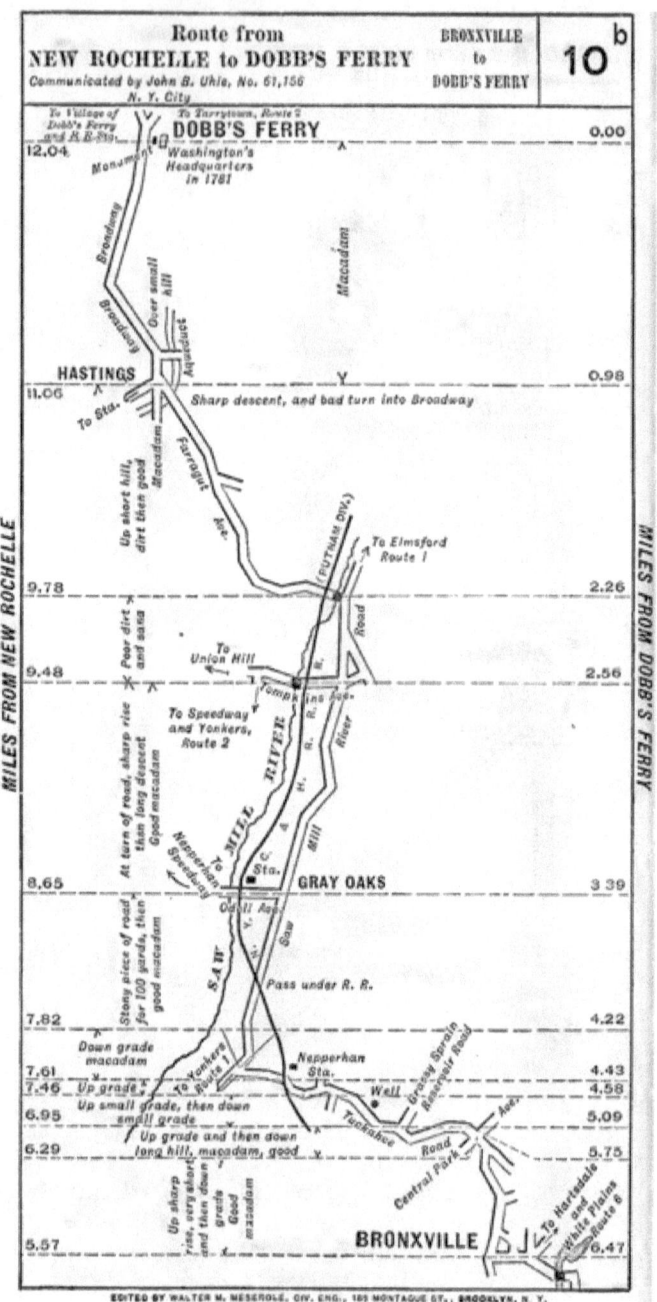

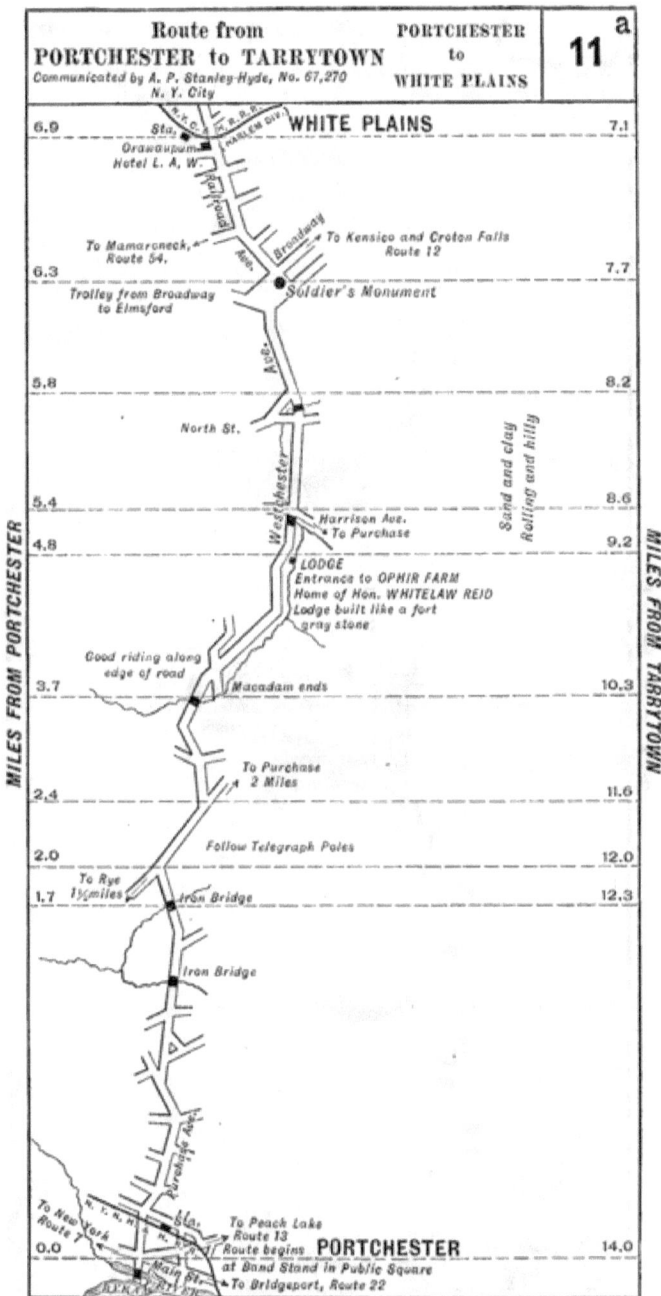

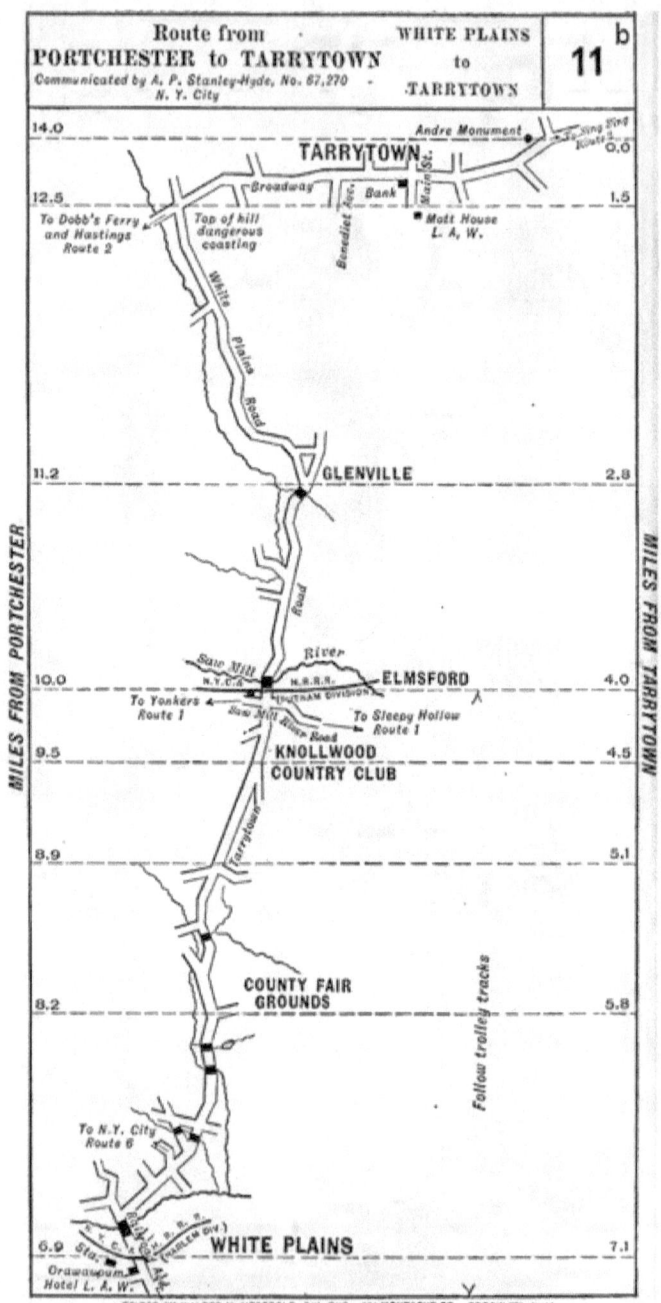

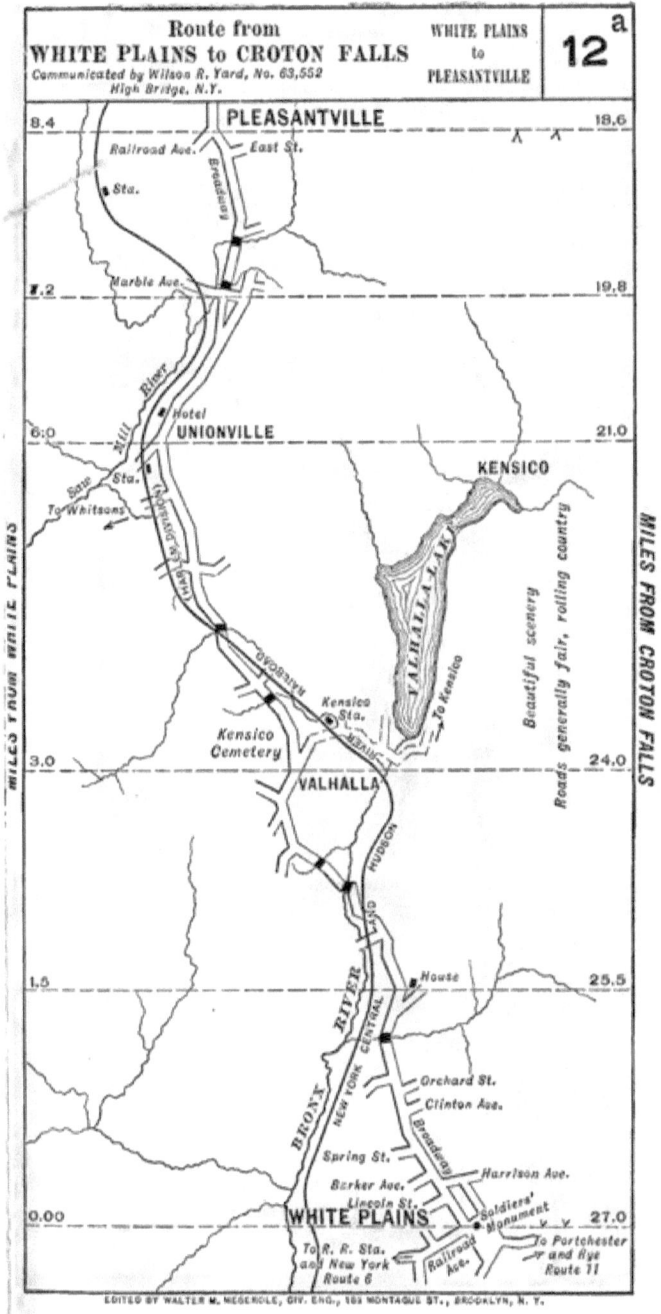

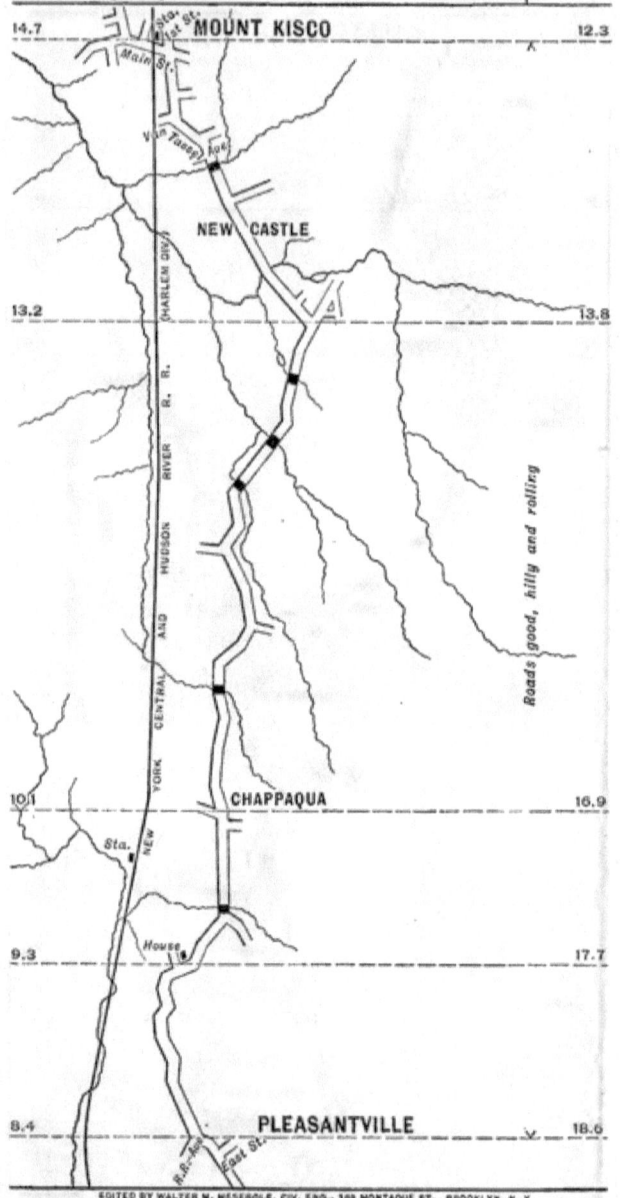

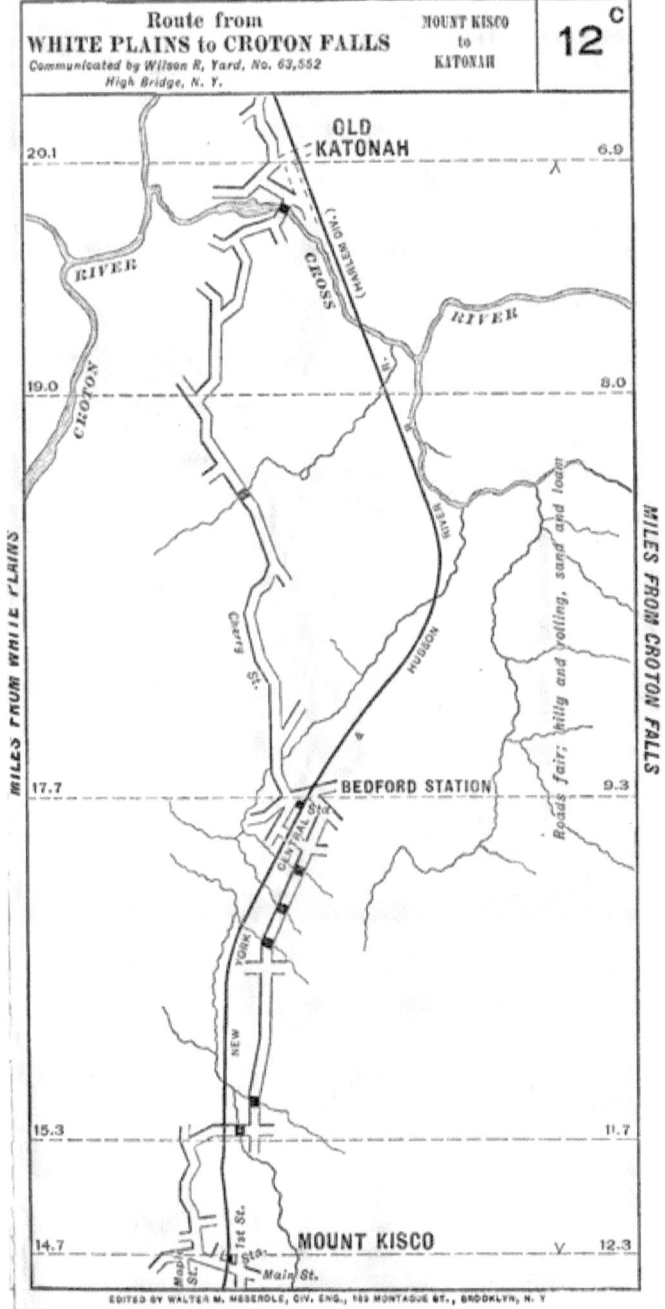

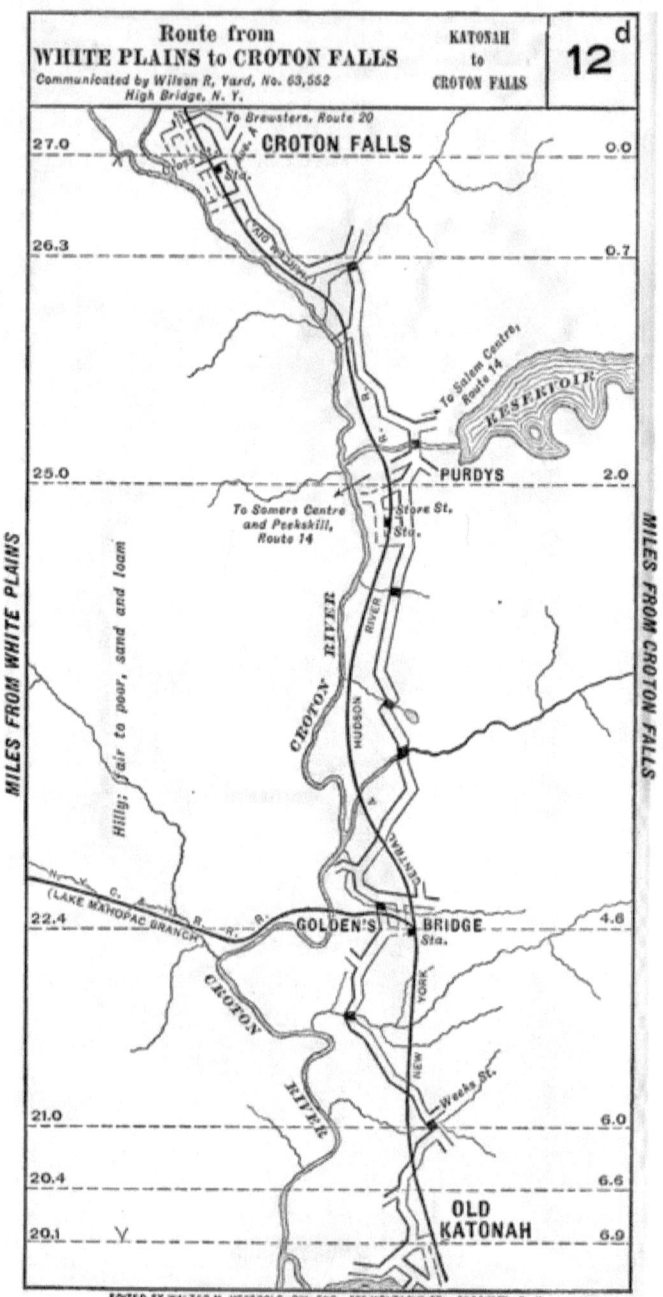

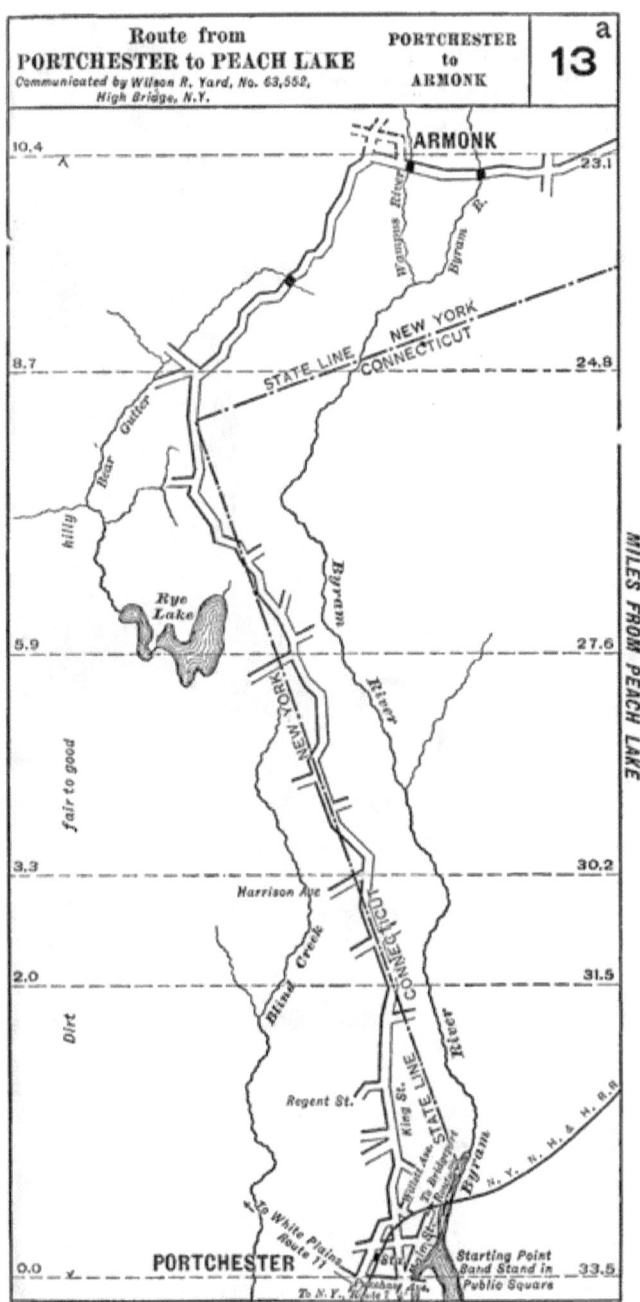

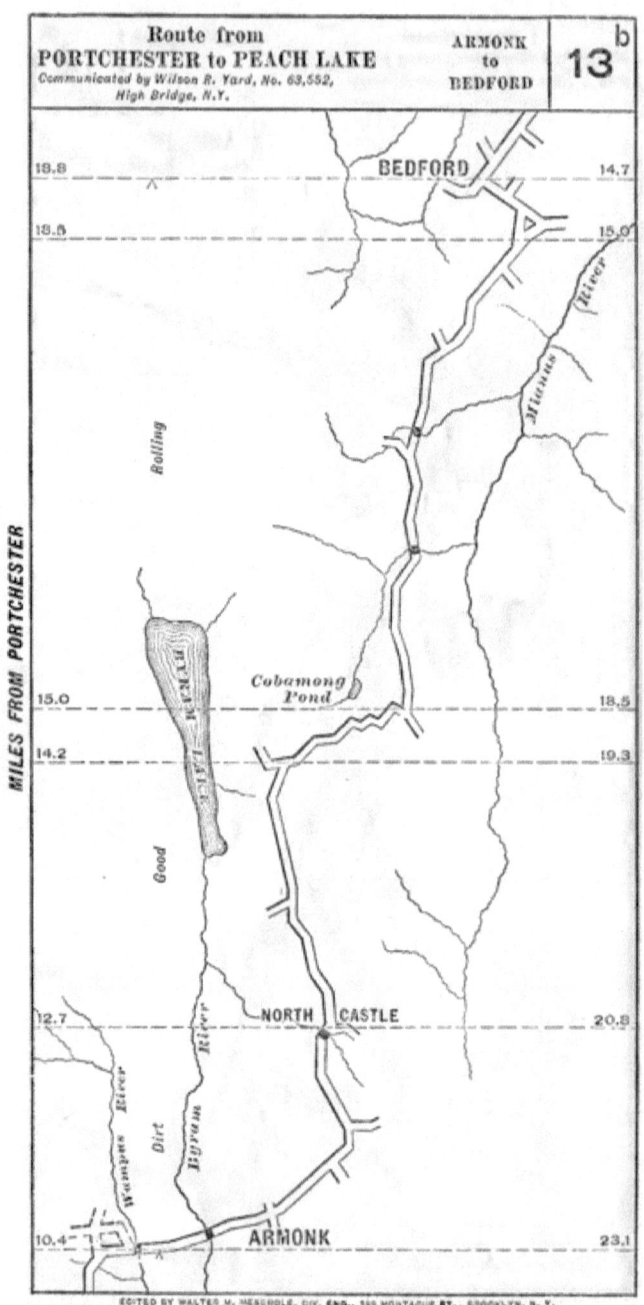

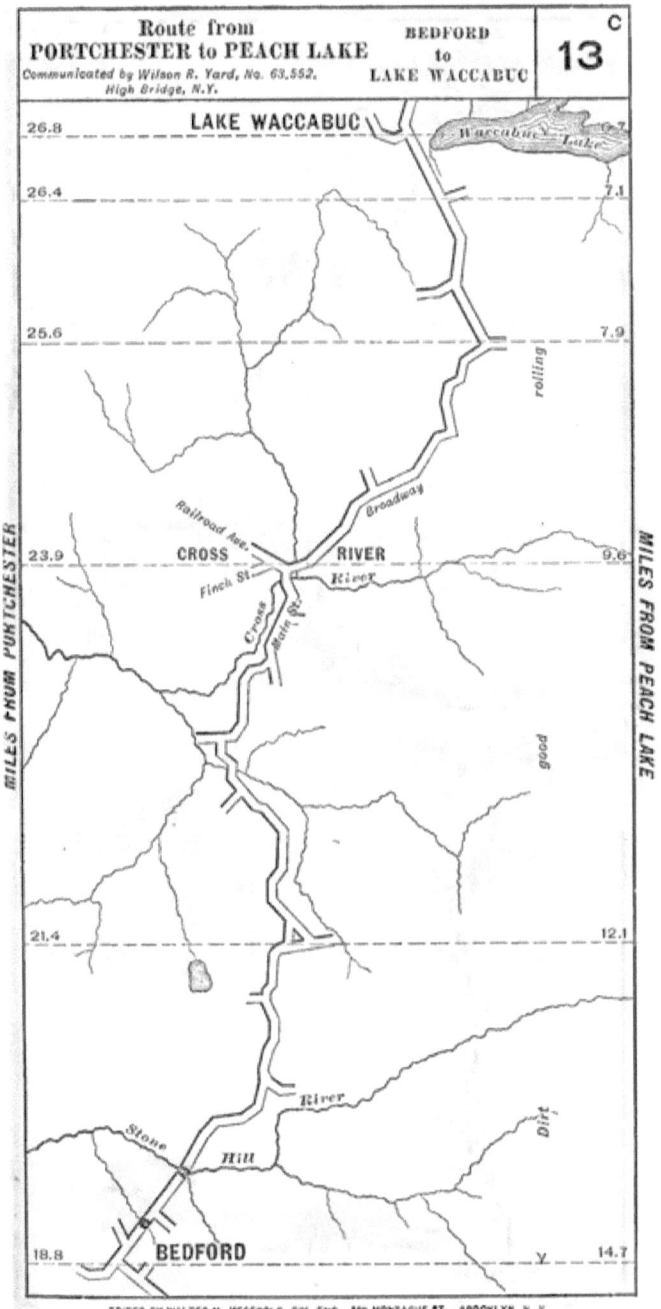

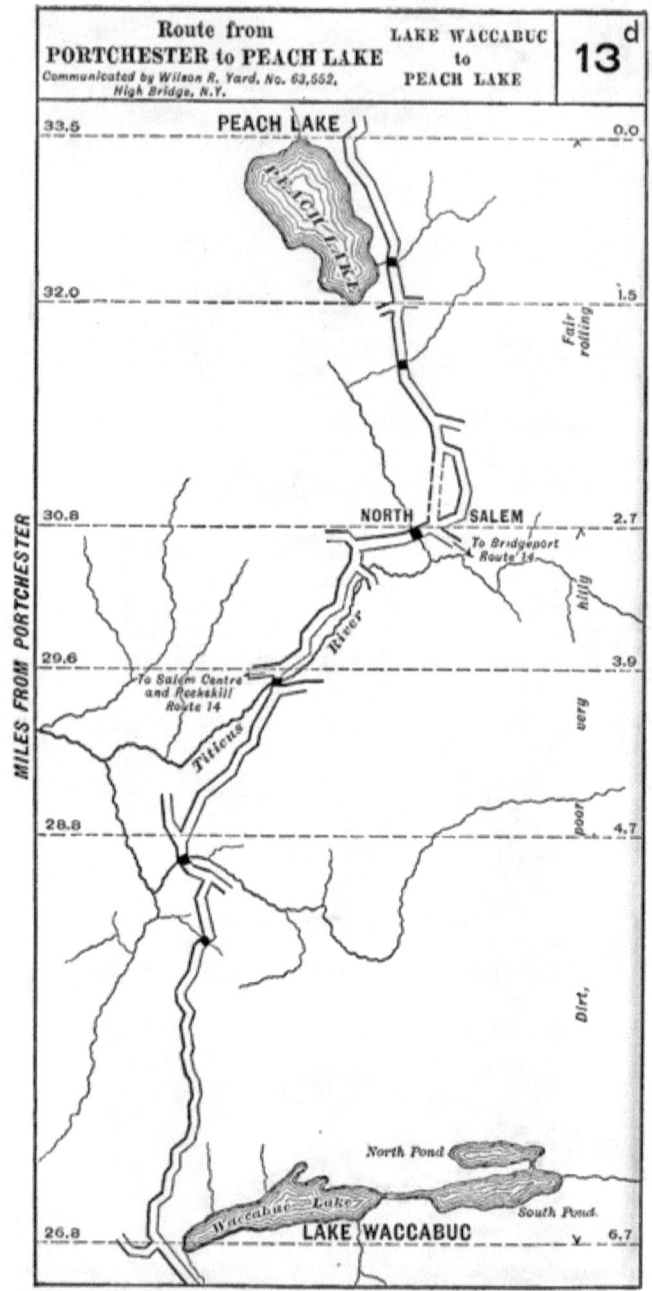

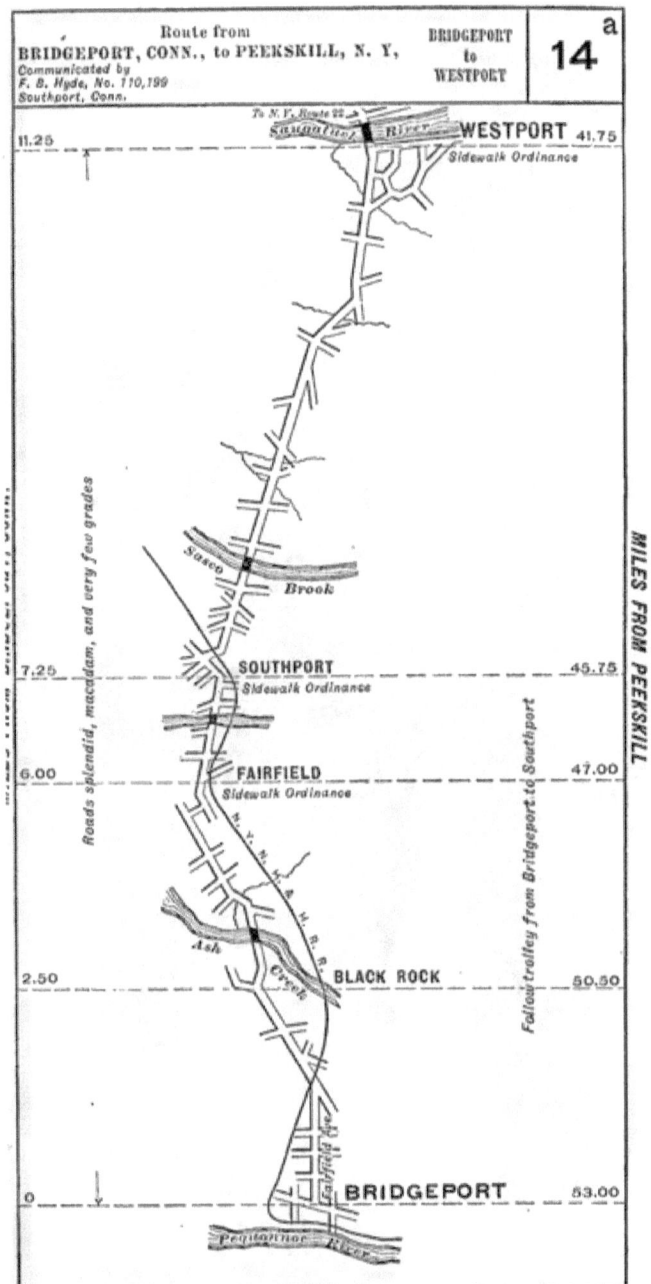

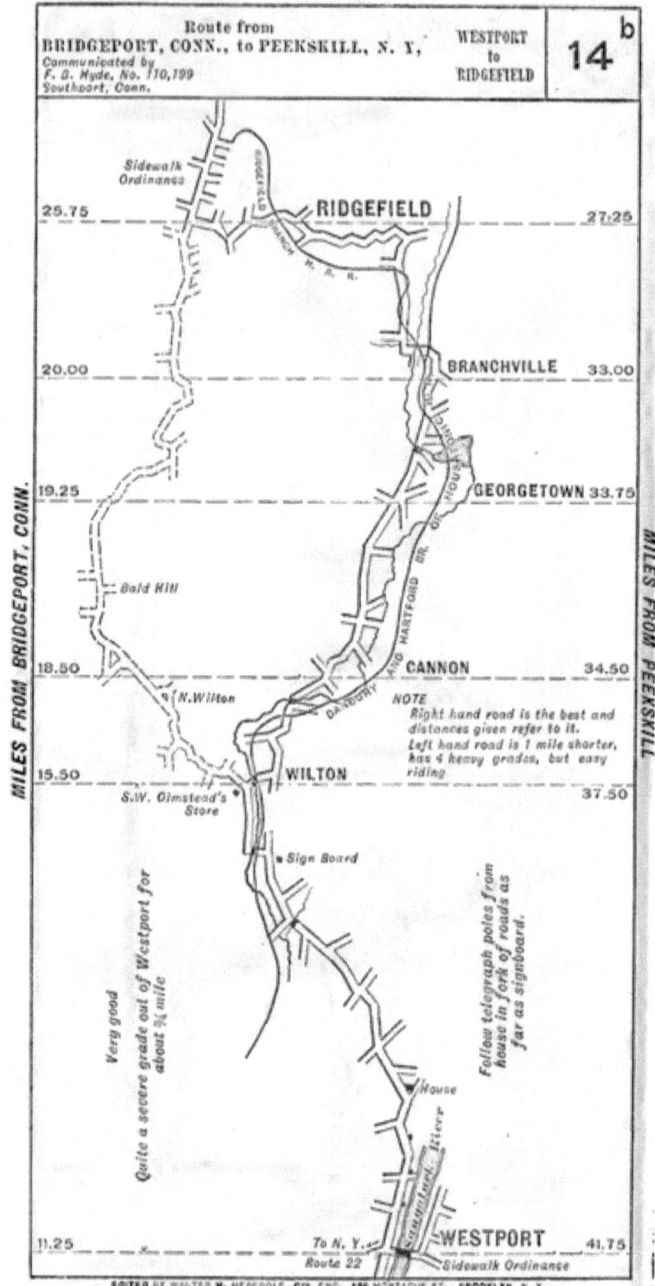

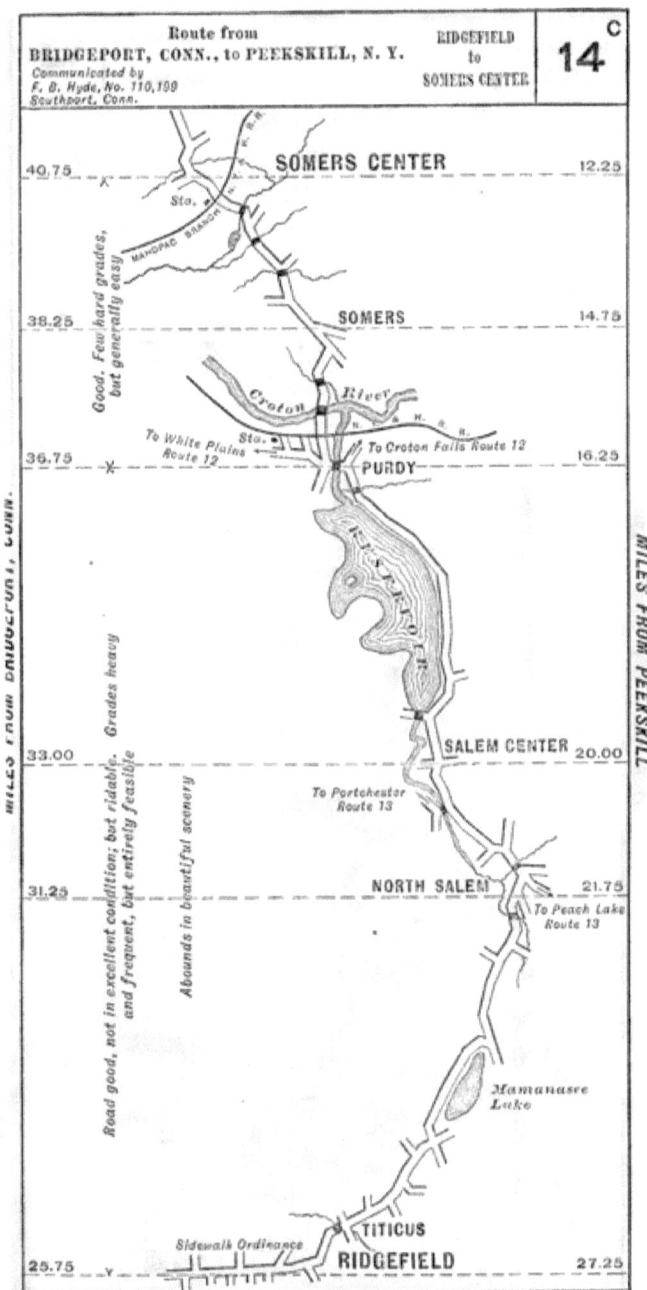

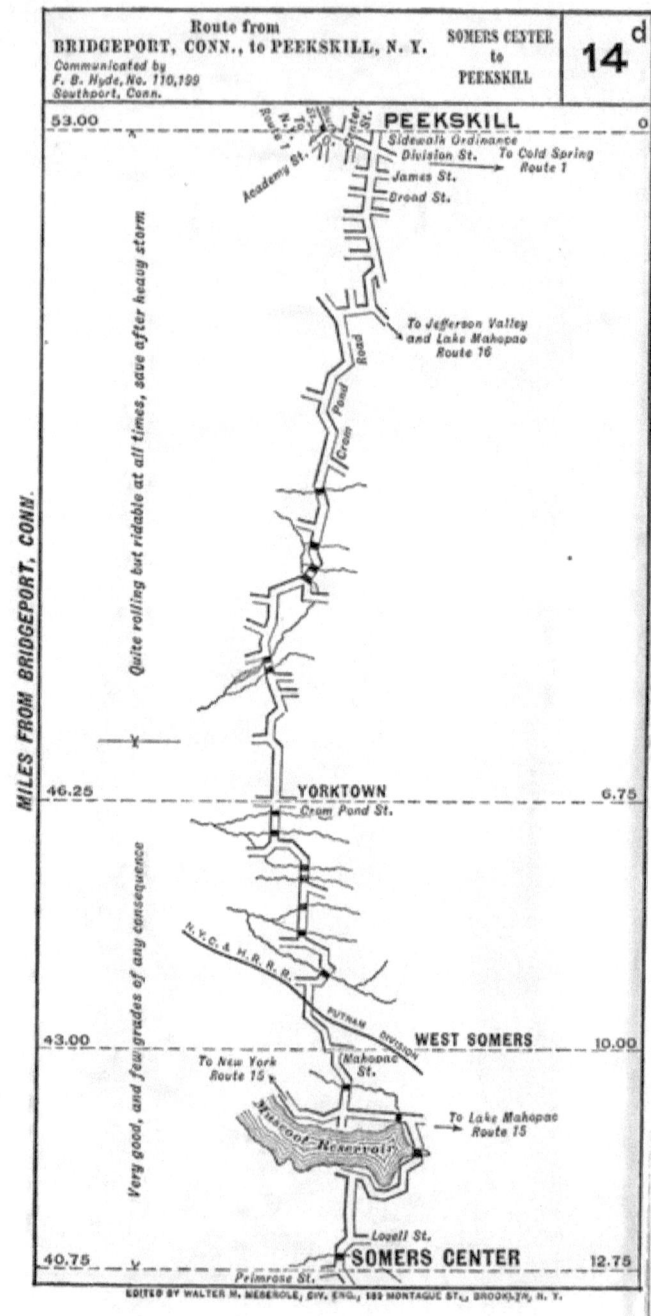

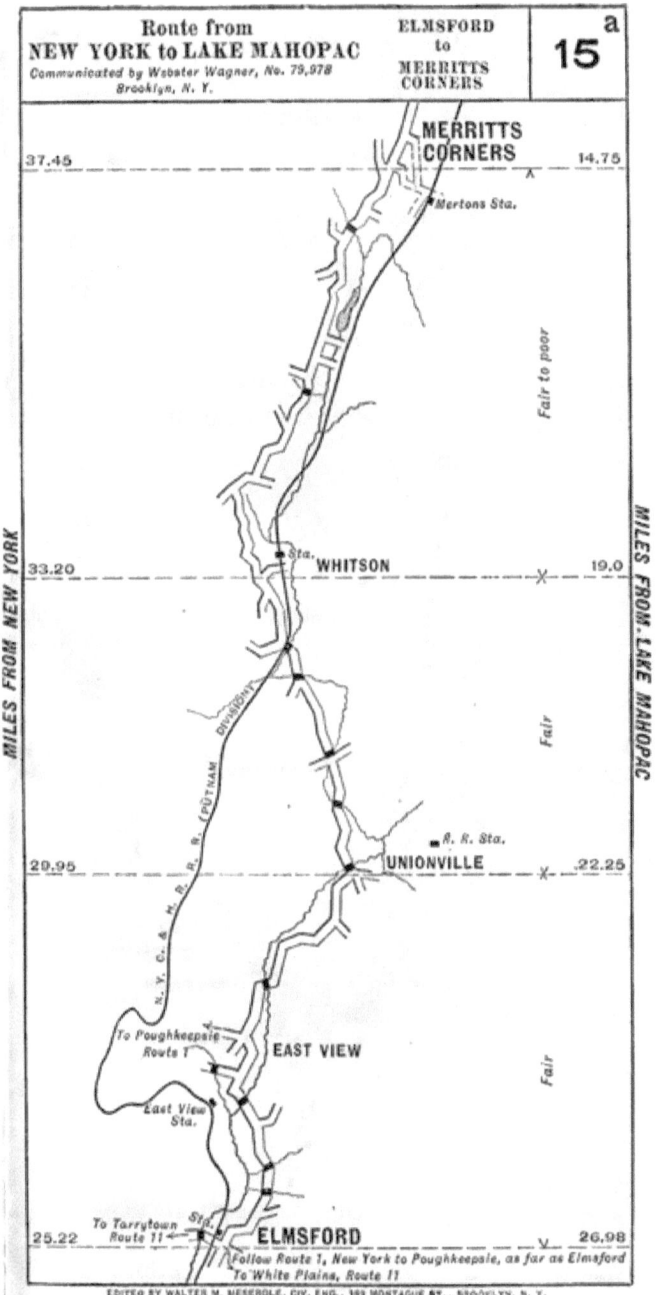

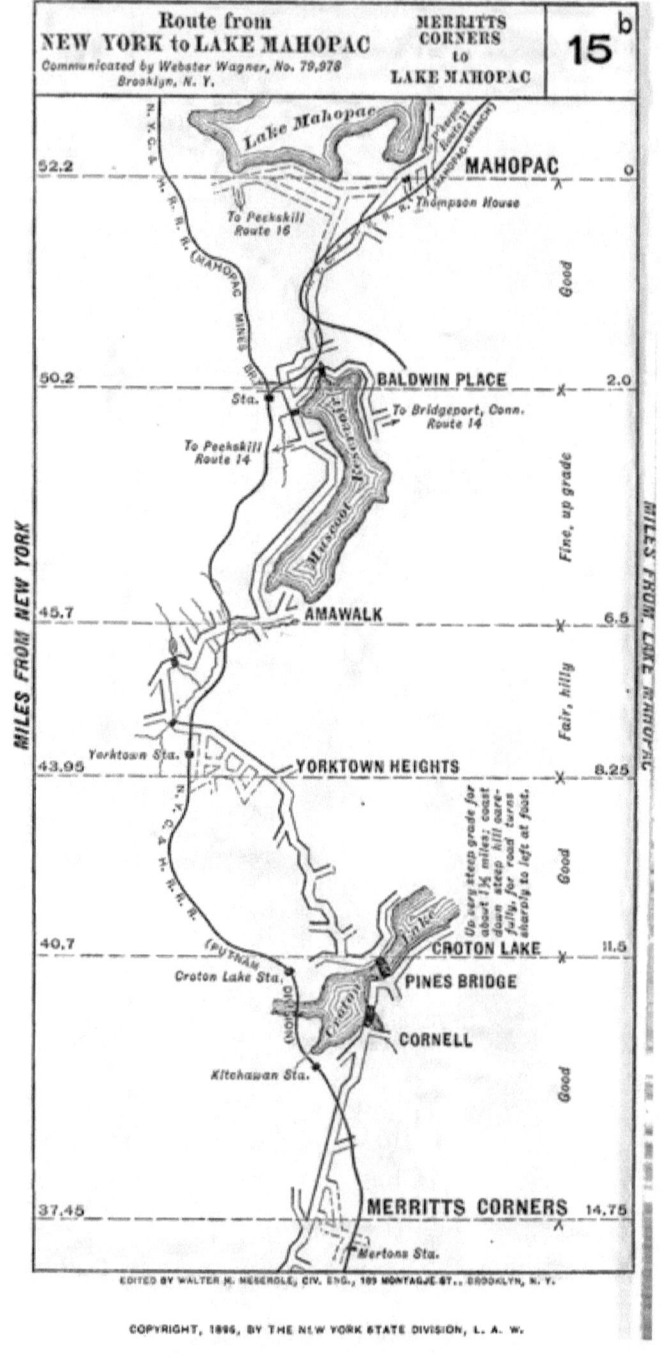

Route from

PEEKSKILL to LAKE MAHOPAC

Communicated by Webster Wagner, No. 79,978
Brooklyn, N. Y.

16

EDITED BY WALTER M. MESEROLE, CIV. ENG., 189 MONTAGUE ST., BROOKLYN, N. Y.

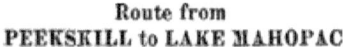

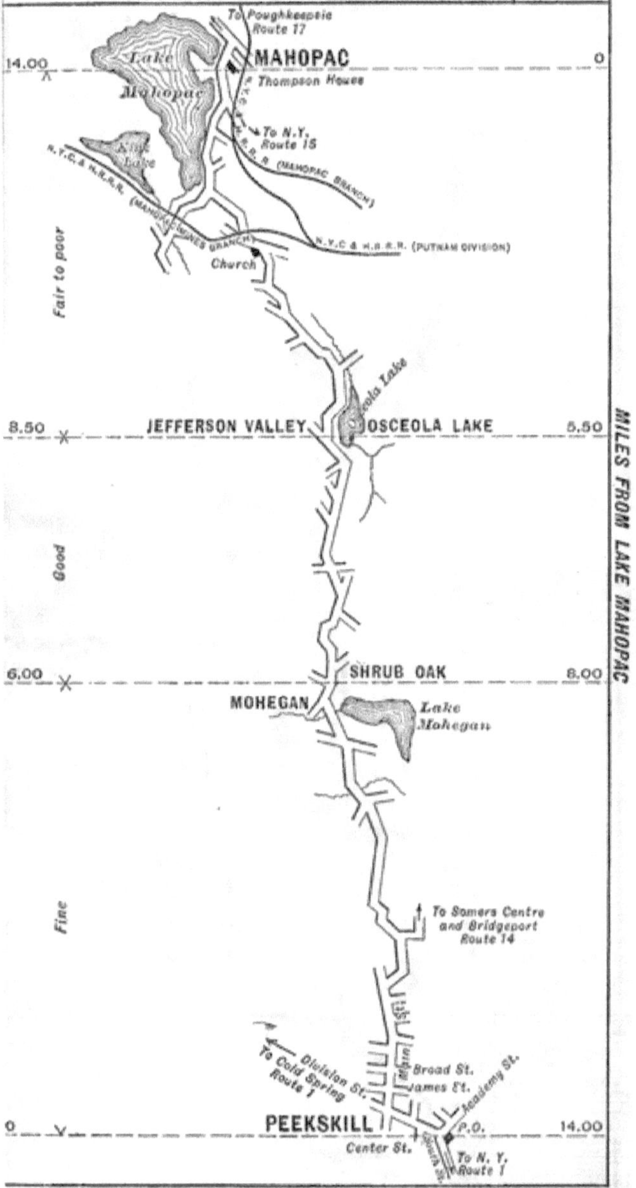

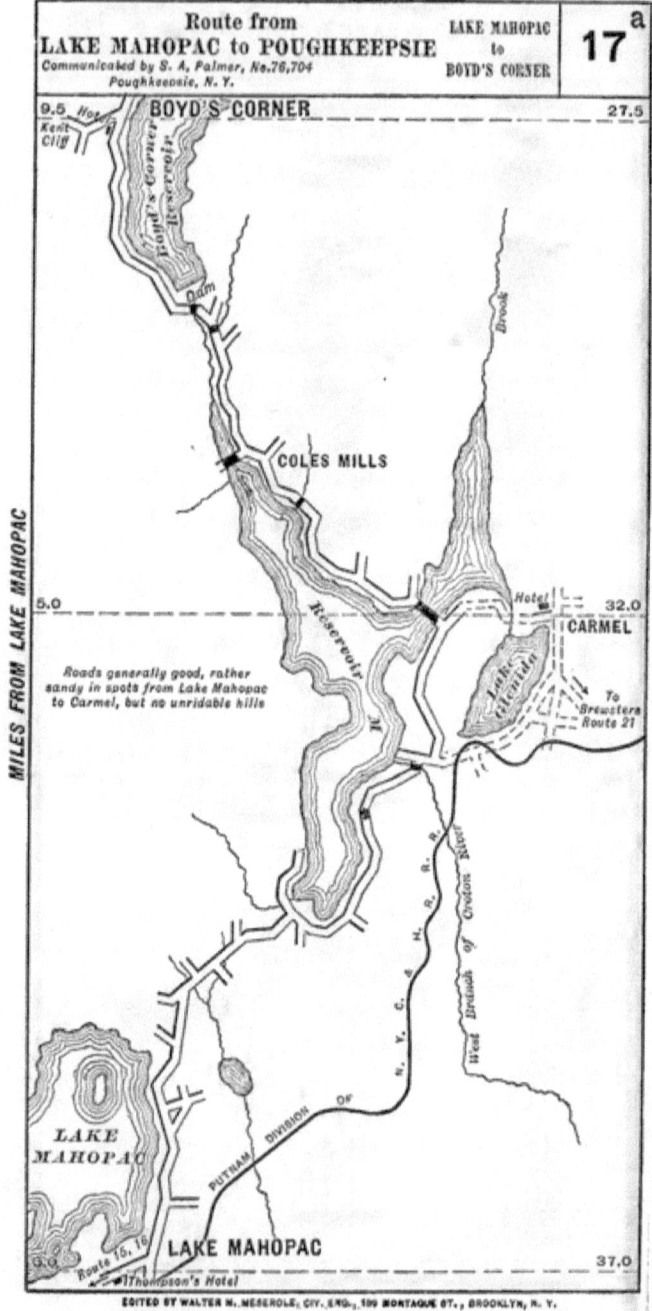

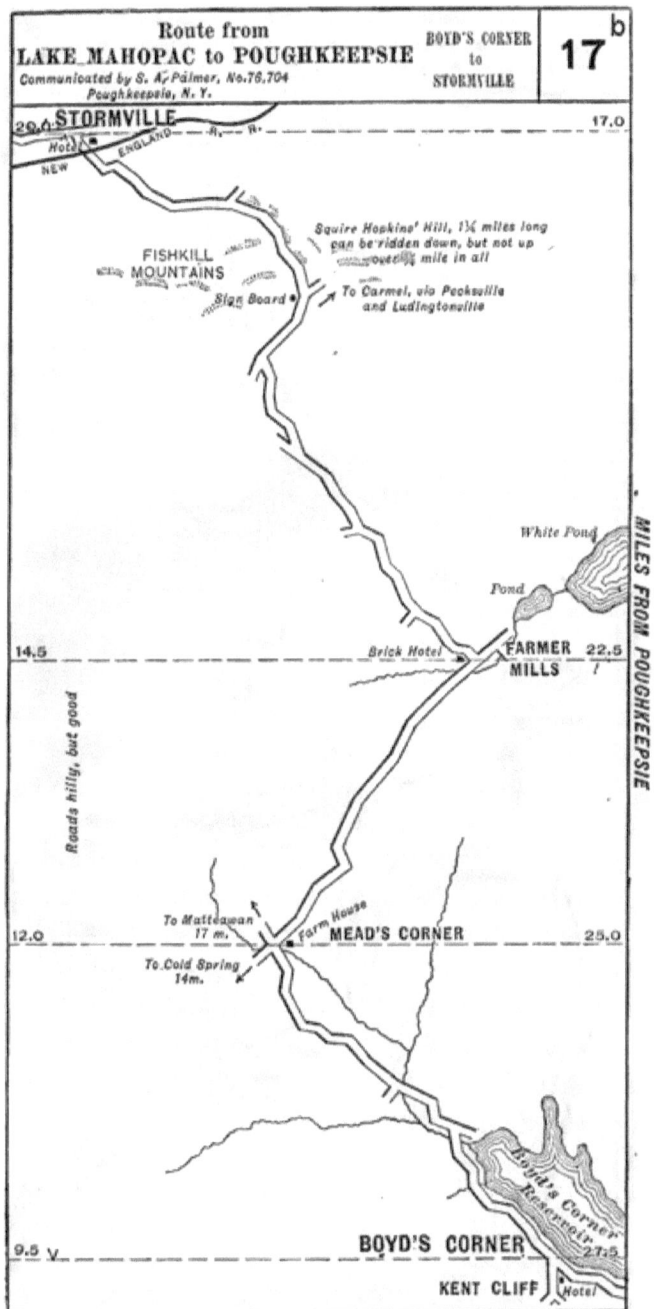

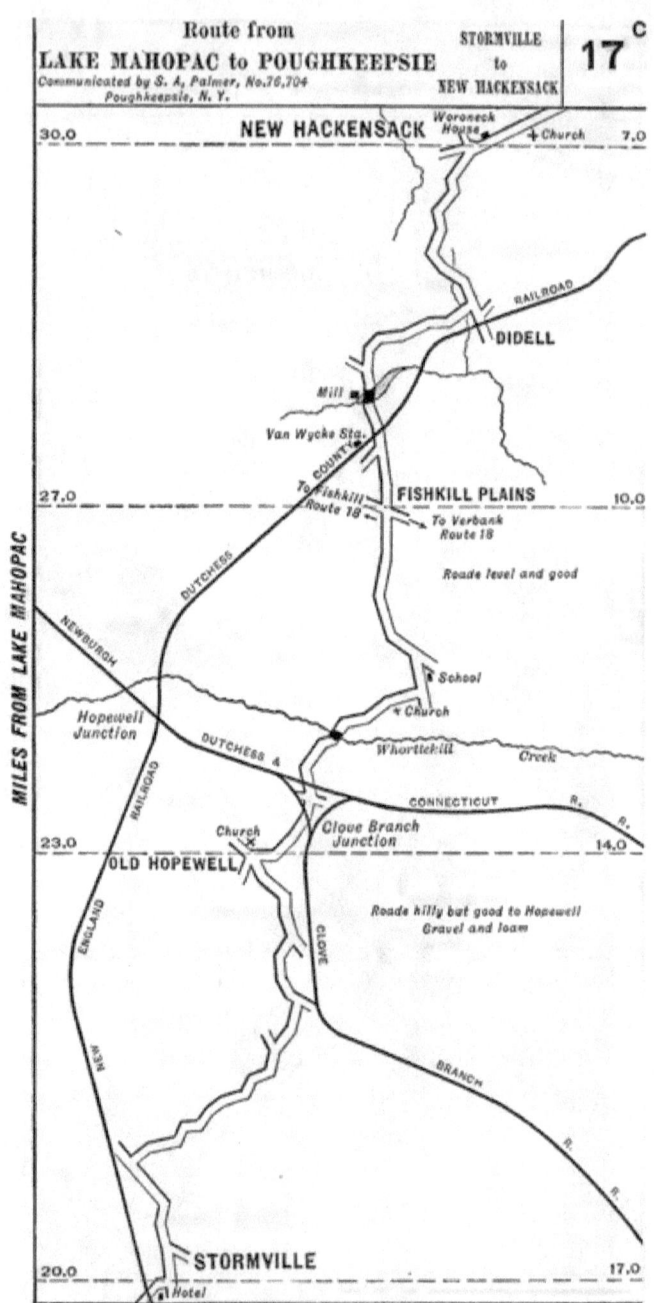

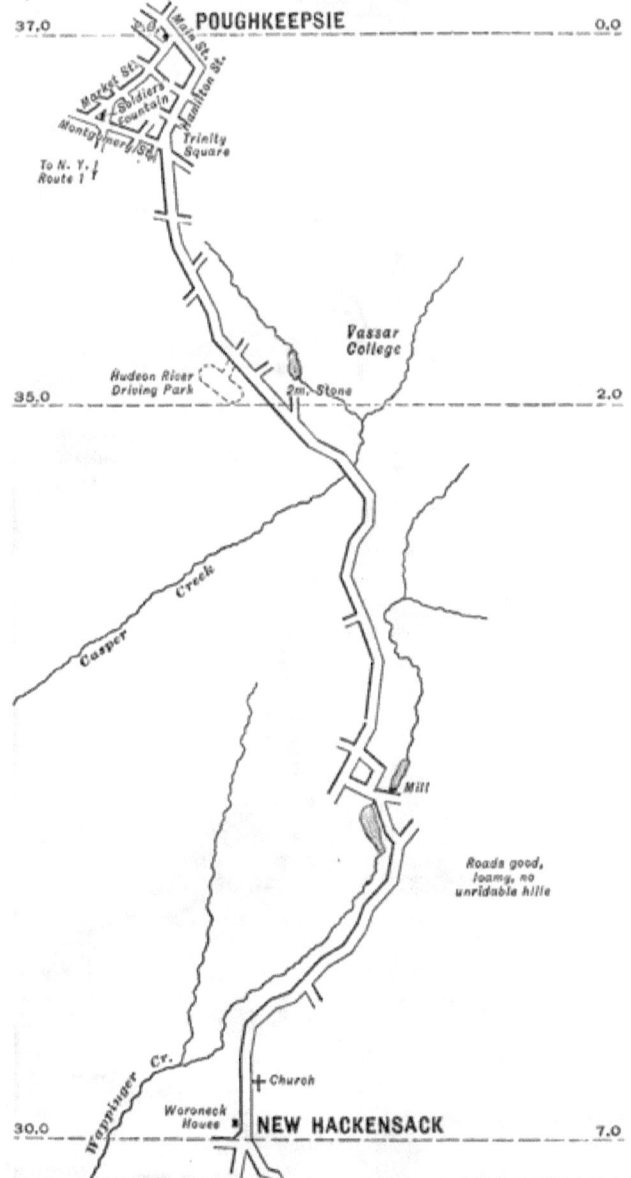

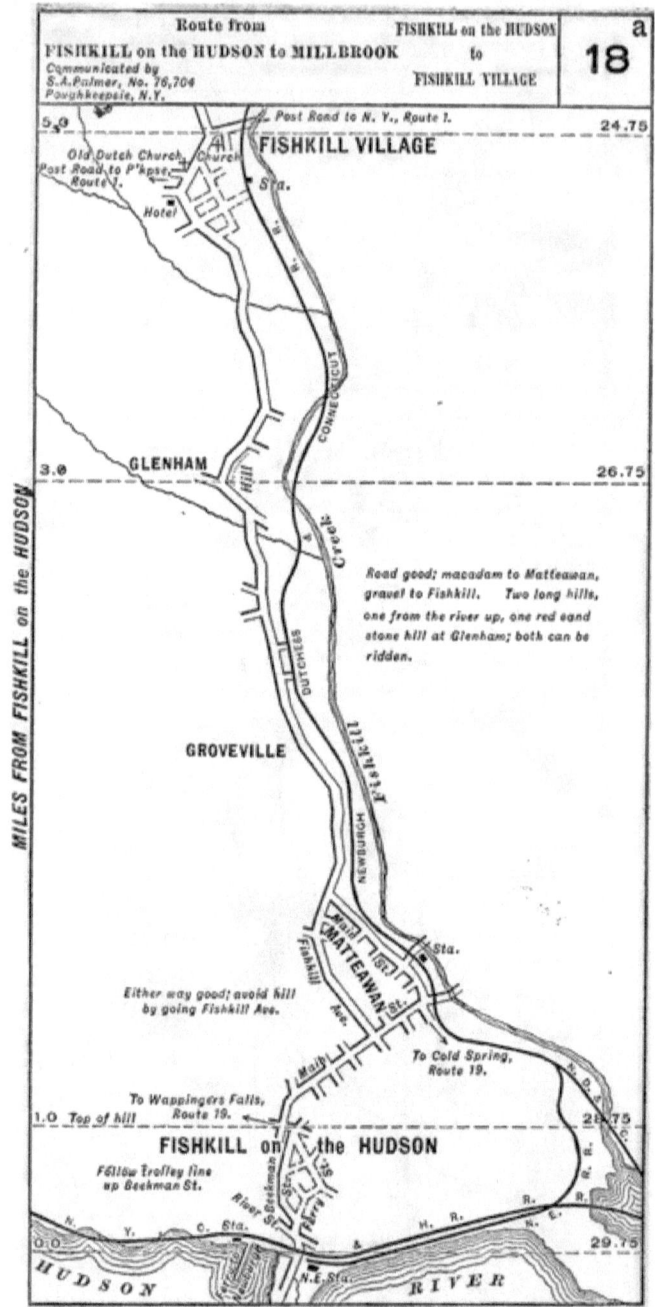

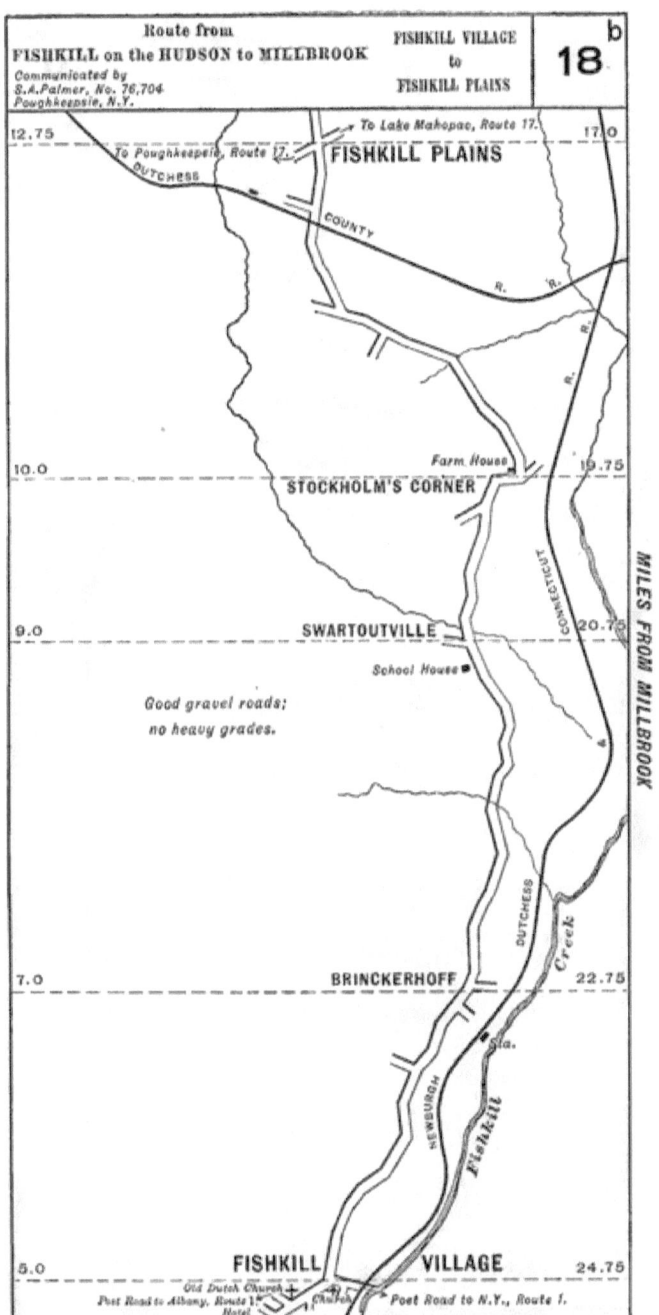

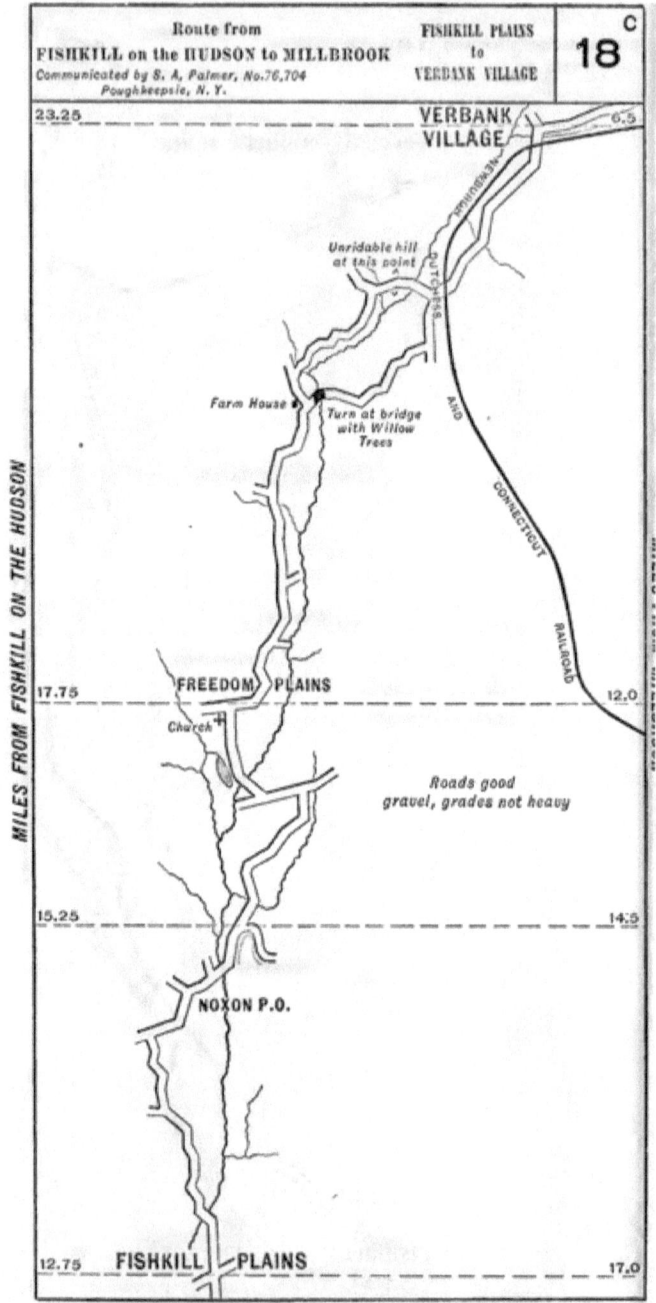

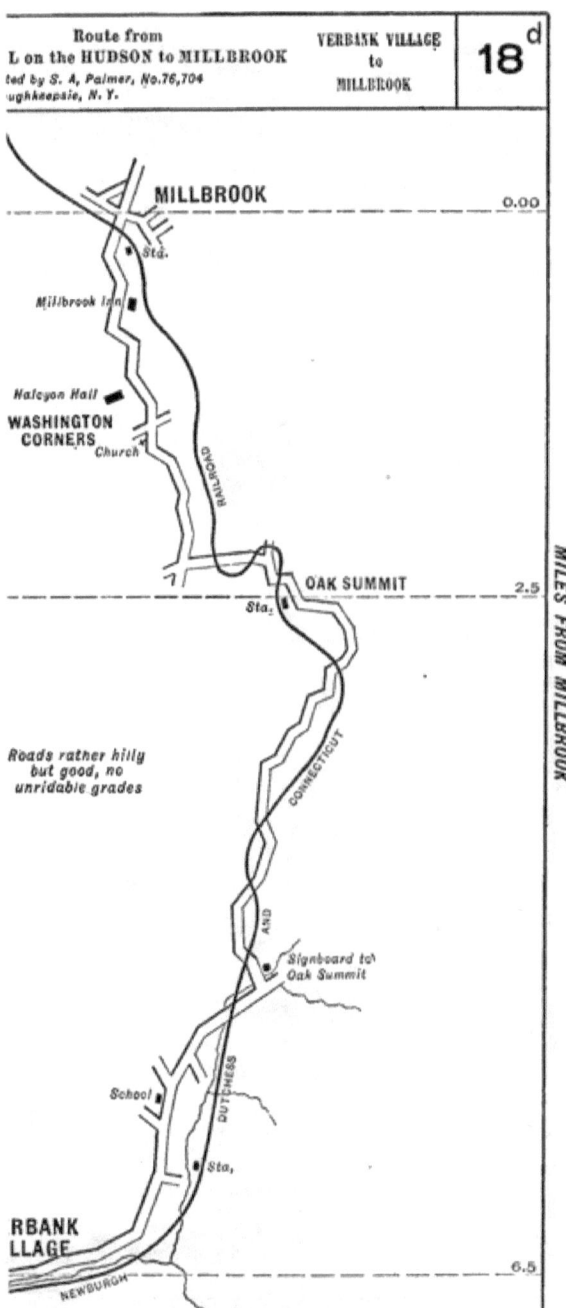

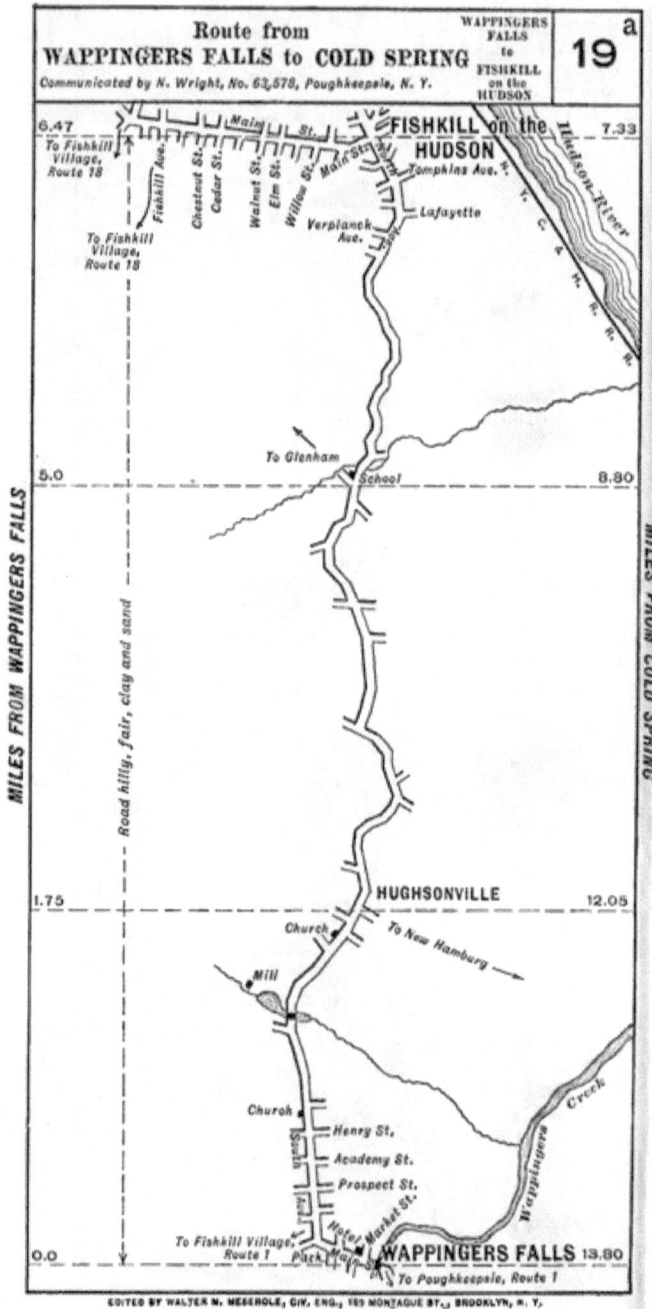

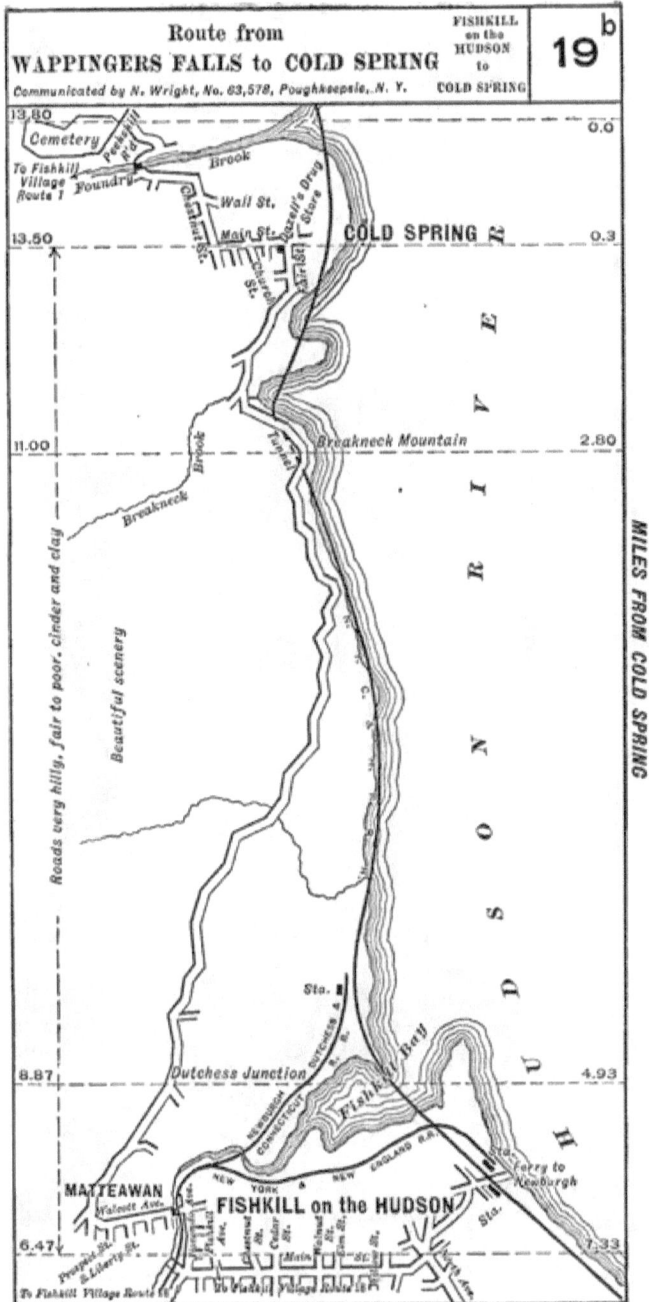

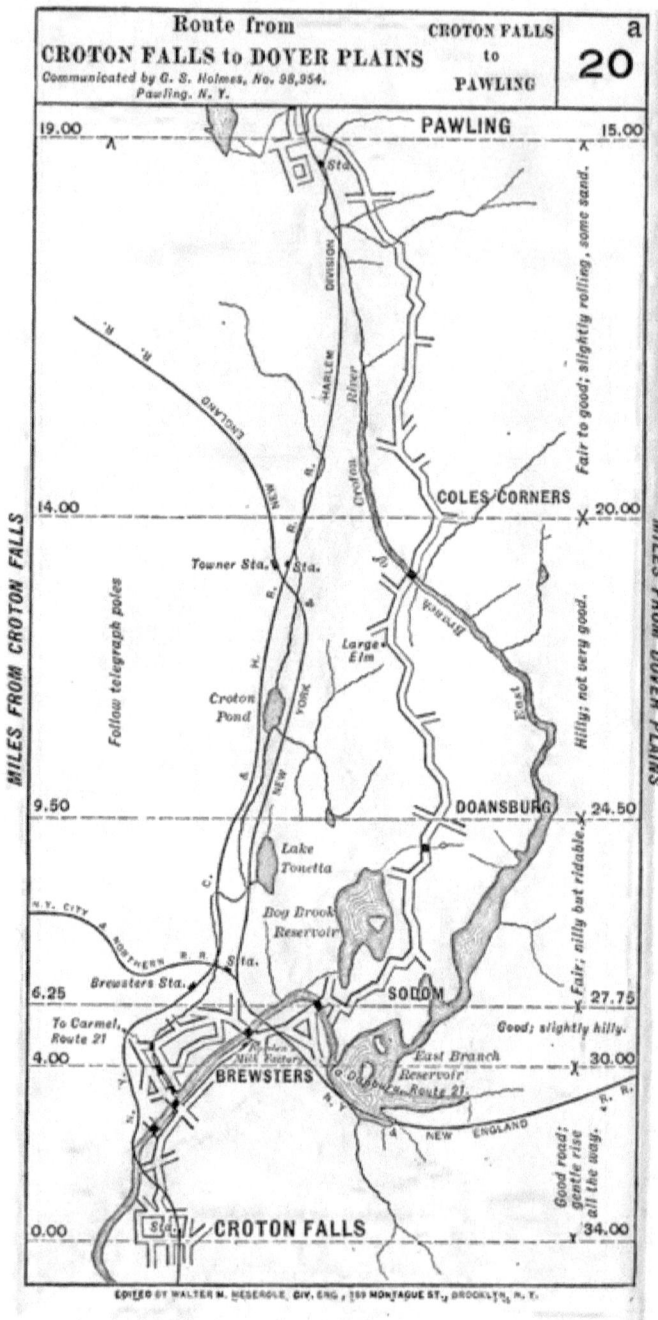

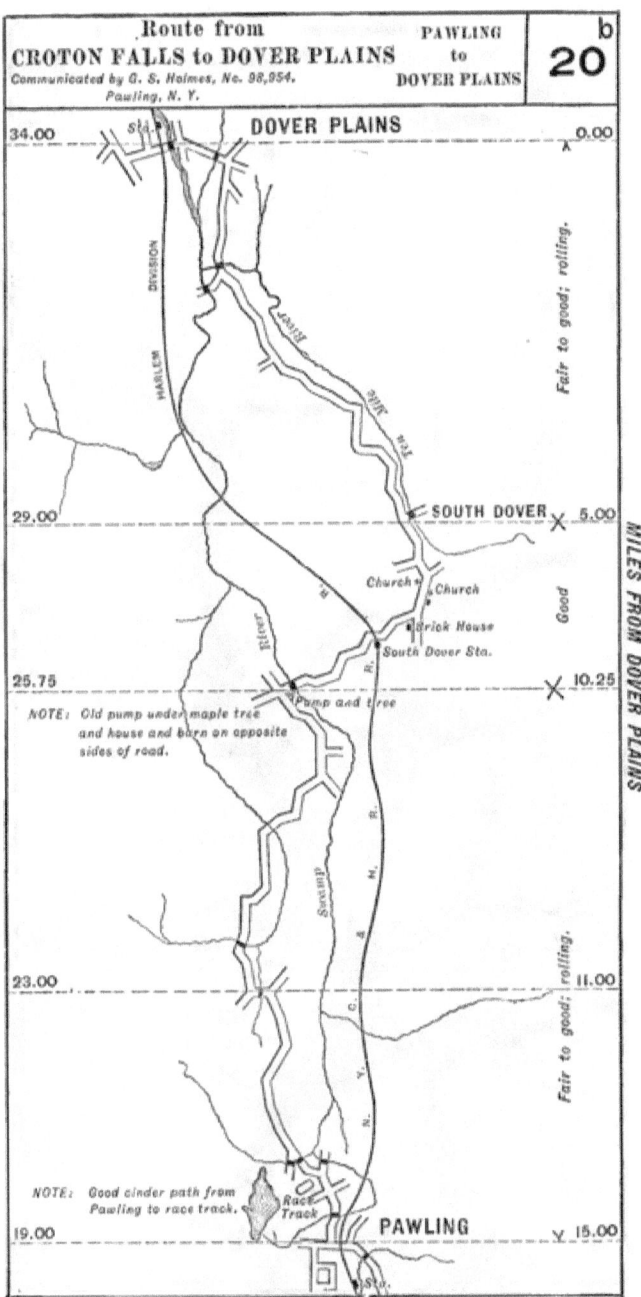

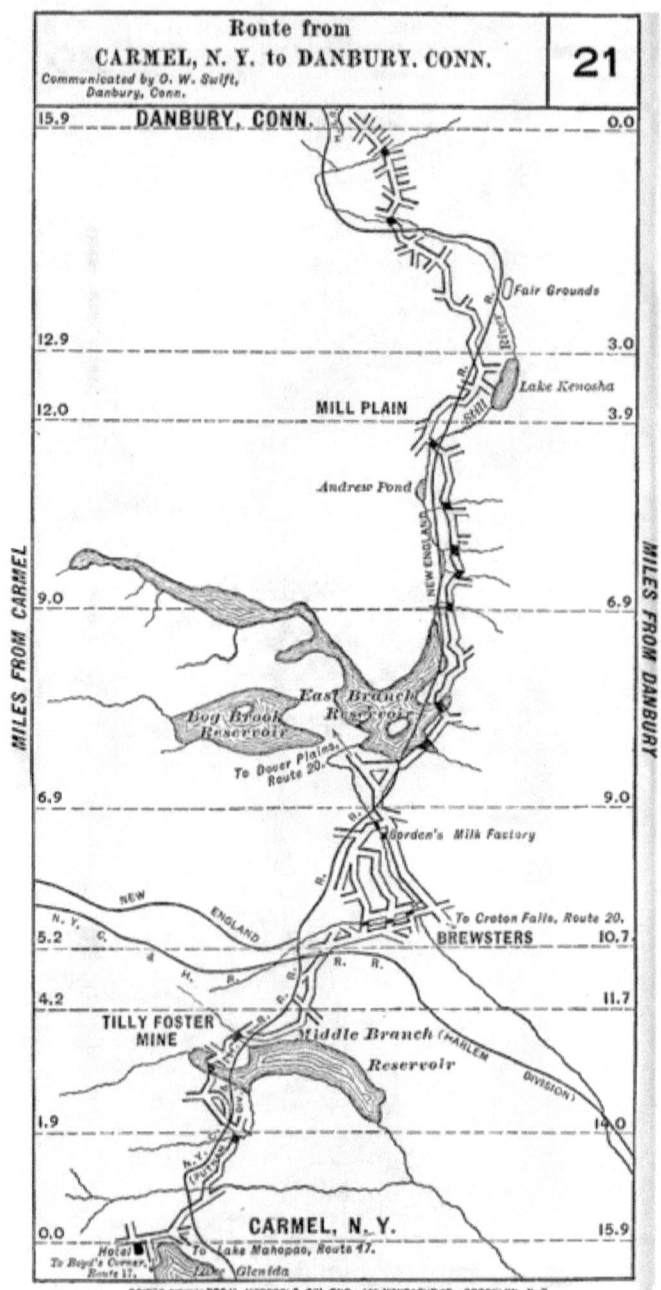

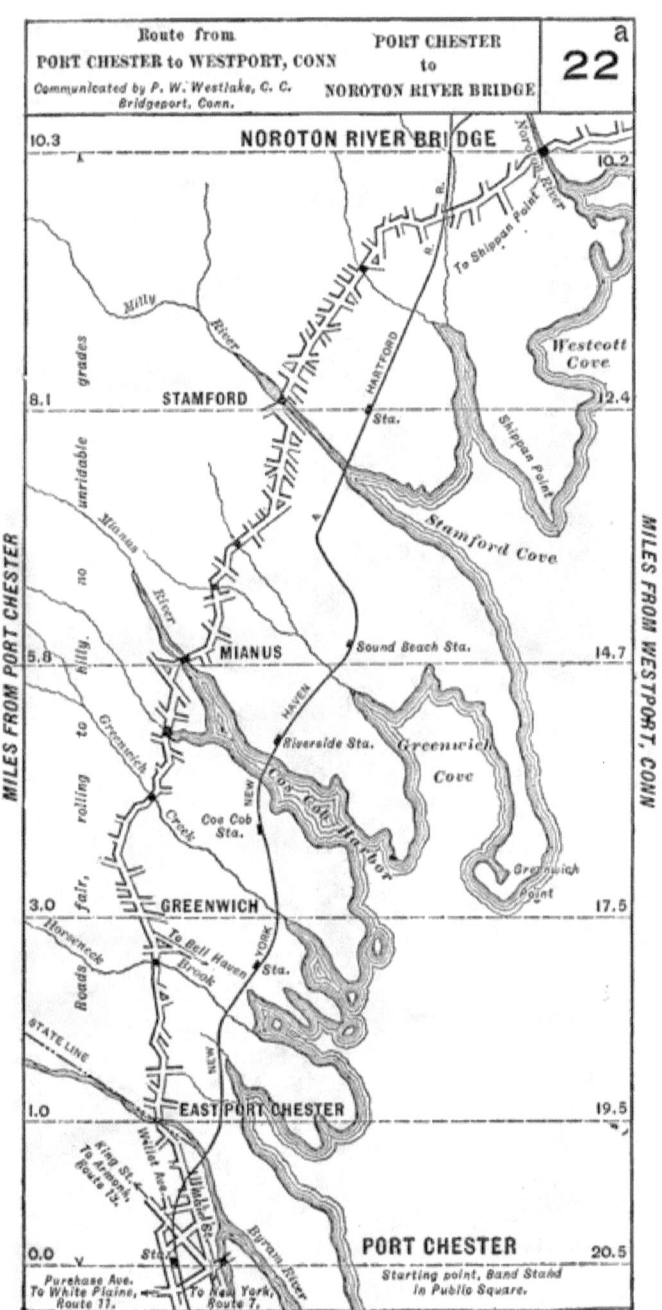

Route from PORT CHESTER to WESTPORT, CONN.
NOROTON RIVER BRIDGE to WESTPORT

22 b

Communicated by P. W. Westlake, C. C. Bridgeport, Conn.

- To Danbury
- To Bridgeport, Route 14.
- To Ridgefield, Route 14.
- **WESTPORT** — 20.5 / 0.0
- Saugatuck River
- To Saugatuck
- To Wilton
- Saugatuck Sta.
- Hilly
- To Weston
- To East Norwalk
- **NORWALK** — 17.5 / 3.0
- Sta.
- Norwalk River
- Norwalk Harbor
- DANBURY & HARTFORD R. R.
- HOUSATONIC R. R.
- To South Norwalk
- Armory Hill
- To New Canaan
- Turnpike
- To Roton Point
- Five Mile River
- Five Mile River Sta.
- To New Canaan
- **DARIEN** — 13.1 / 7.4
- Stang Brook
- Noroton Sta.
- N. Y. N. H. & H. R. R.
- Noroton River
- NEW CANAAN BRANCH R. R.
- **NOROTON RIVER BRIDGE** — 10.3 / 10.2
- Sta.
- Noroton Bay

Roads fair to middling, rolling to hilly. Norwalk River, grades ridable.

EDITED BY WALTER M. MESEROLE, DIV. ENG., 189 MONTAGUE ST., BROOKLYN, N. Y.
COPYRIGHT, 1896, BY THE NEW YORK STATE DIVISION, L. A. W.

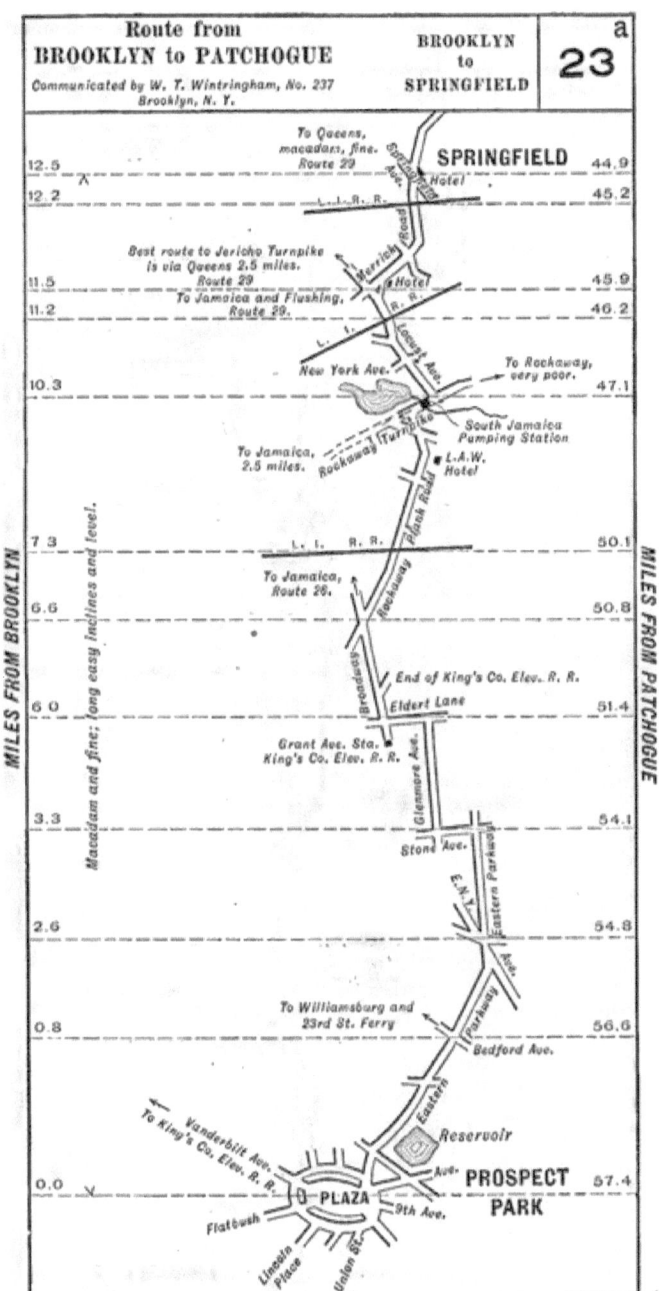

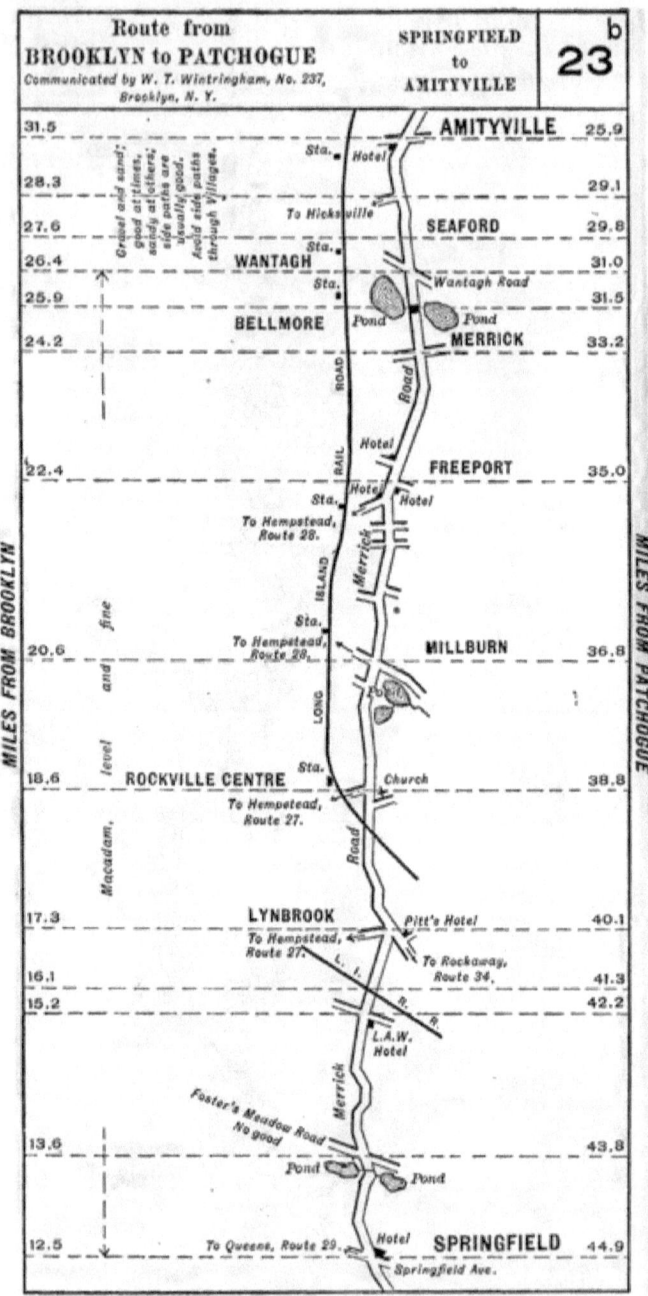

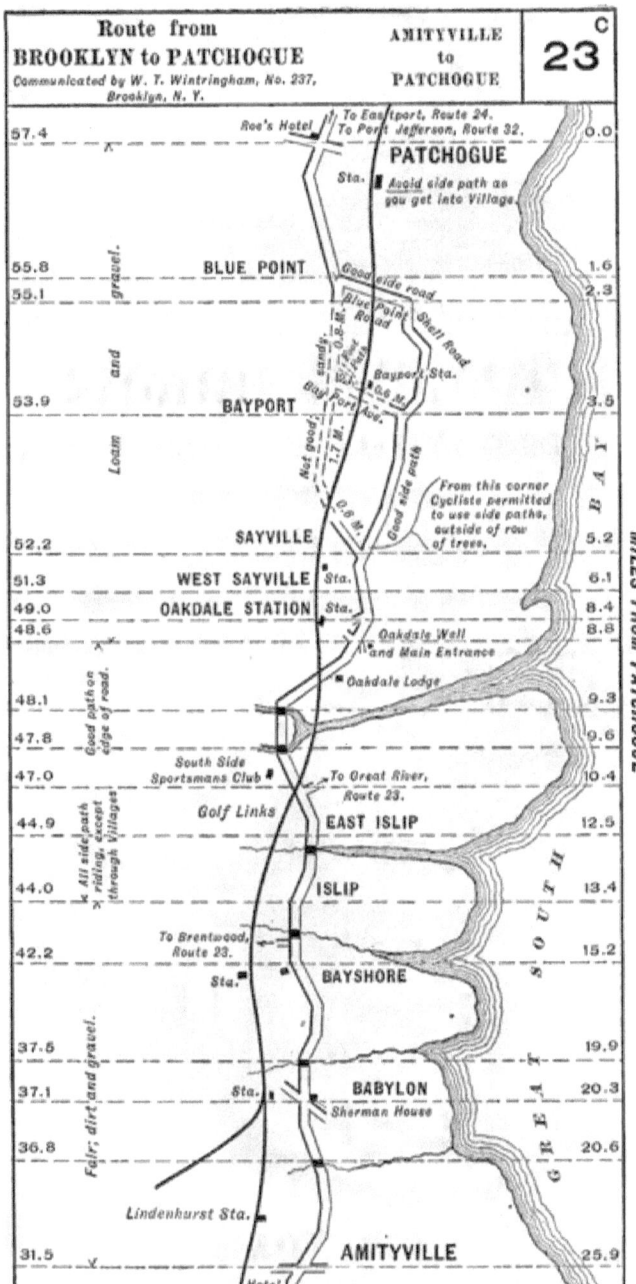

Hotel Newpoint
AMITYVILLE, L. I.

30 miles from New York; OPENS JUNE 24. Alway cool; 150 feet from Great South Bay; table and service of the best; electric lights; rooms with private baths. SPECIAL RATES FOR YOUNG MEN; good roads for bicycling; man in attendance; accommodations for 40 horses. Reasonable terms.

E. HATHAWAY

·· Hotel Kenmore ··
LEADING HOTEL OF ALBANY, N. Y.
... Strictly First=Class ...

Centrally Located. Convenient to State Capitol, other public buildings and places of interest.

HEADQUARTERS FOR WHEELMEN

H. J. ROCKWELL & SON

Crescent Bicycles

... TOM WARD ...
65 BARCLAY STREET   NEW YORK

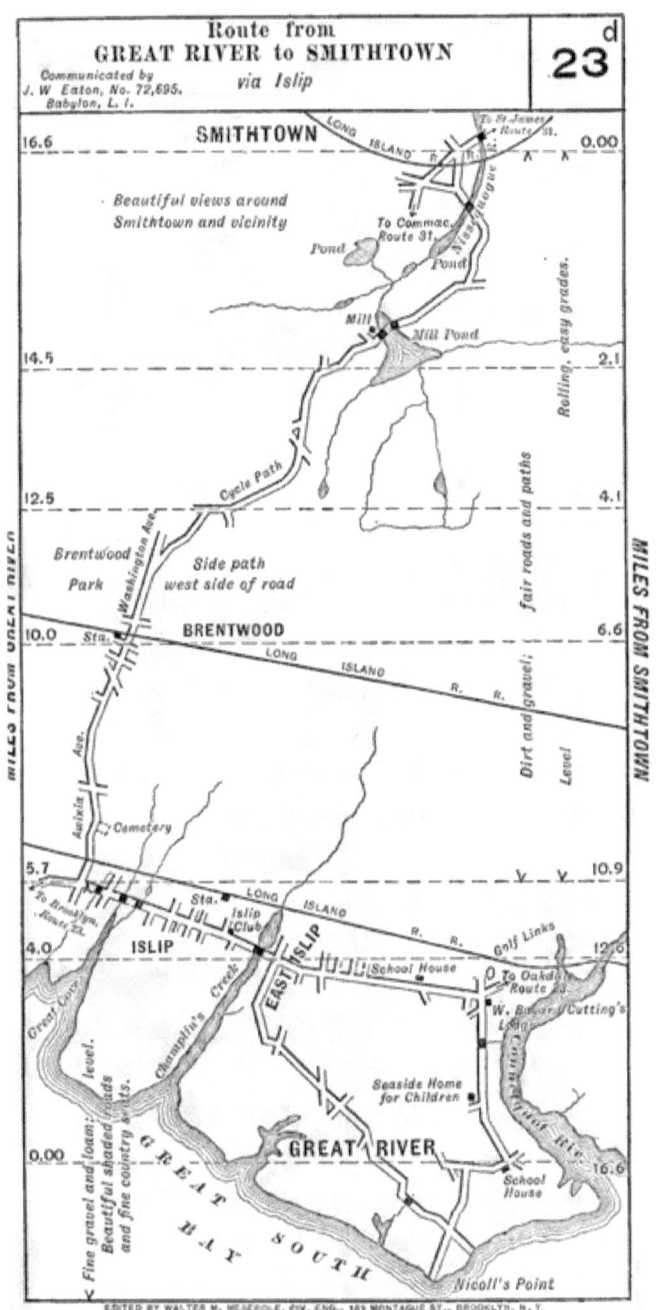

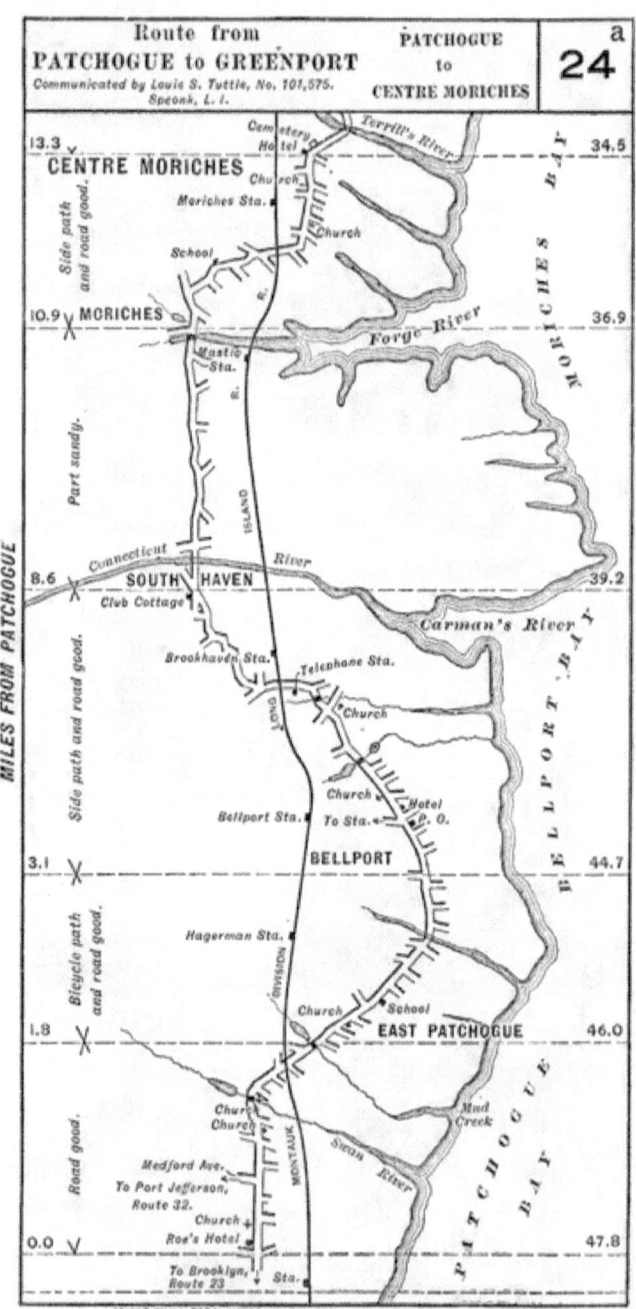

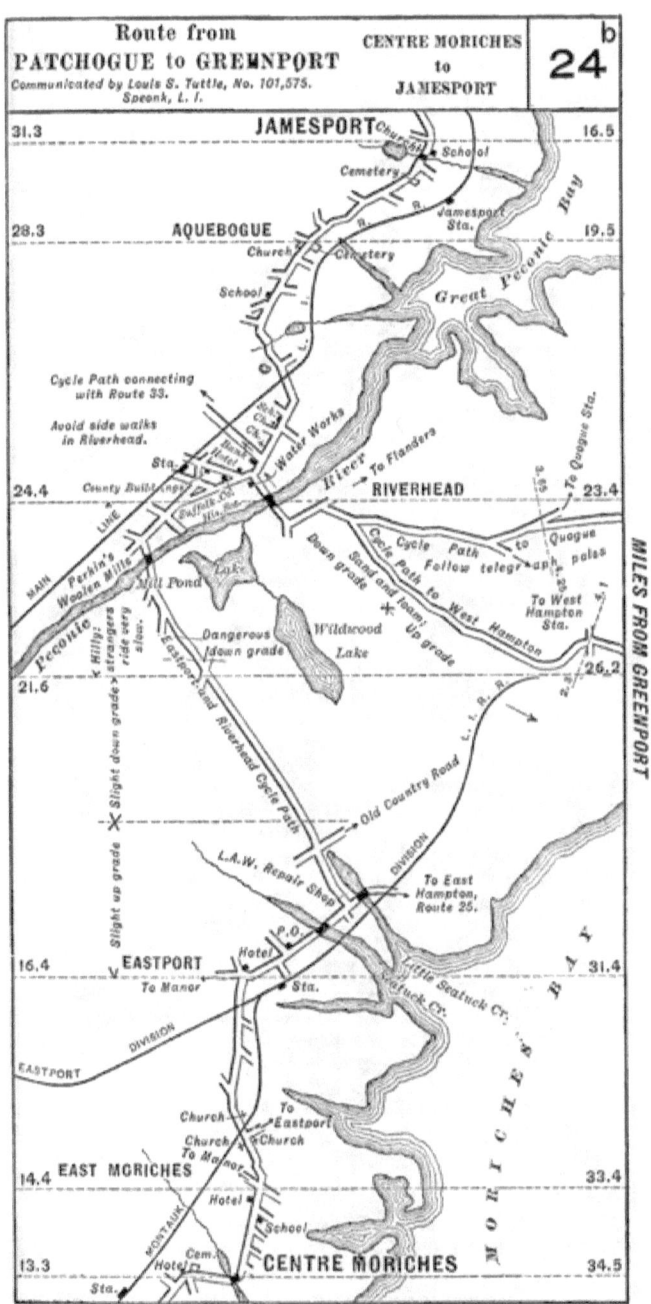

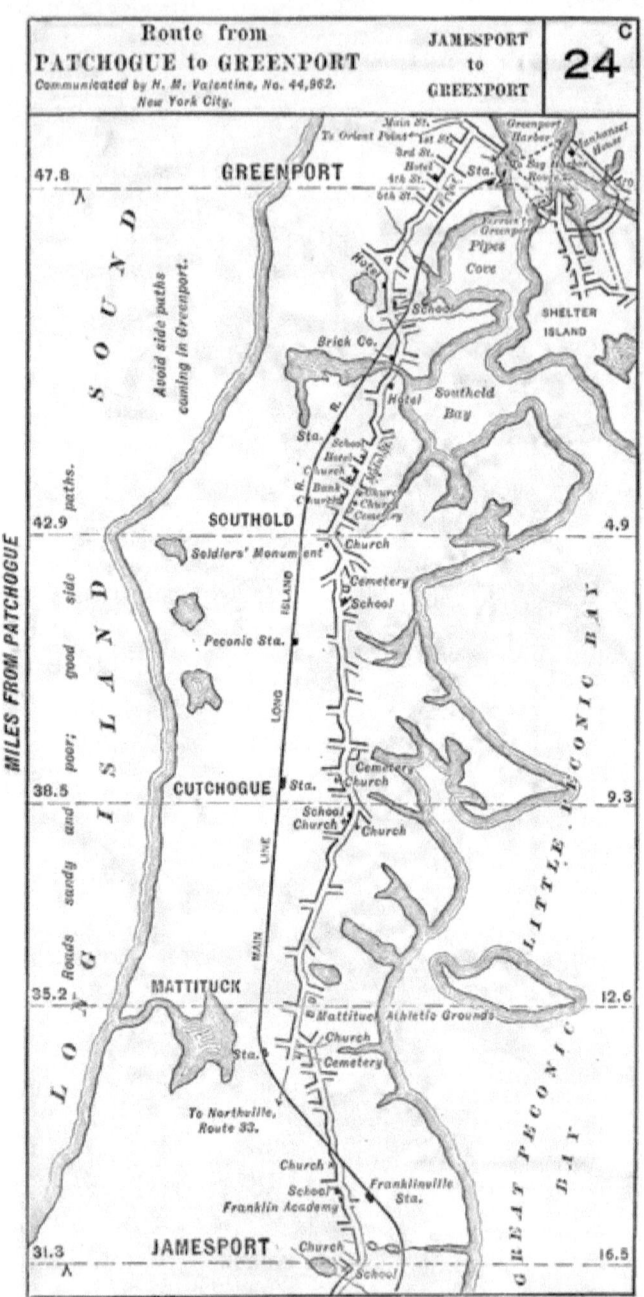

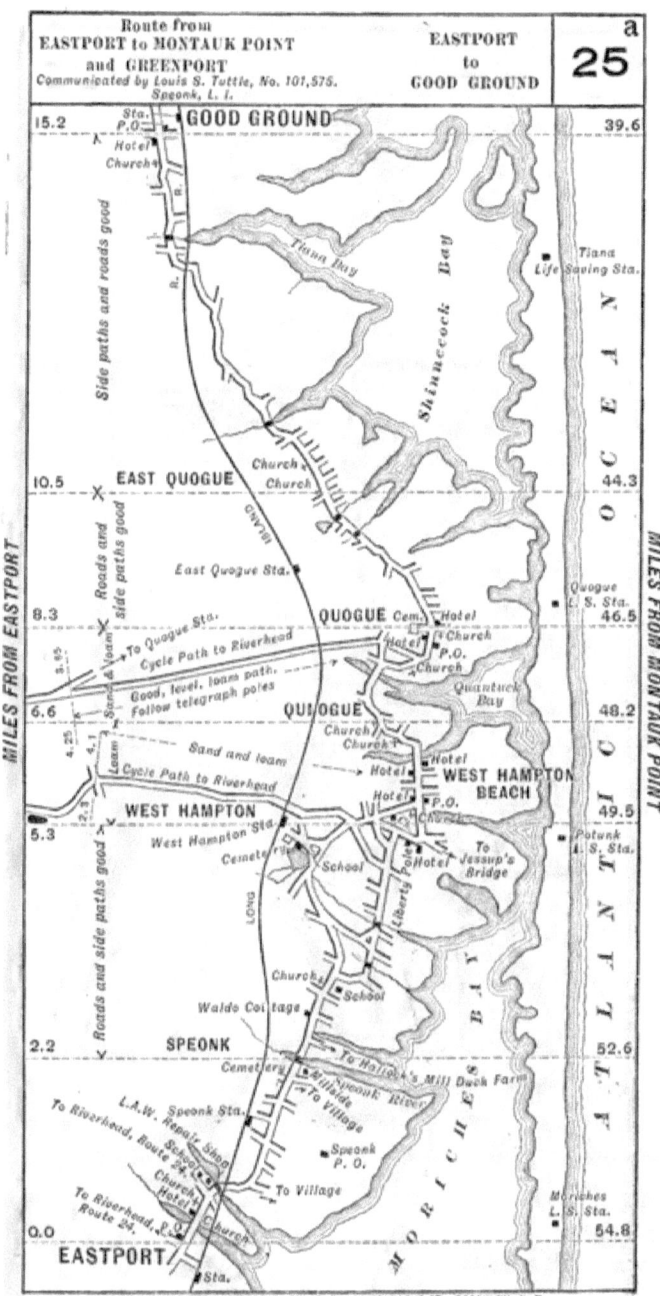

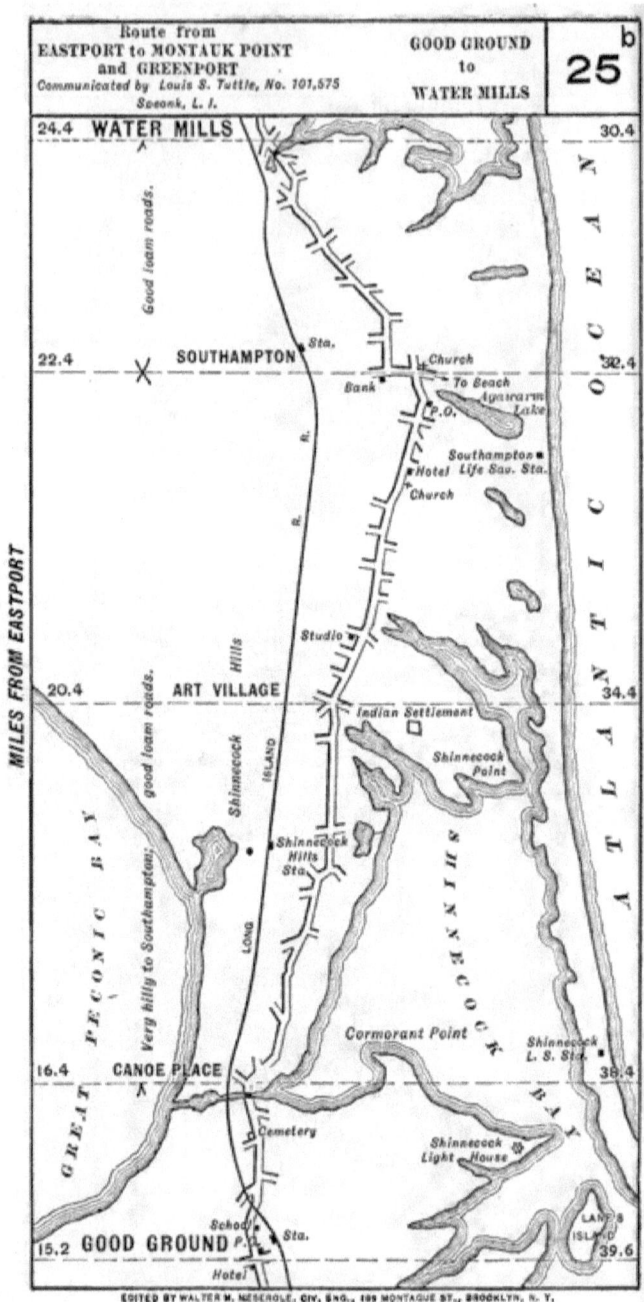

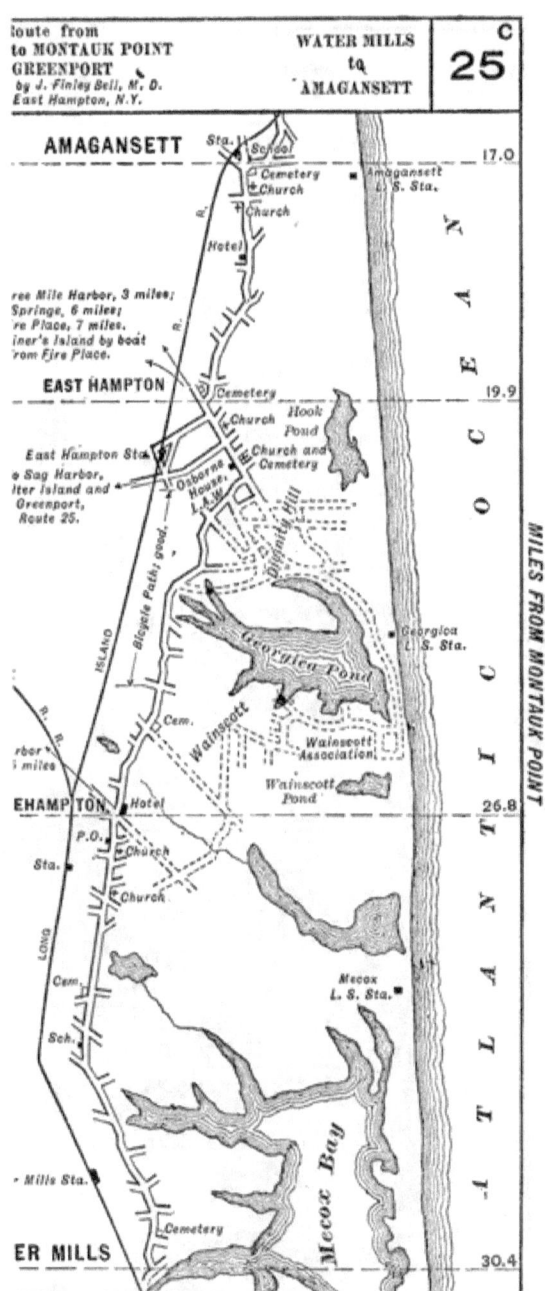

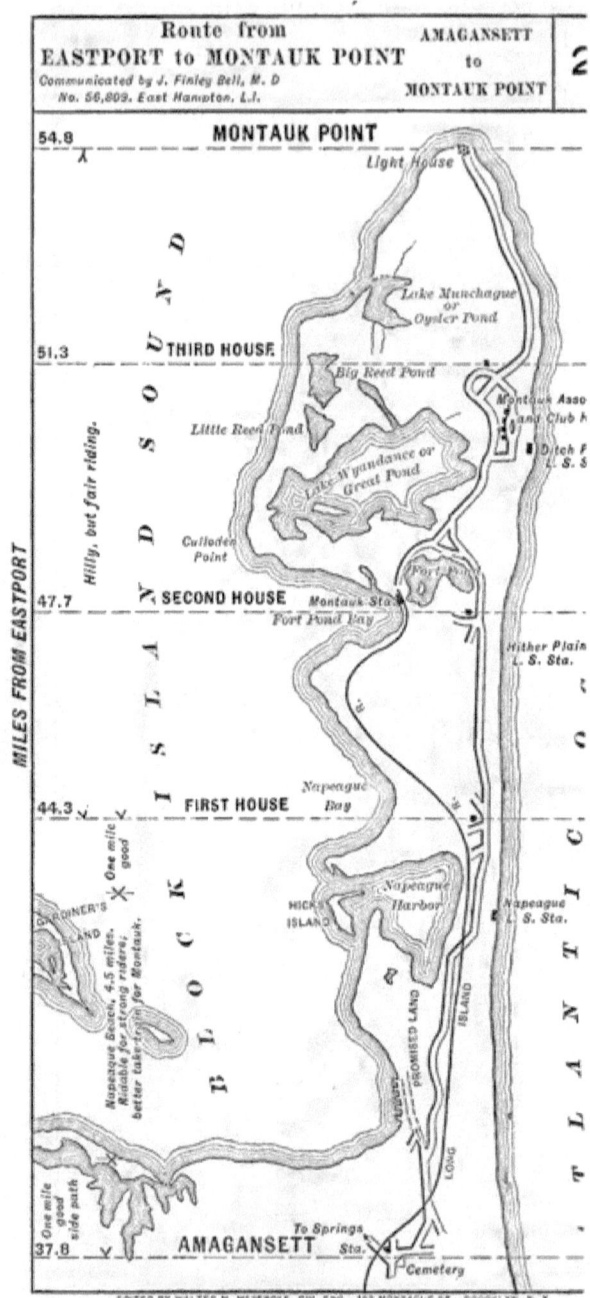

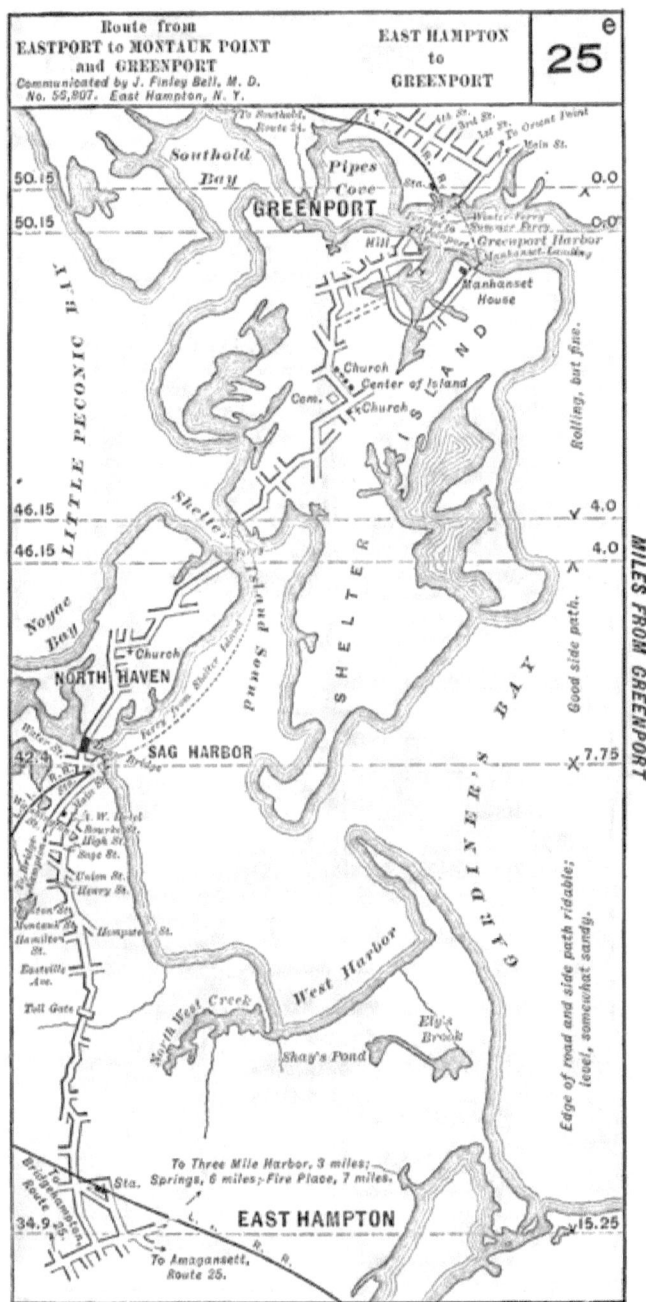

Route from BROOKLYN to JERICHO

Communicated by Dr. Robt. L. Dickinson, No. 67,287, Brooklyn, N. Y.

BROOKLYN to QUEENS — 26 a

Miles from Grant Ave. Station	Description		Miles
7.90	QUEENS — To Willets Point, Route 29.	To Springfield, Route 29.	11.35
7.40		To Hempstead (Trolley) / Wagon Factory	11.85
		(level) / Macadam	
6.35	Hollis Inn Estab. 1710 / Church / HOLLIS / Sta.		12.90
5.85	Keep on main road left fork.		13.40
5.75	Sign forbidding side path riding toward Jamaica from this point.	Jamaica: stringent side path regulations extending nearly to Hollis.	13.50
4.65	End of cobble stone pavement		14.60
4.60	Smith St. or Merrick Road, Route 29.		14.65
4.25	Town Hall / Flushing Ave. / To Flushing, Route 29.	Sta.	15.00
	JAMAICA — Fulton St. level, trolley; cobble stones, covered well with dirt; poor riding.	Pond	
4.00	Rockaway		15.25
3.70		To Rockaway	15.55
3.50	L.A.W. Hotel	Liberty Hotel	15.75
2.30	To Richmond Hill and Morris Park	Liberty Ave.	16.95
1.35	OZONE PARK	L.I.R.R.	17.90
0.85	WOODHAVEN	Sta. / To Merrick Road and Babylon, Route 23.	18.40
	Rockaway Plank Road / Broadway, level, fair; macadam.	End of Elev. structure	
0.08	Take left fork.		19.17
	Under Elevated Rail Road to fork.	Eldert's Lane	
0.00	Last Sta. Kings Co. Elev. R. R. / Follow Route 23 from Park Plaza to Eldert's Lane.	Grant Ave. / Liberty / Glenmore Ave.	19.25

EDITED BY WALTER M. MESEROLE, CIV. ENG., 596 MONTAGUE ST., BROOKLYN, N. Y.

COPYRIGHT, 1898, BY THE NEW YORK STATE DIVISION, L. A. W.

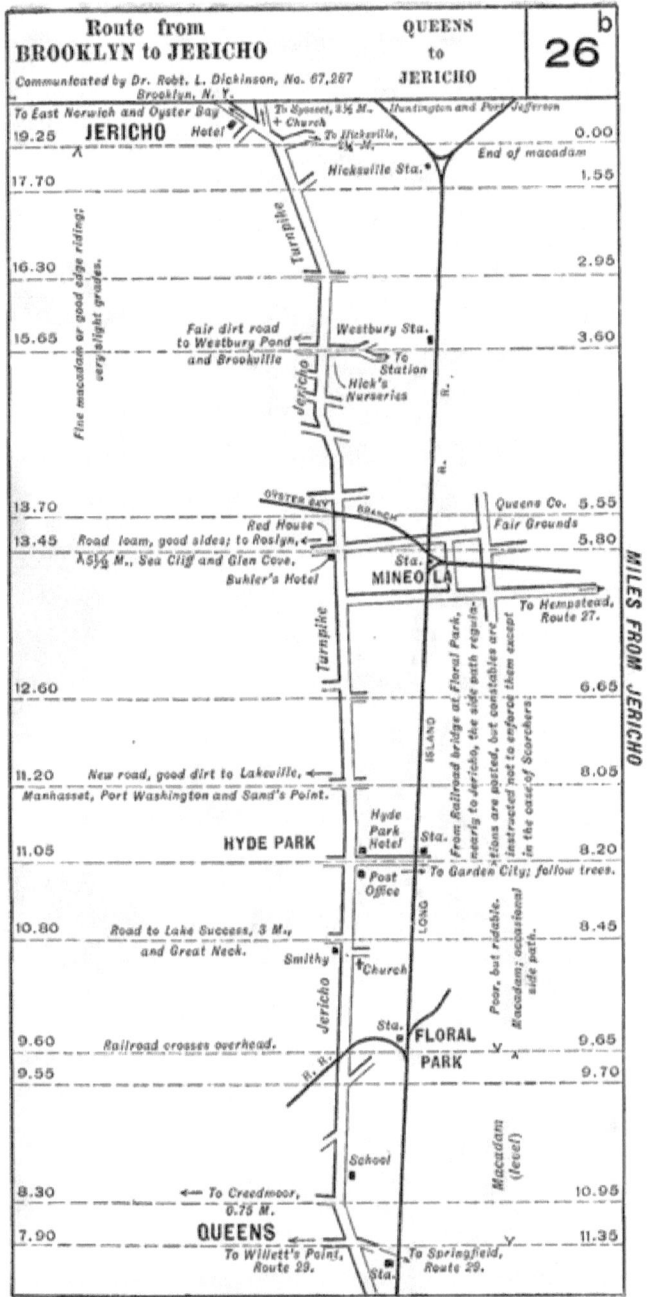

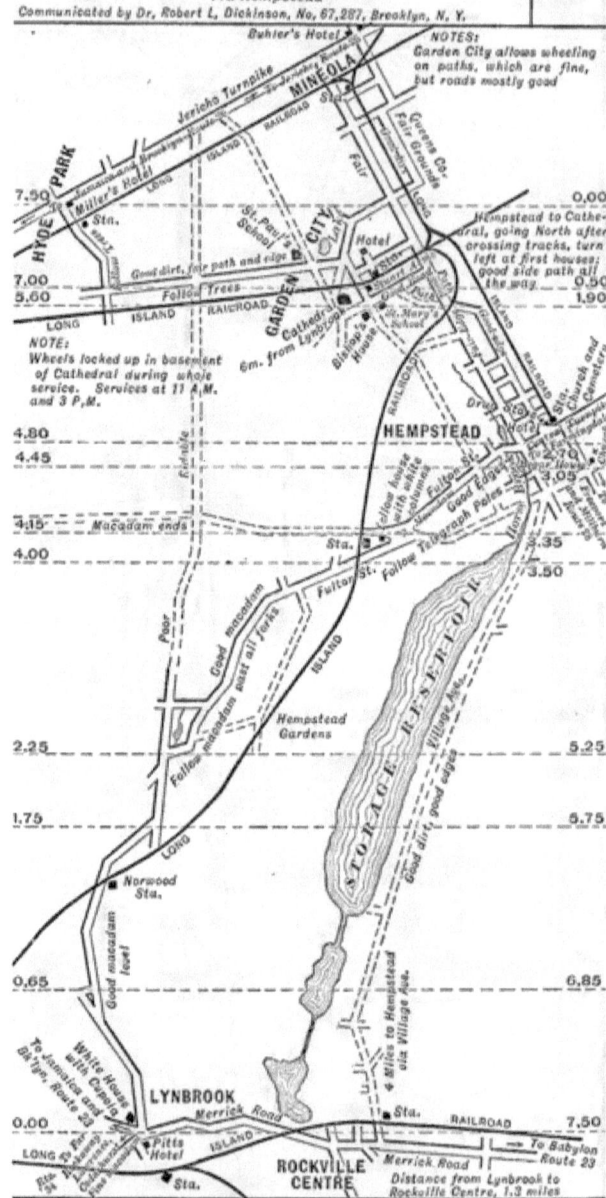

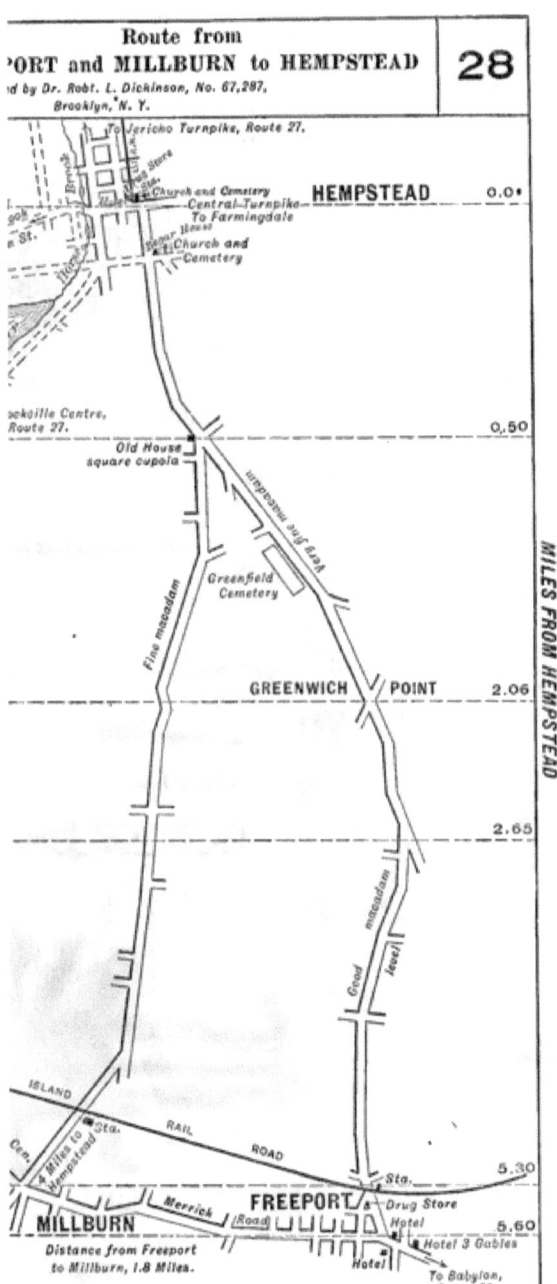

"The Pines," (Fulton Street, corner St. Paul's Road), Hempstead, L. I.
"L. A. W." OFFICIAL HOUSE.

A select, strictly temperance house, which caters to ladies and gentlemen only. All refreshments are of the best quality. "The Pines" affords ladies the quiet of a refined home, and is entirely free from the annoyances accompanying a "Road House."

A HOME IN HEALTHY, ARISTOCRATIC HEMPSTEAD.

$500.00 cash, balance monthly, buys a fine, new residence, (built by days' work), on large plot, in cream Hempstead Village, near two stations, and Garden City Schools, houses have open, sanitary, nickel-plated plumbing, enamelled iron bath, cabinet oak trim, open fire-places, tiled hearths, etc. Frequent city trains, from 5.30 A.M. until midnight, also rapid transit, commutation, 10 cents. Hempstead has public water (pronounced "absolutely pure," by Prof. Chandler, of New York), is lighted by large electric lights, and just outside Greater New York.

Address F. W. CRANDELL, (Owner), Hempstead, L. I.

YOUR TRIP

will not be spoiled by

DUST OR RAIN

If you use OUR GEAR CASE.

WRITE US
or
YOUR DEALER
or
YOUR MAKER

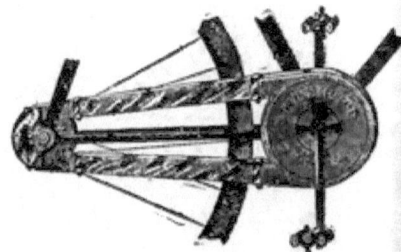

PRICE, $5.00

The Frost Gear Case Co.,
253 BROADWAY, NEW YORK.

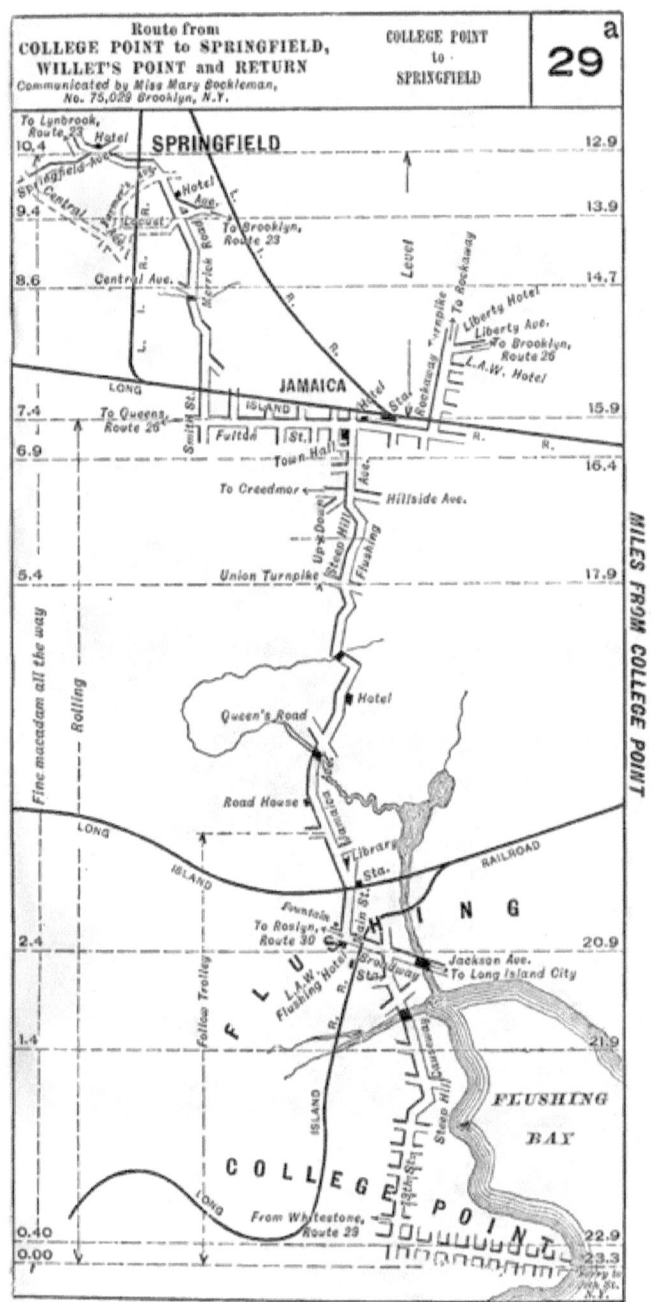

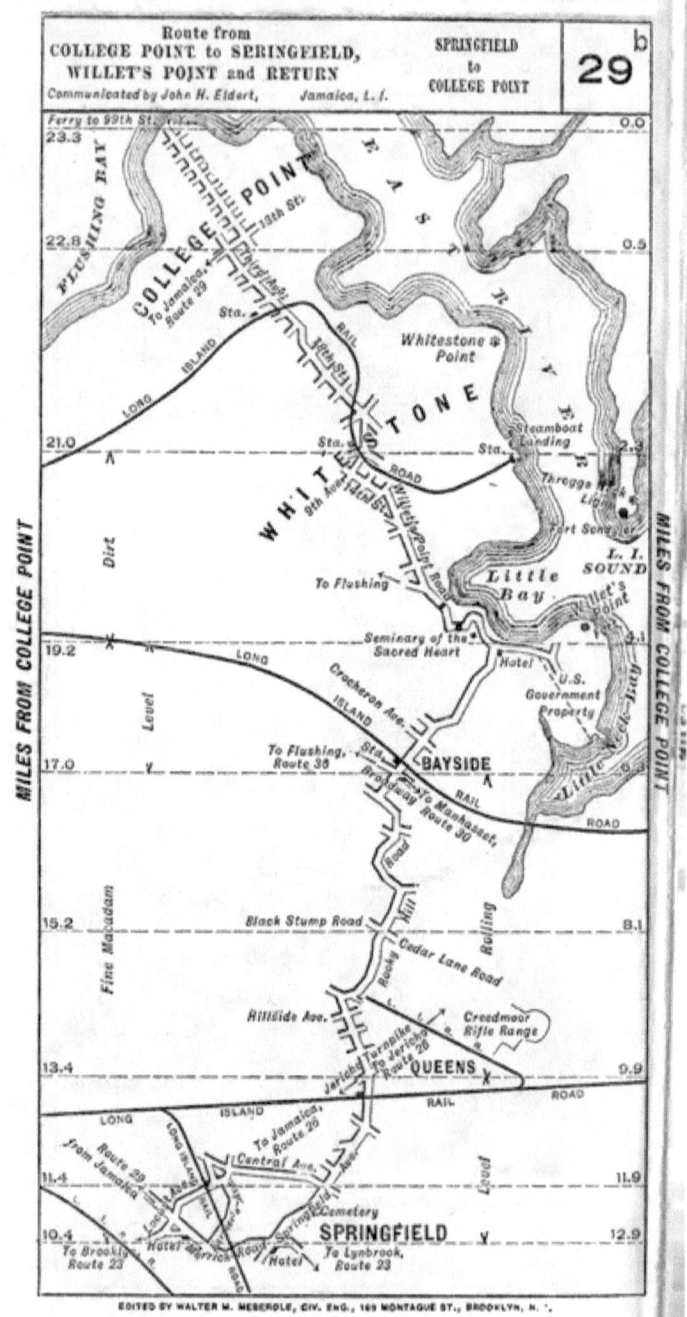

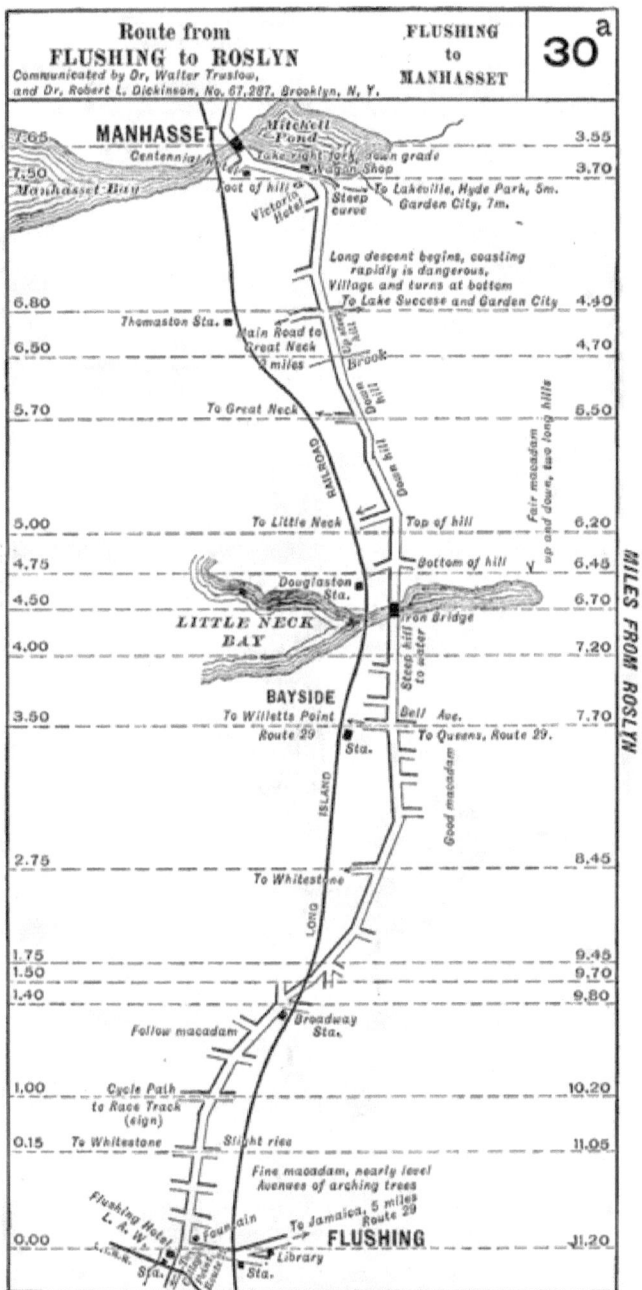

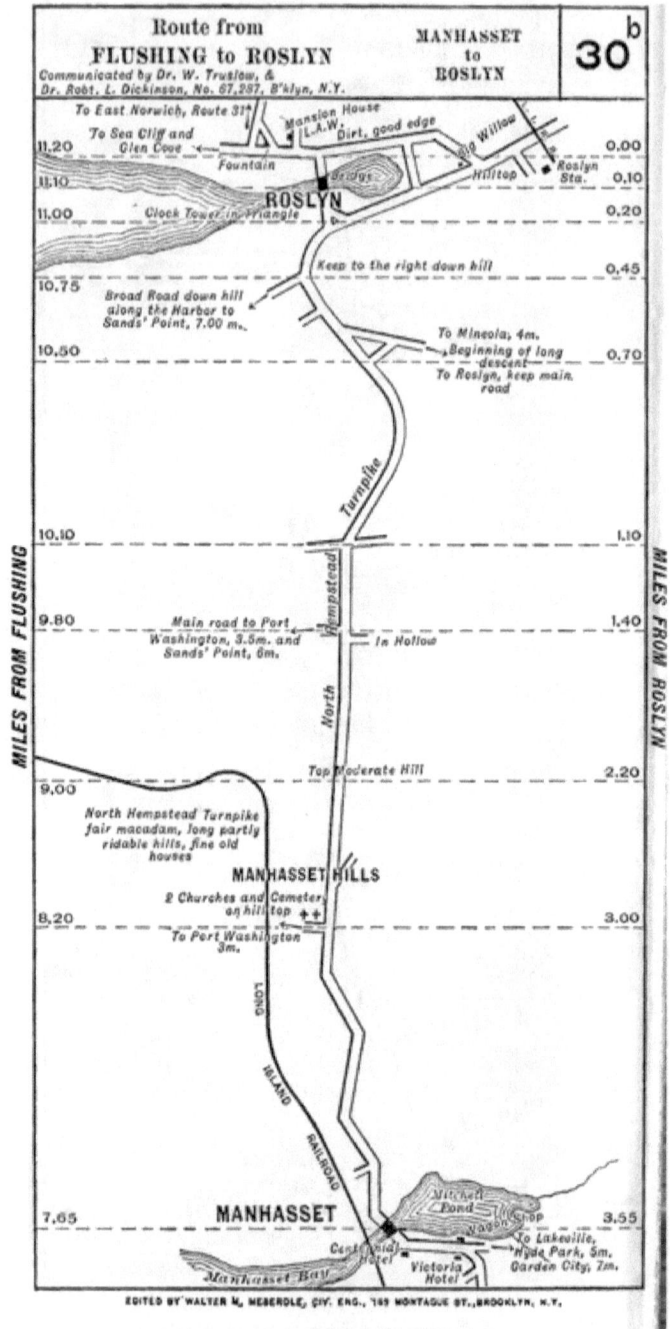

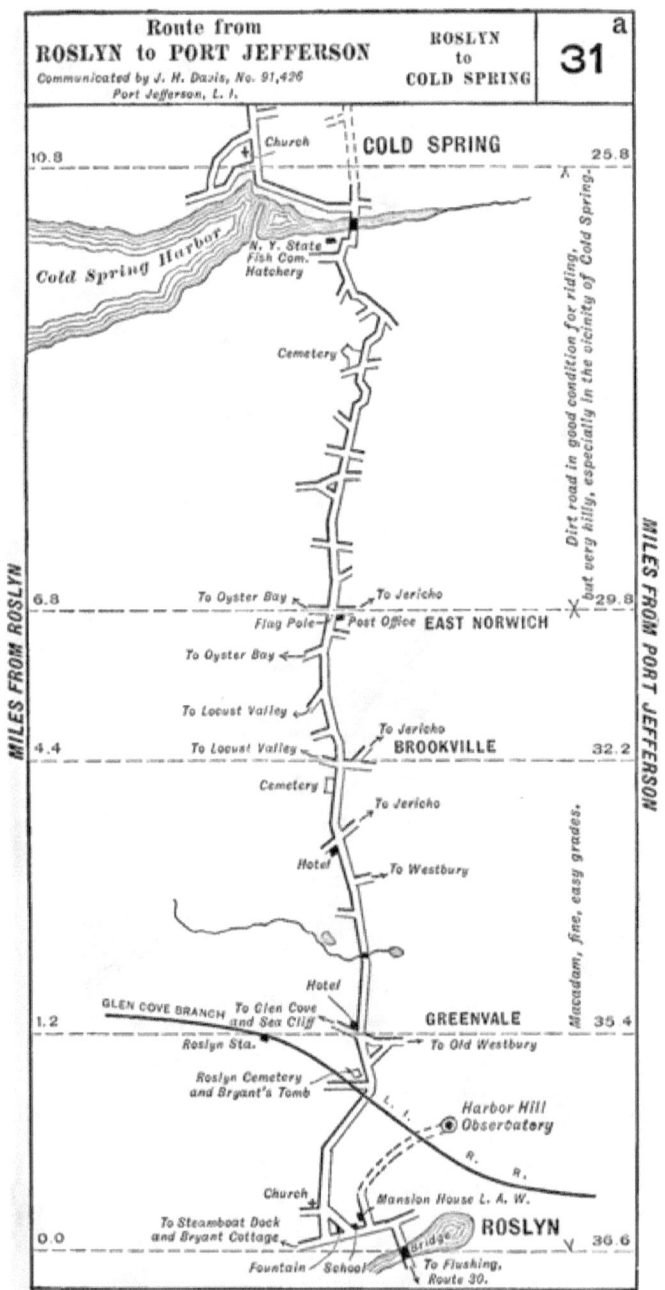

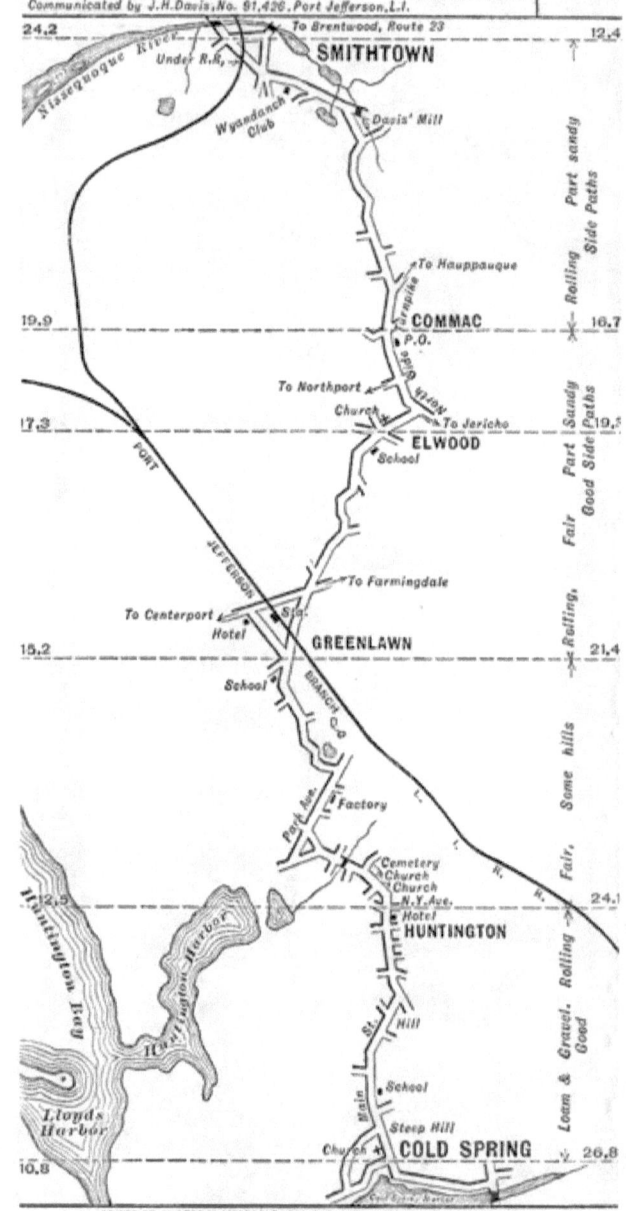

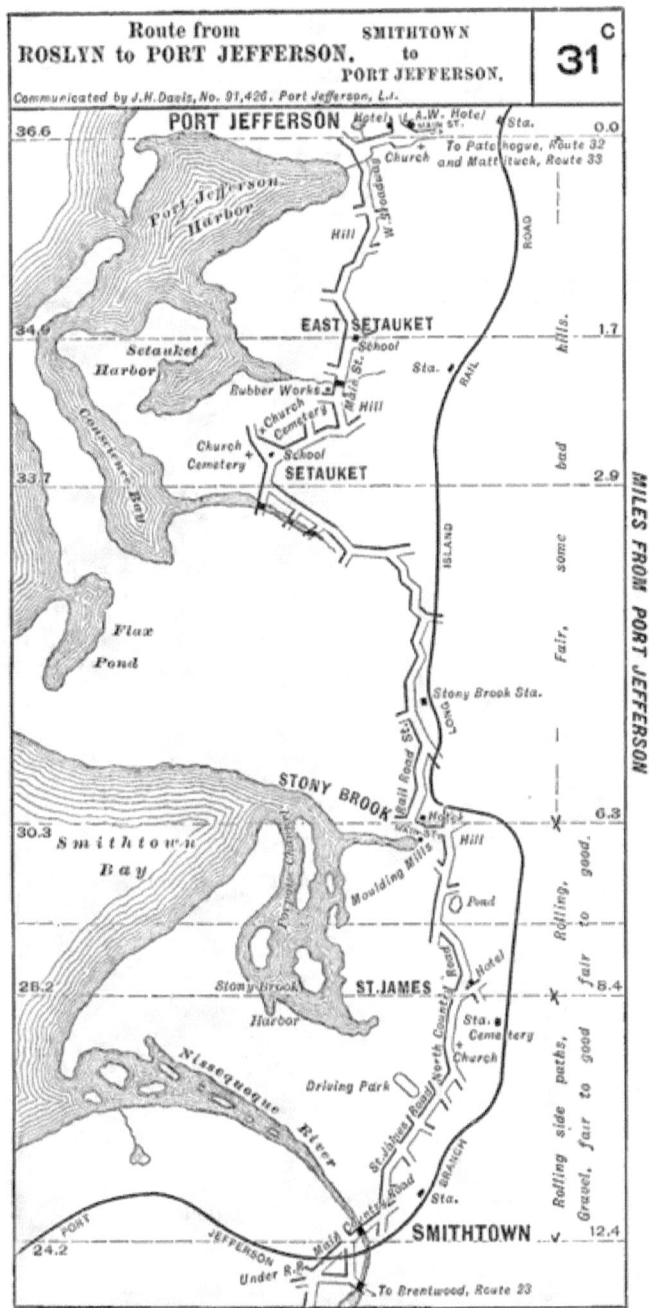

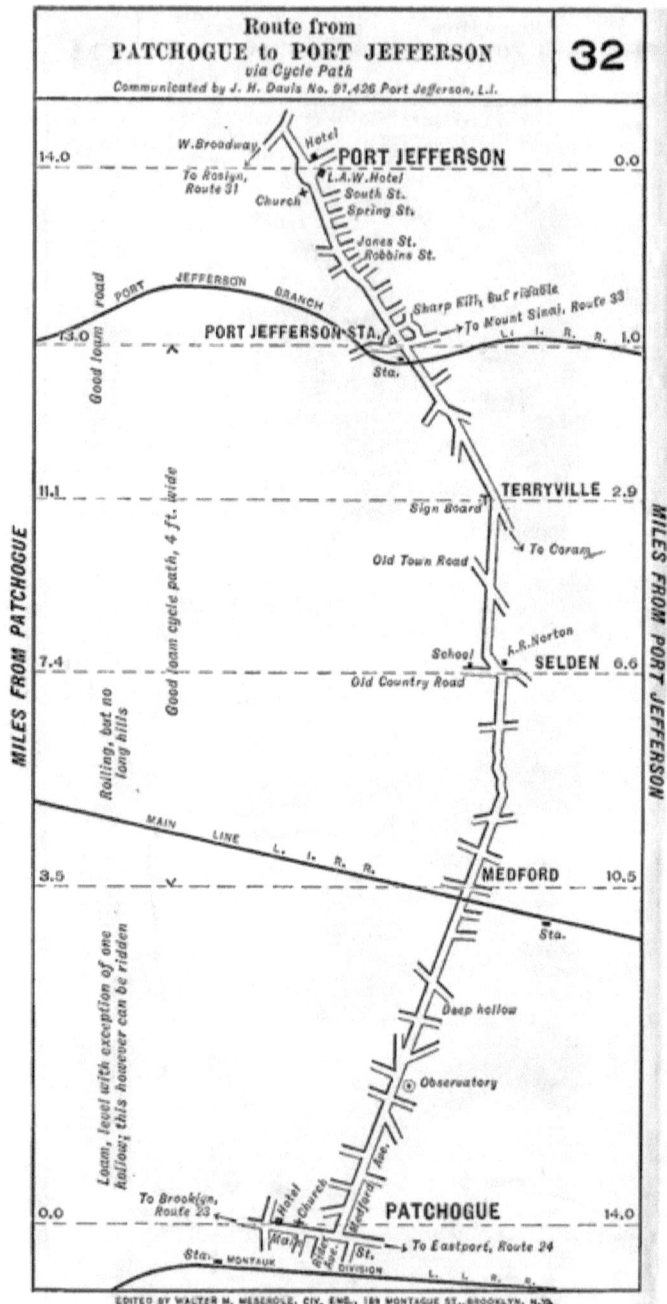

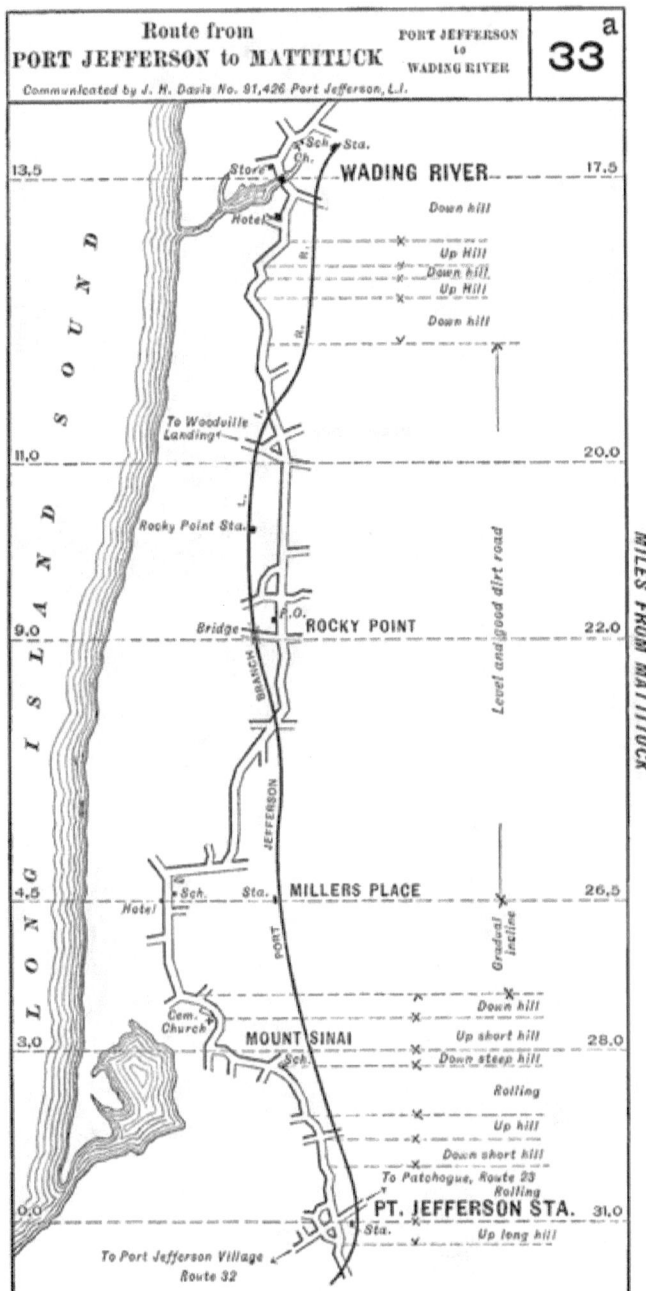

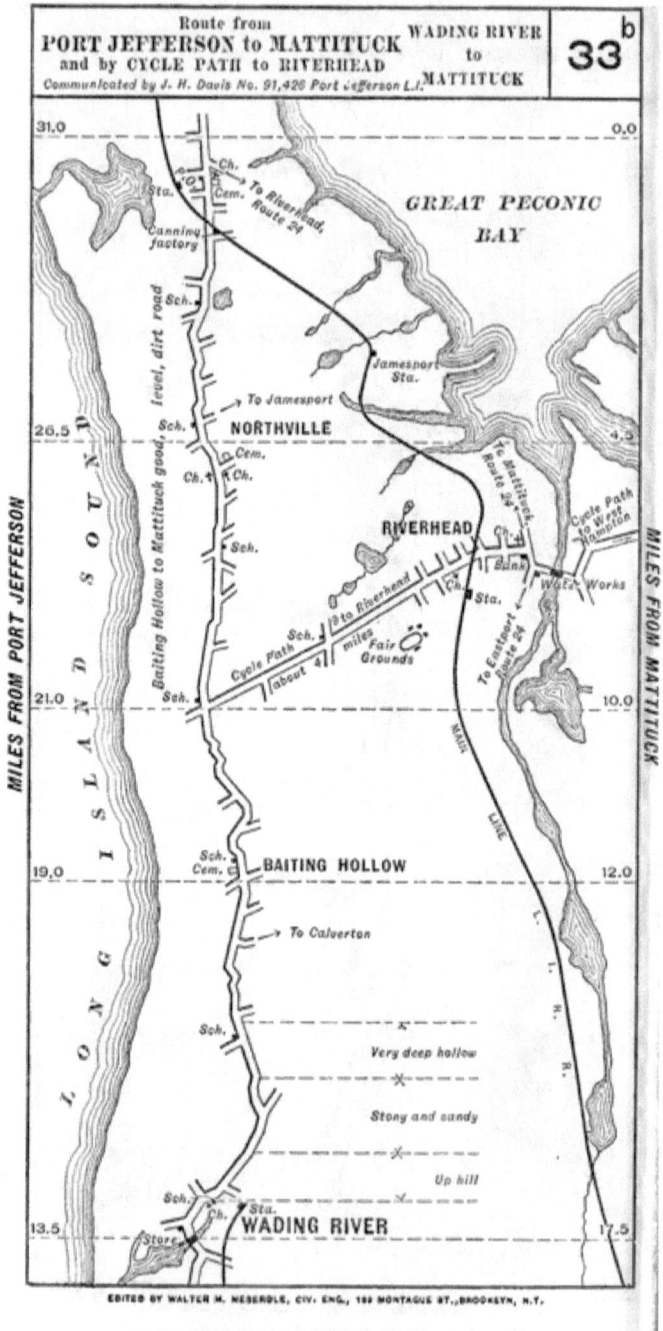

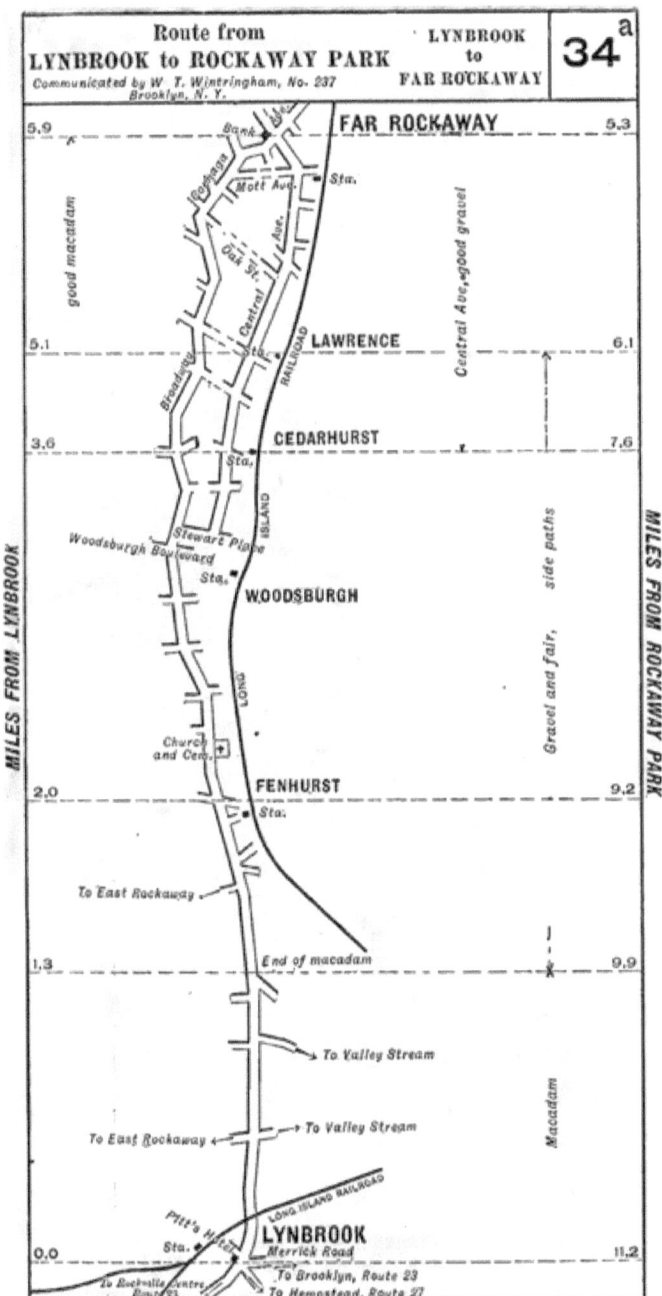

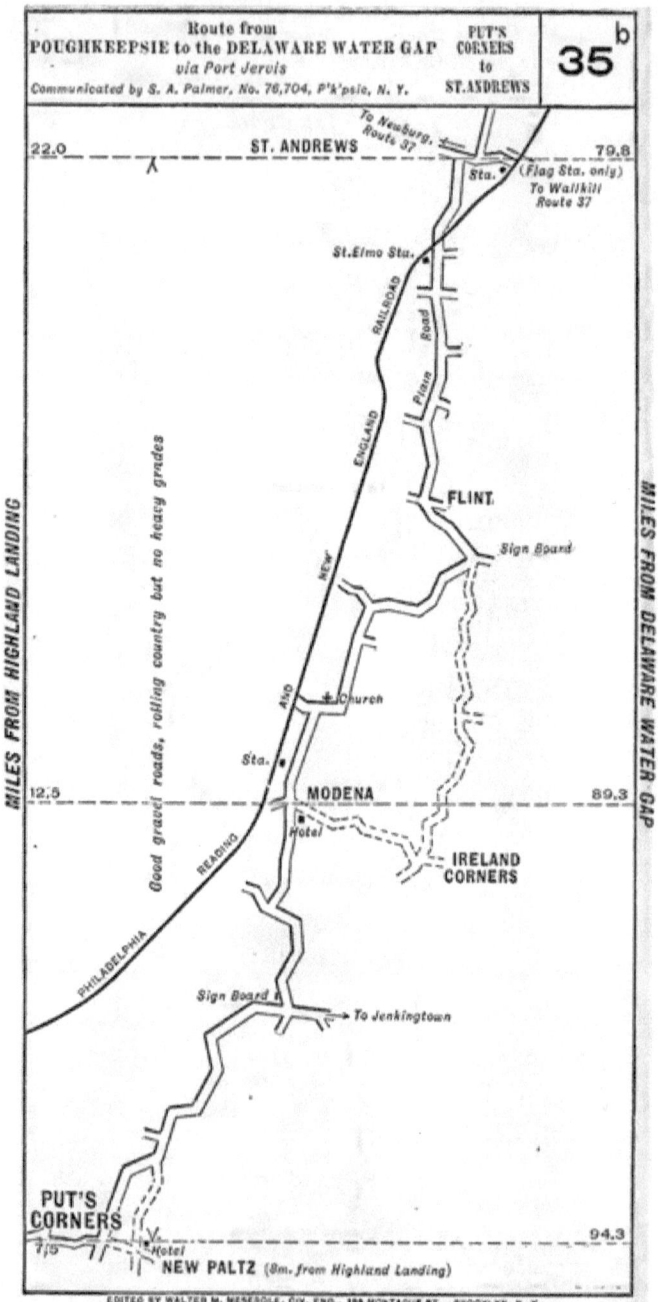

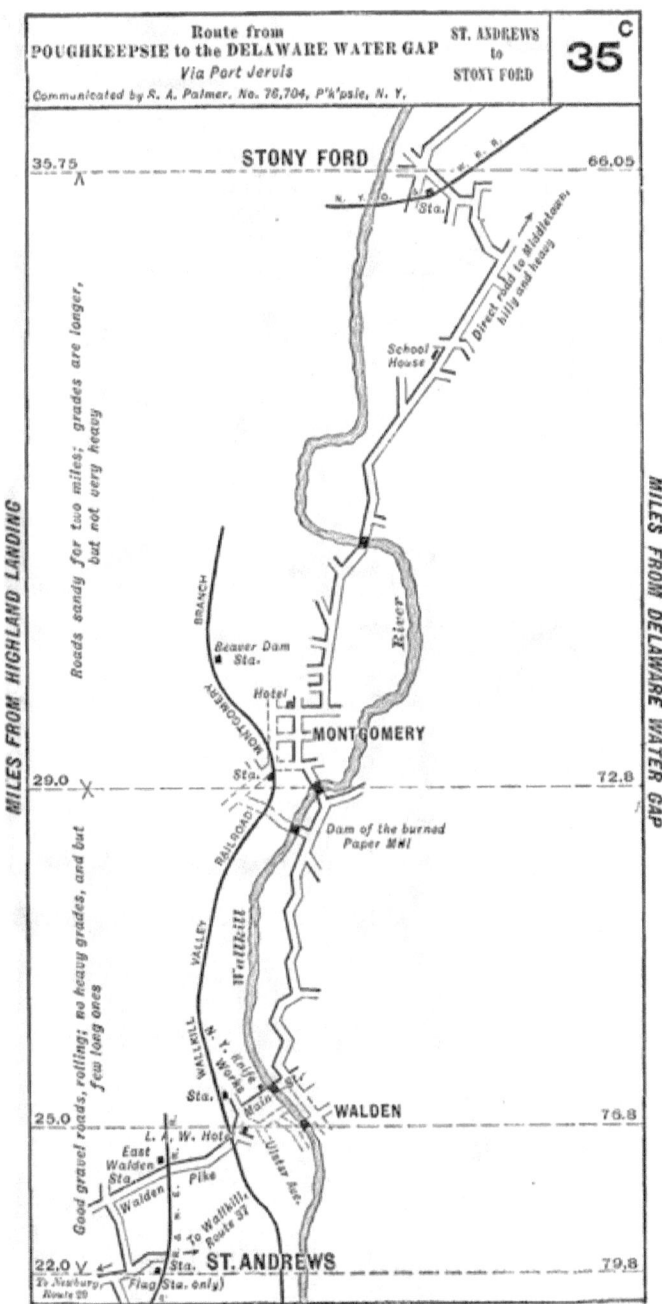

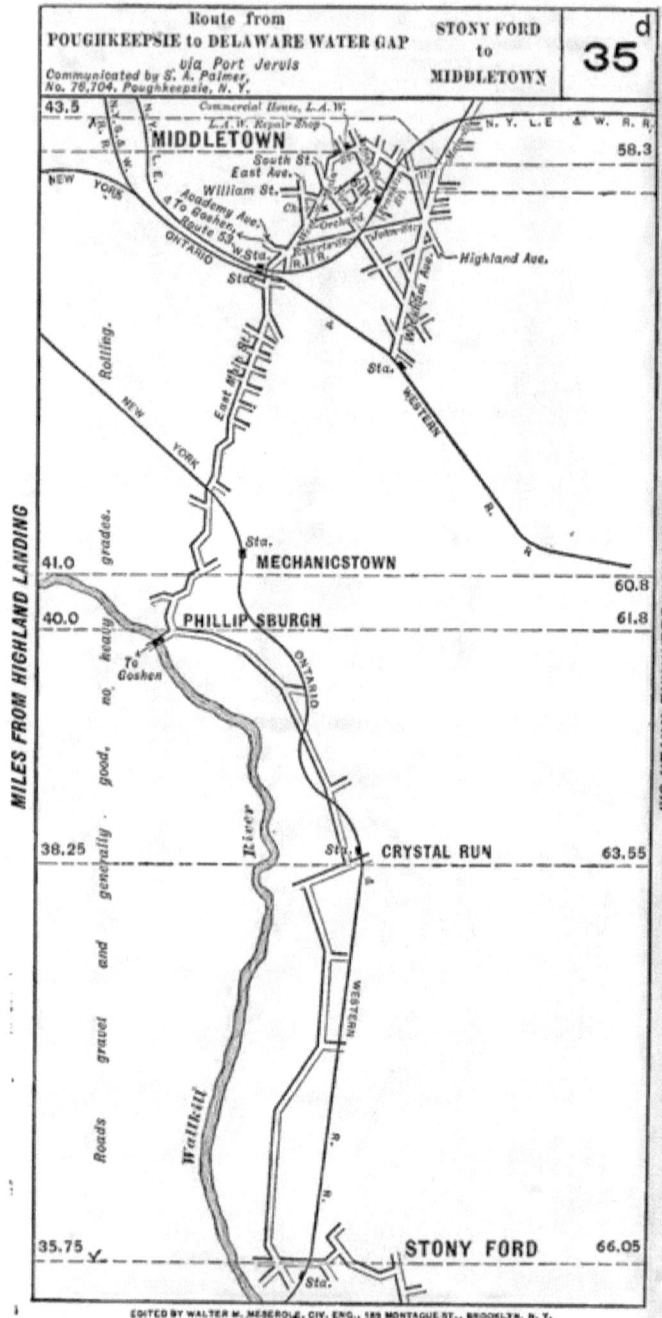

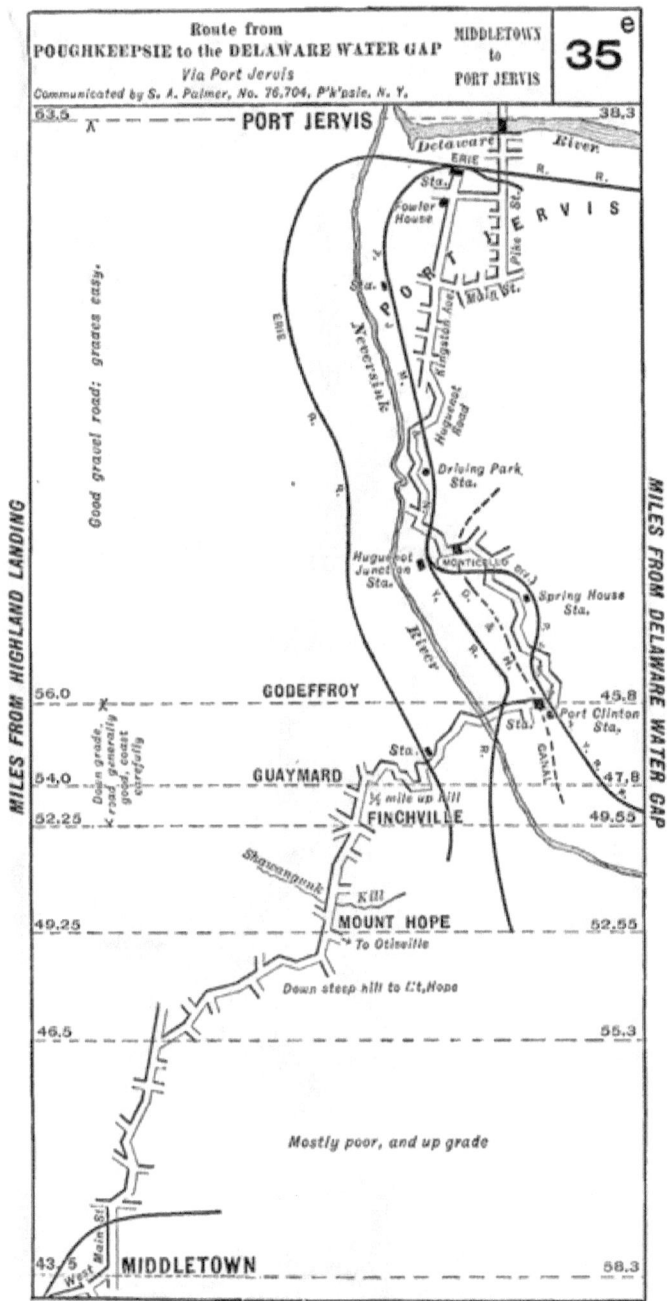

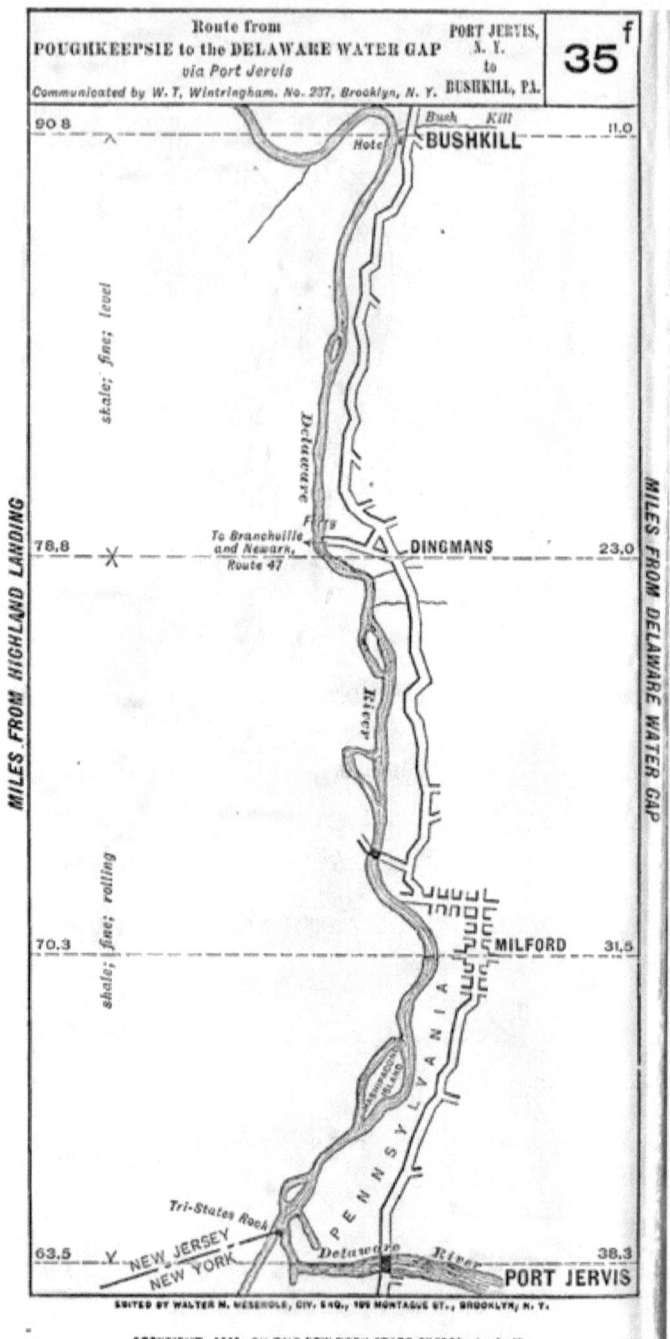

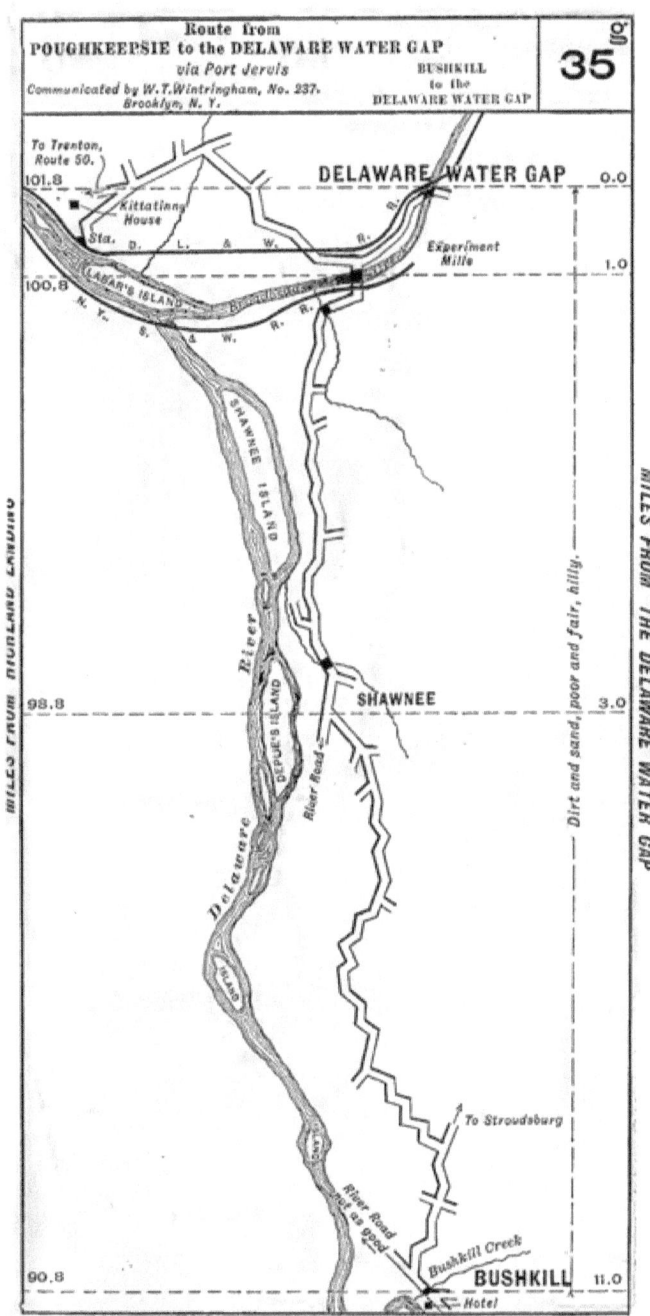

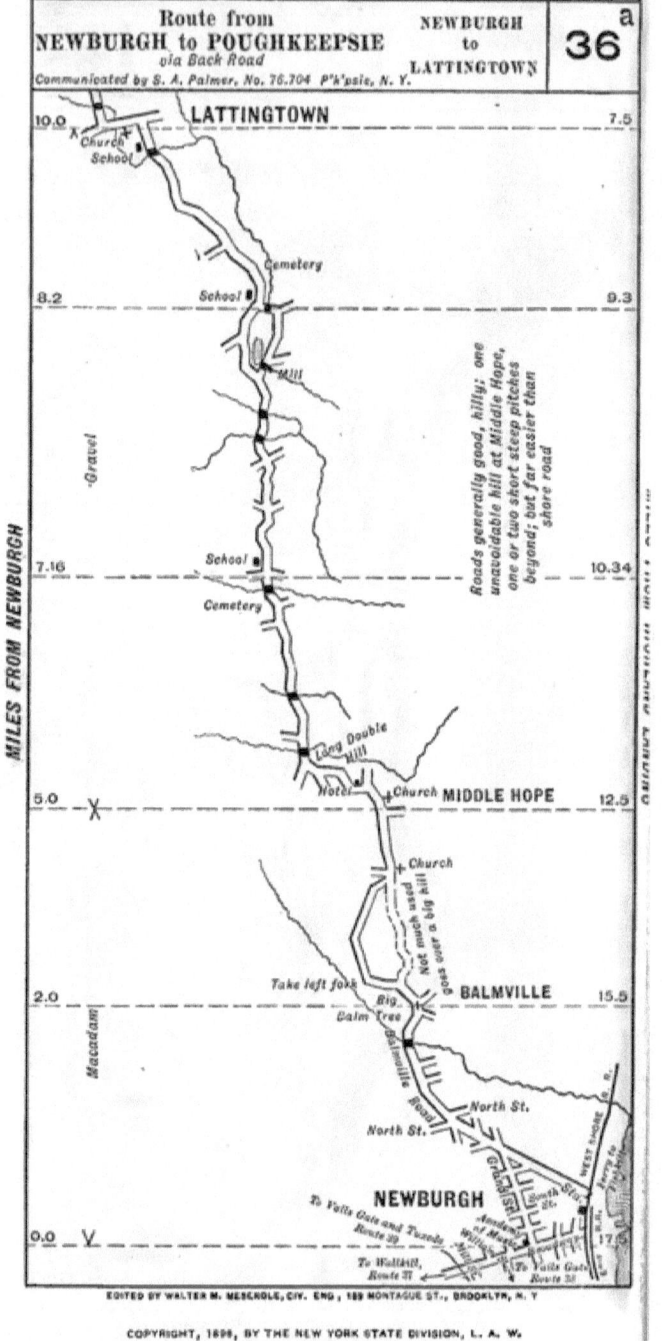

Route from
NEWBURGH to POUGHKEEPSIE
via Back Road
Communicated by S. A. Palmer, No. 76,704, P'k'psie, N. Y.

LATTINGTOWN to POUGHKEEPSIE

36 b

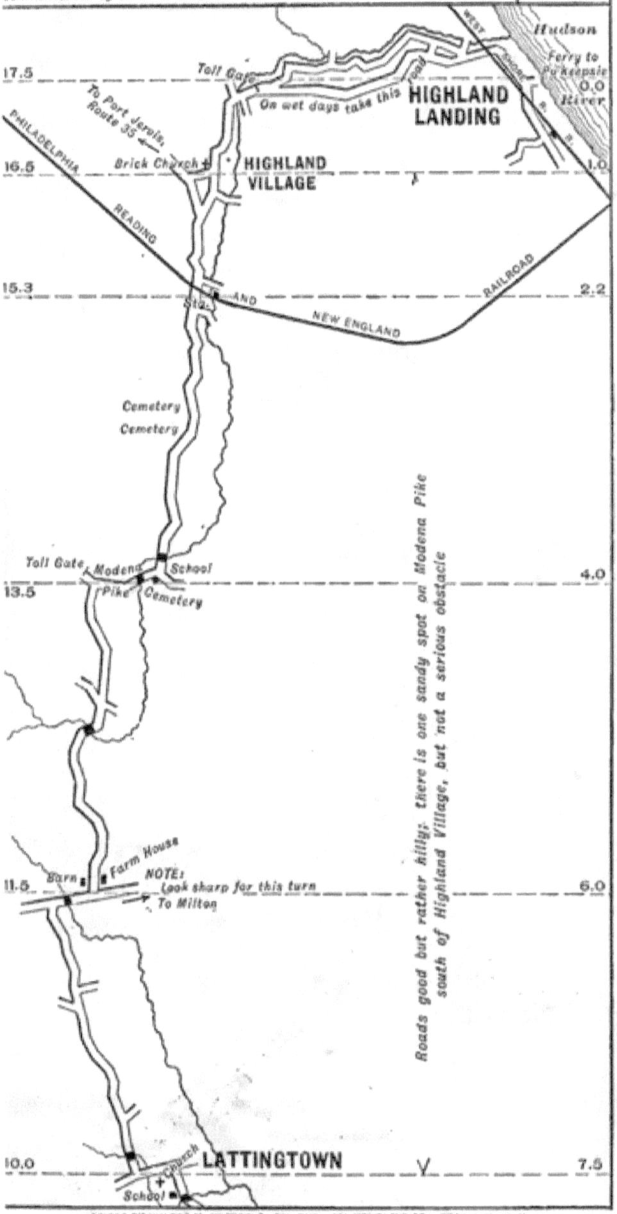

17.5 — Toll Gate

To Port Jervis, Route 35

On wet days take this

HIGHLAND LANDING

Hudson Ferry to P'keepsie

West Shore R. R.

River

0.0

PHILADELPHIA

16.5 — Brick Church

HIGHLAND VILLAGE

1.0

READING

15.3 — Sta.

AND NEW ENGLAND RAILROAD

2.2

Cemetery Cemetery

Toll Gate, Modena, School

13.5 — Pike, Cemetery

4.0

Roads good but rather hilly; there is one sandy spot on Modena Pike south of Highland Village, but not a serious obstacle

MILES FROM HIGHLAND LANDING

Farm House

11.5 — Barn

NOTE: Look sharp for this turn
To Milton

6.0

10.0 — Church LATTINGTOWN
School

7.5

EDITED BY WALTER M. MESEROLE, CIV. ENG., 103 MONTAGUE ST., BROOKLYN, N. Y.

COPYRIGHT, 1896, BY THE NEW YORK STATE DIVISION, L. A. W.

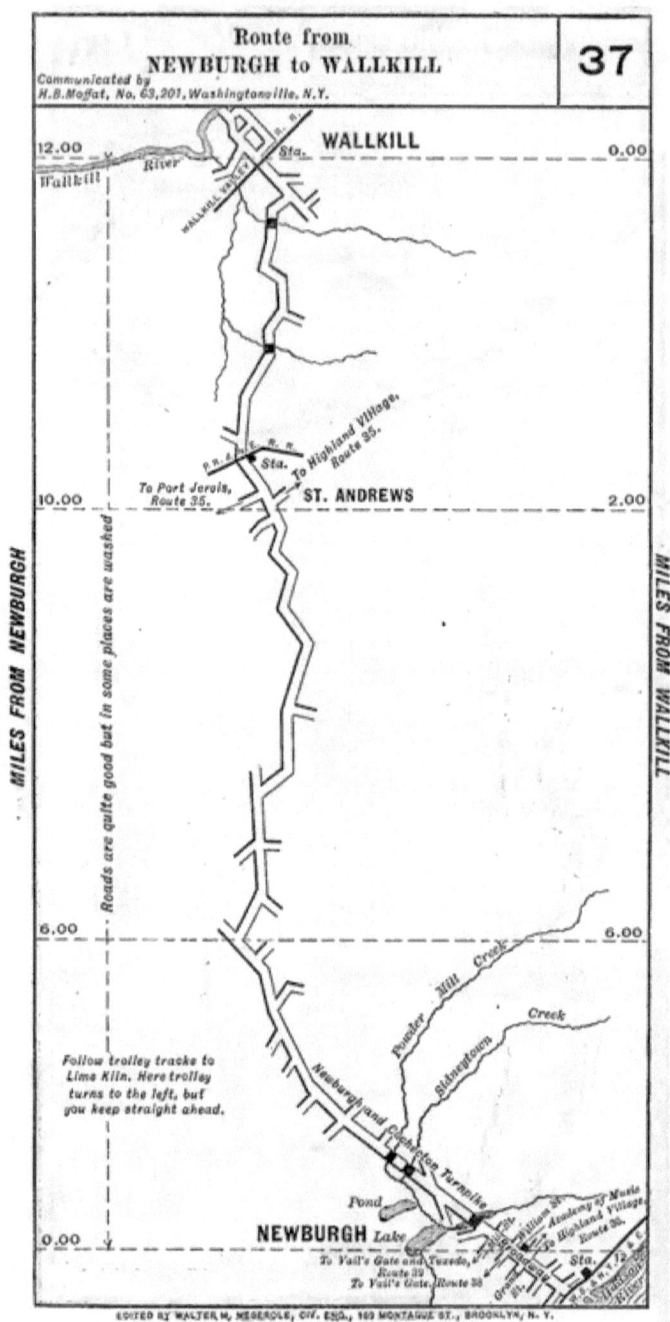

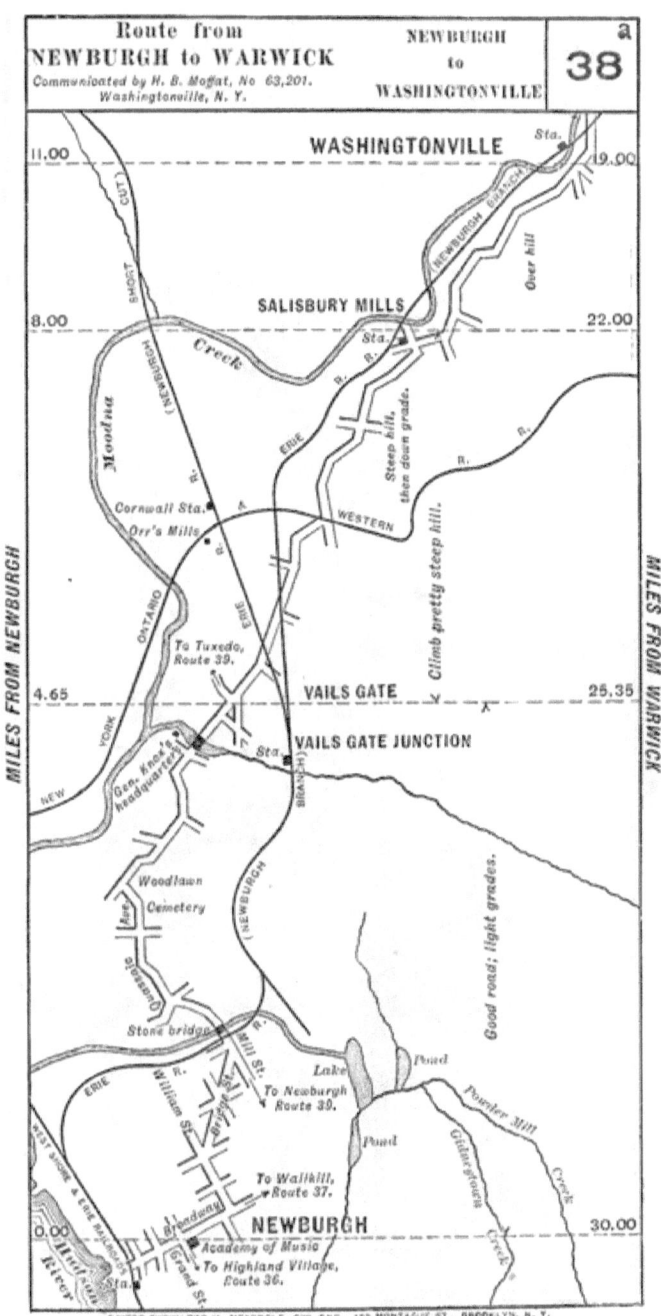

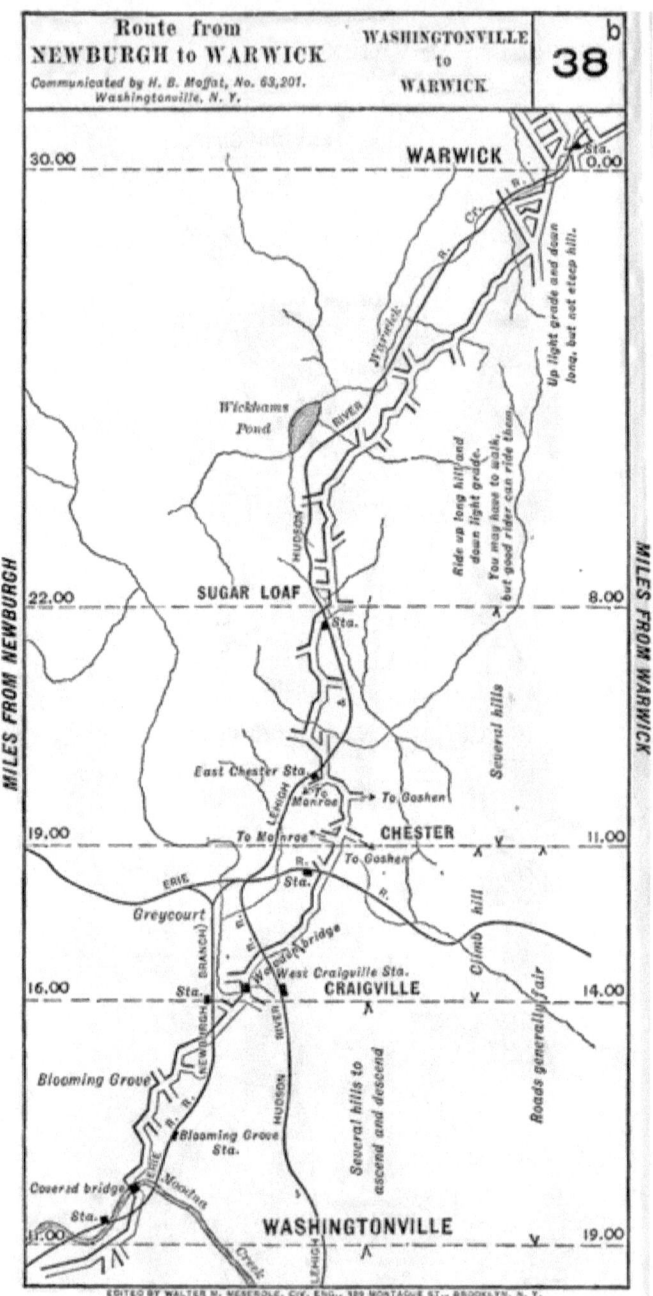

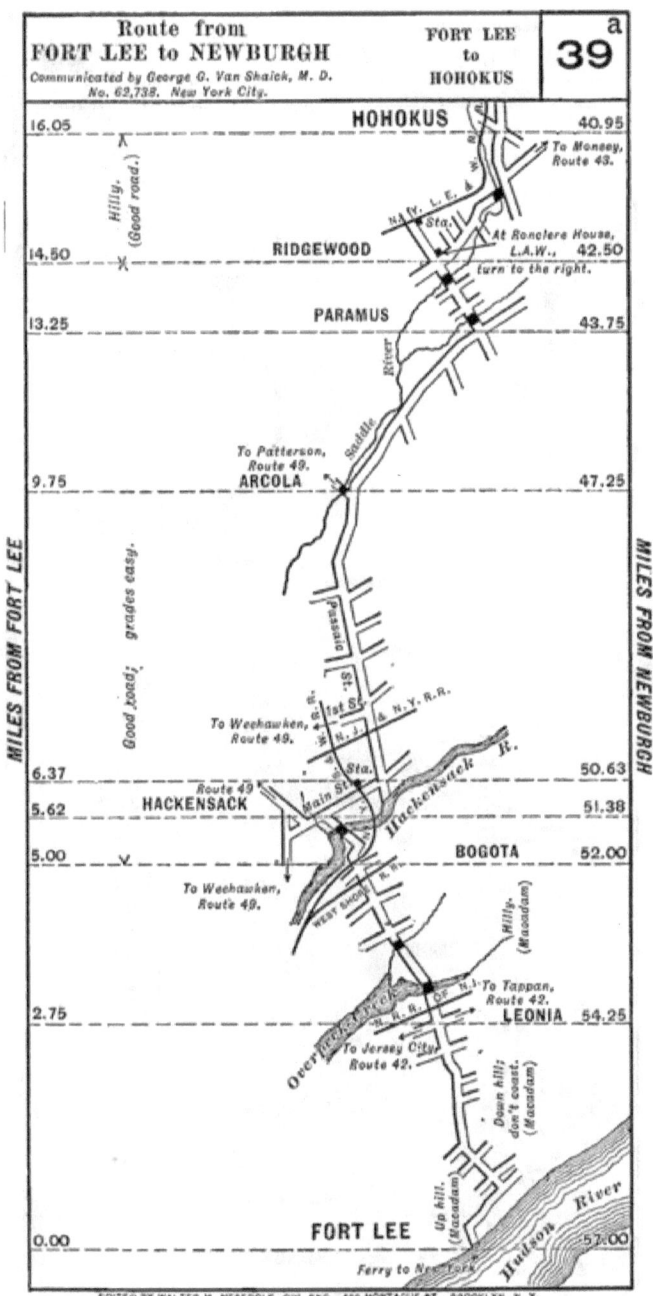

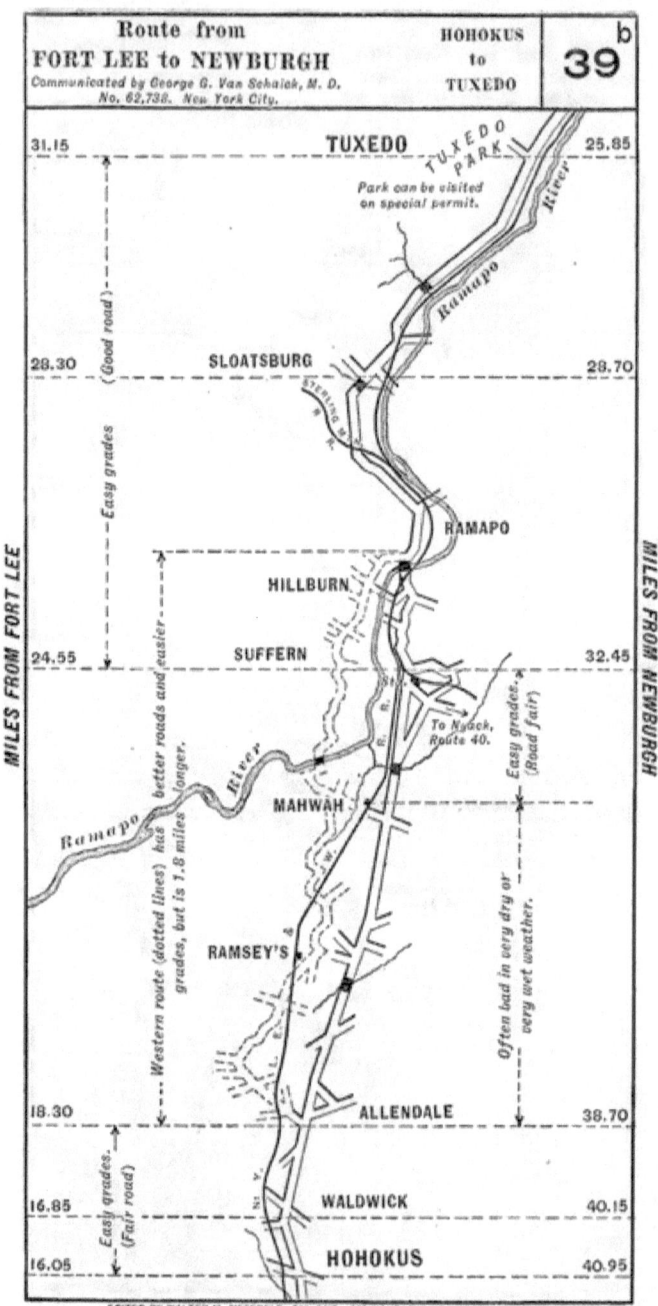

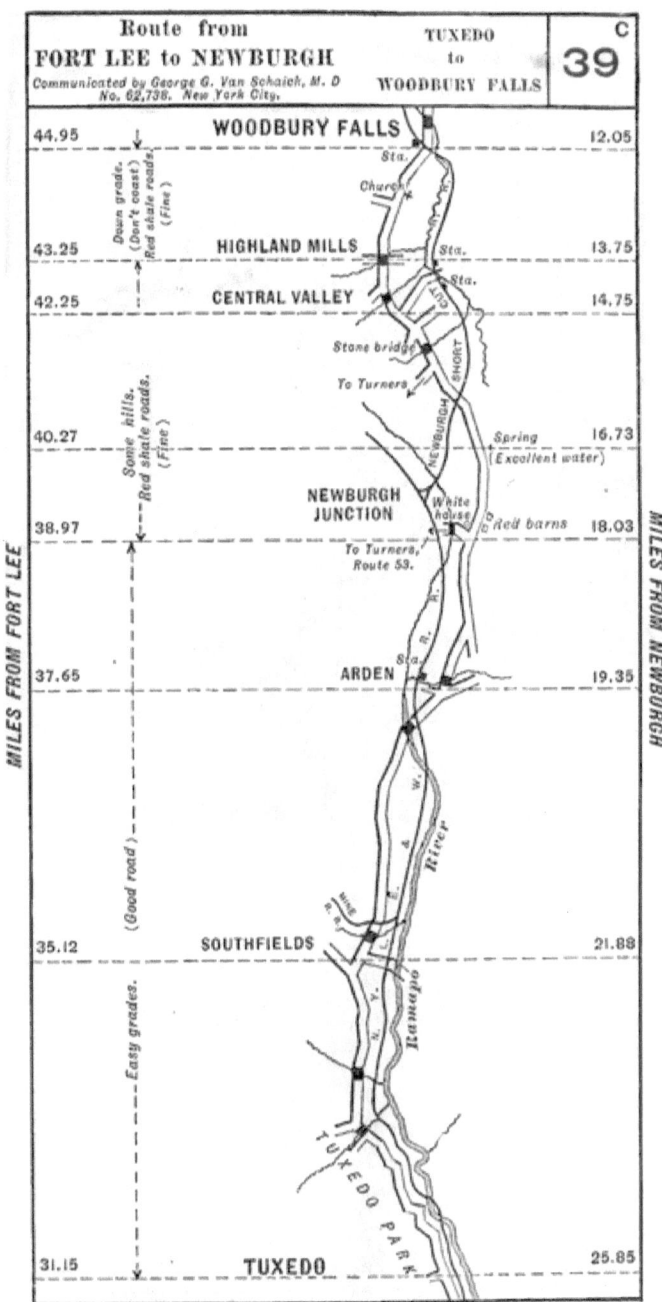

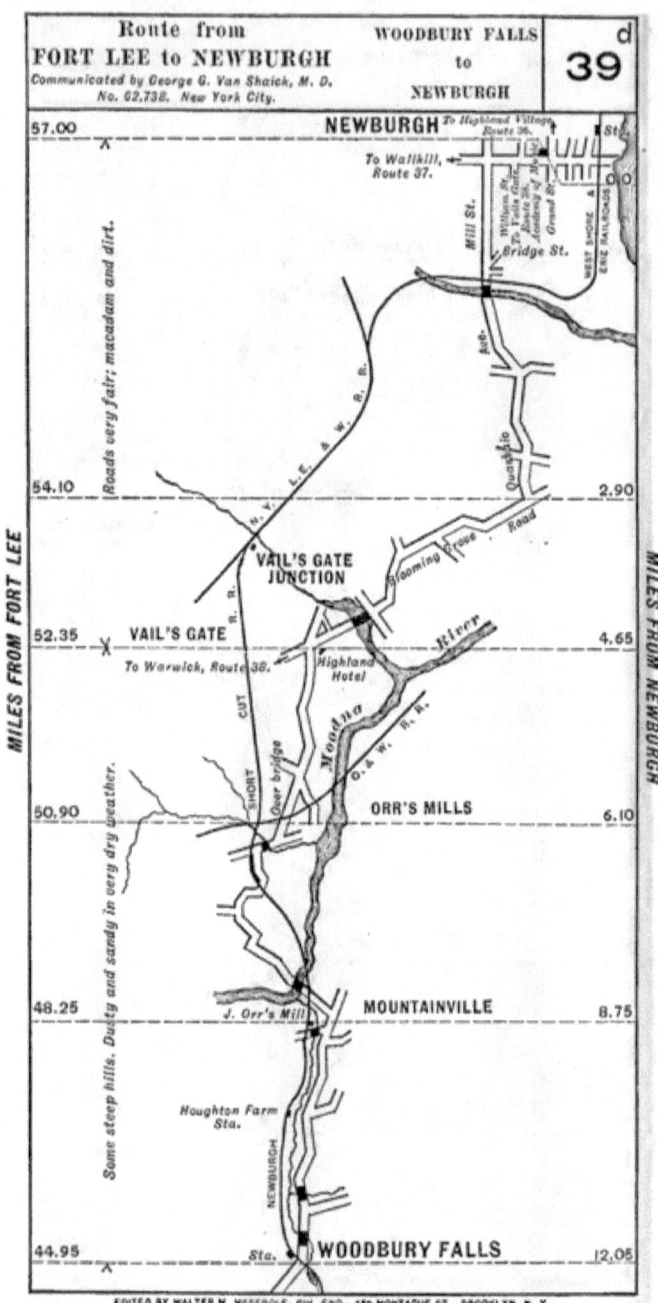

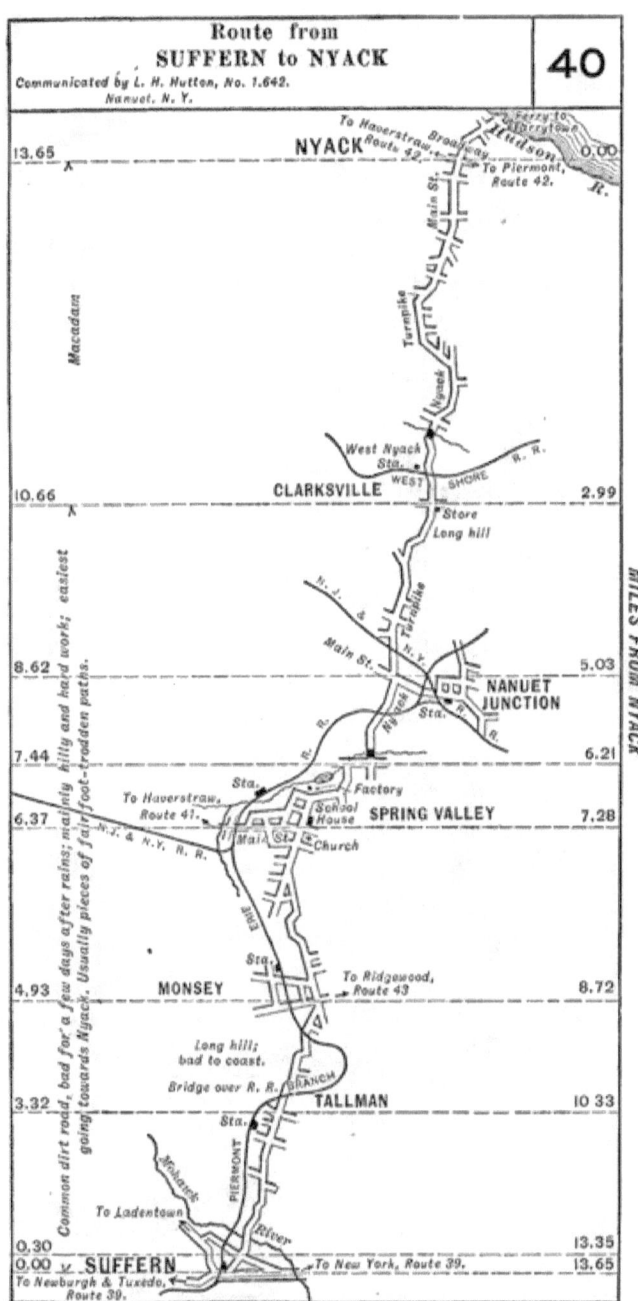

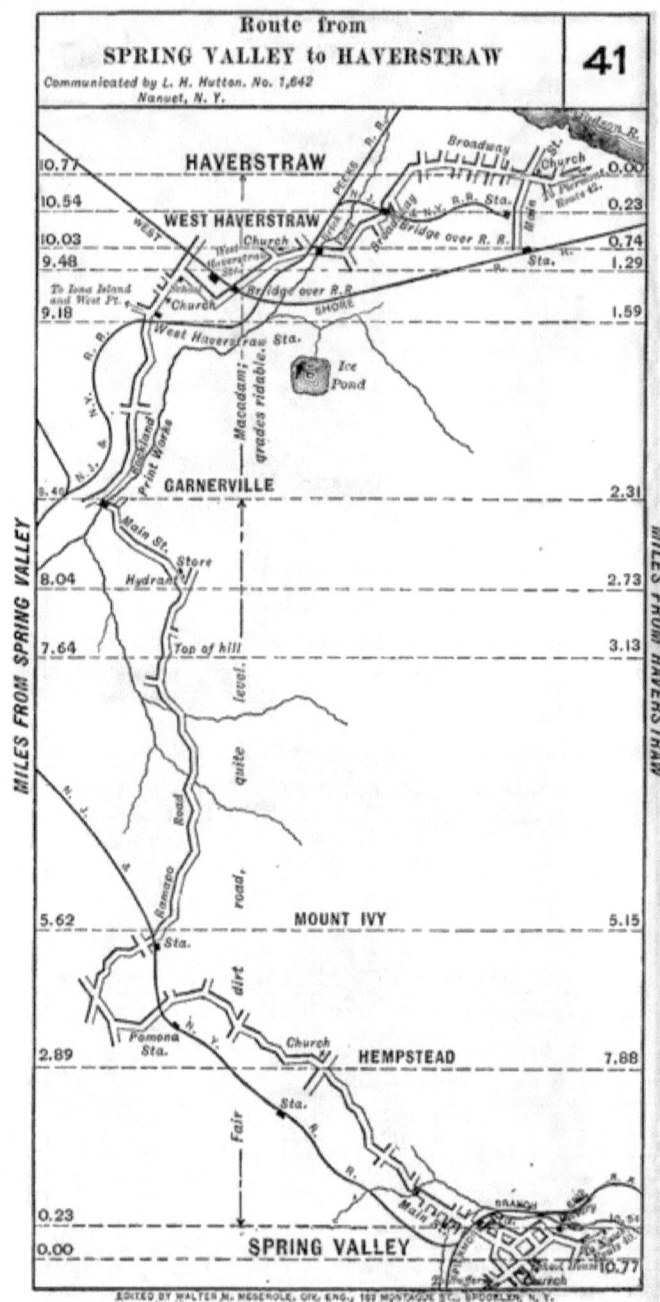

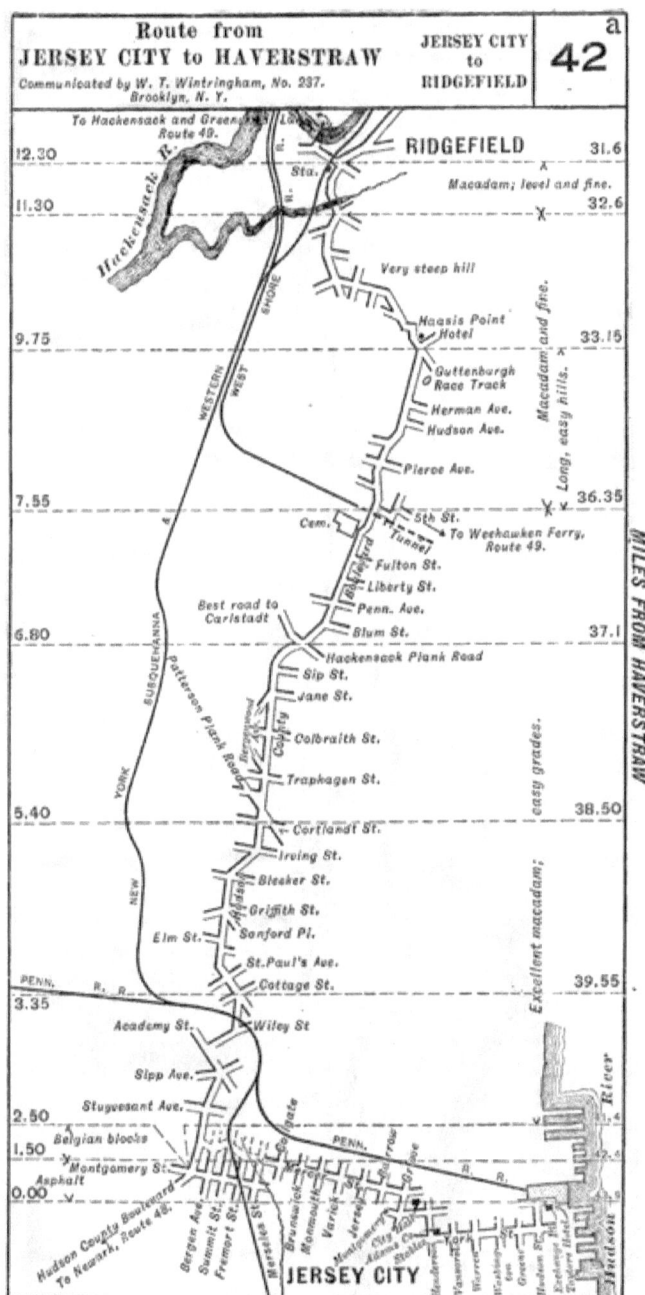

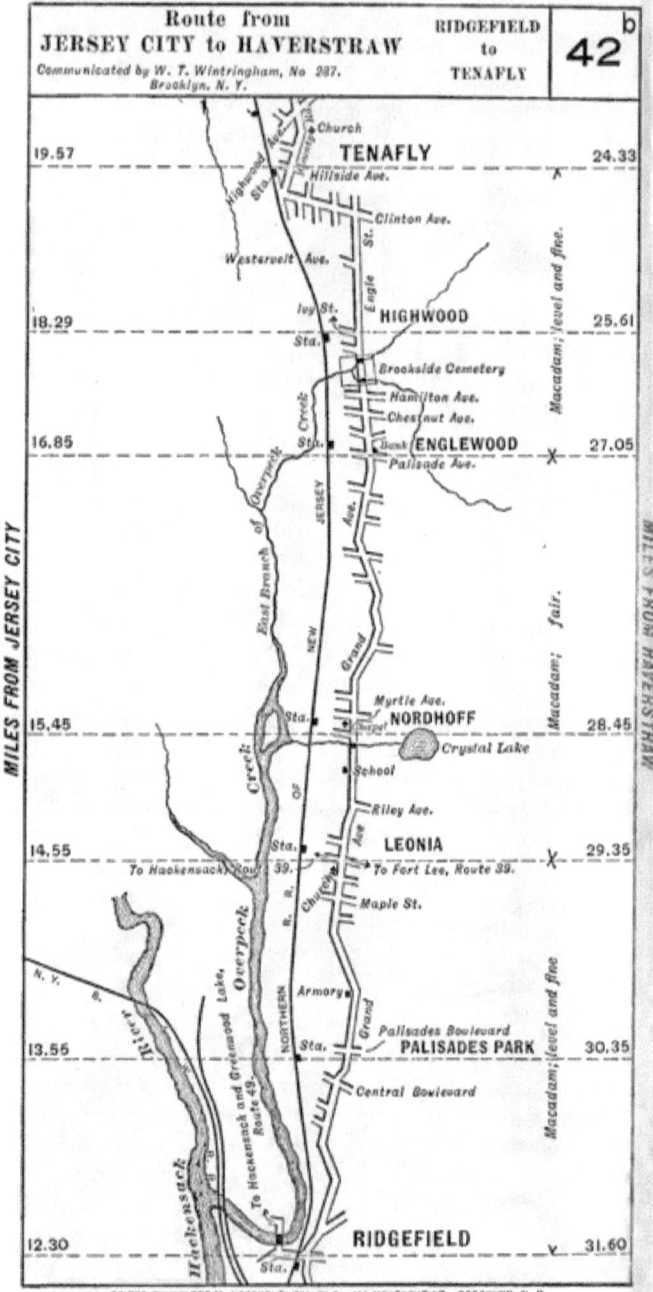

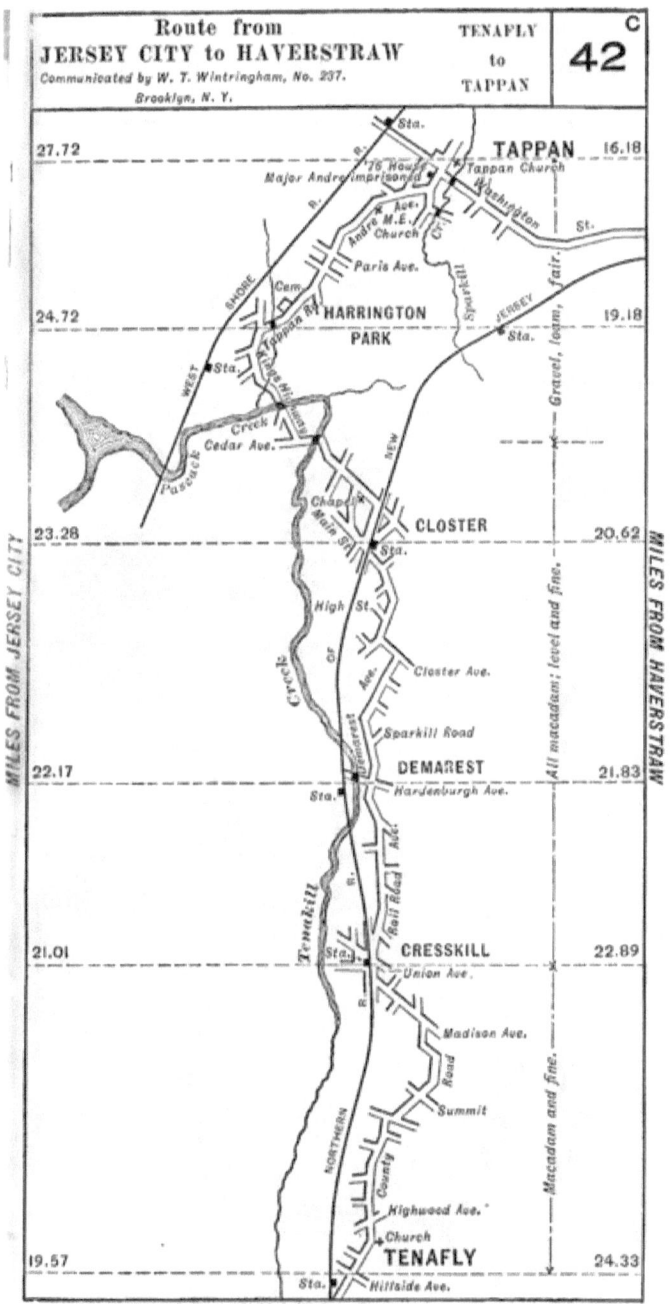

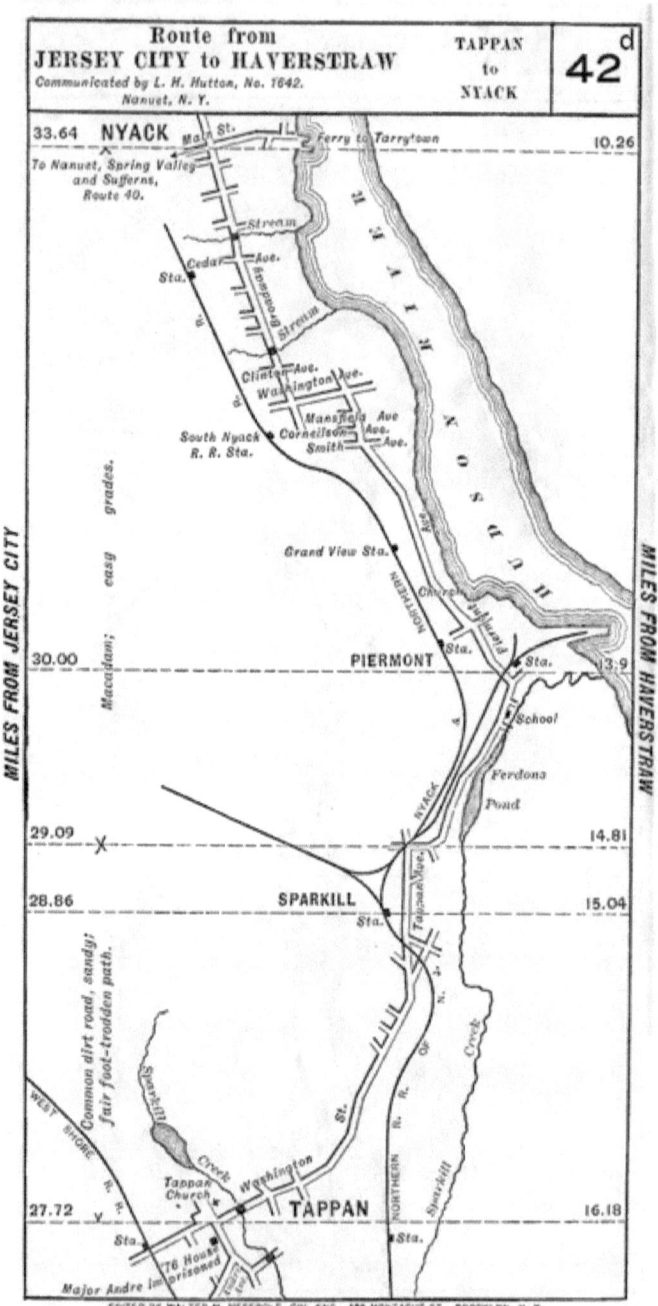

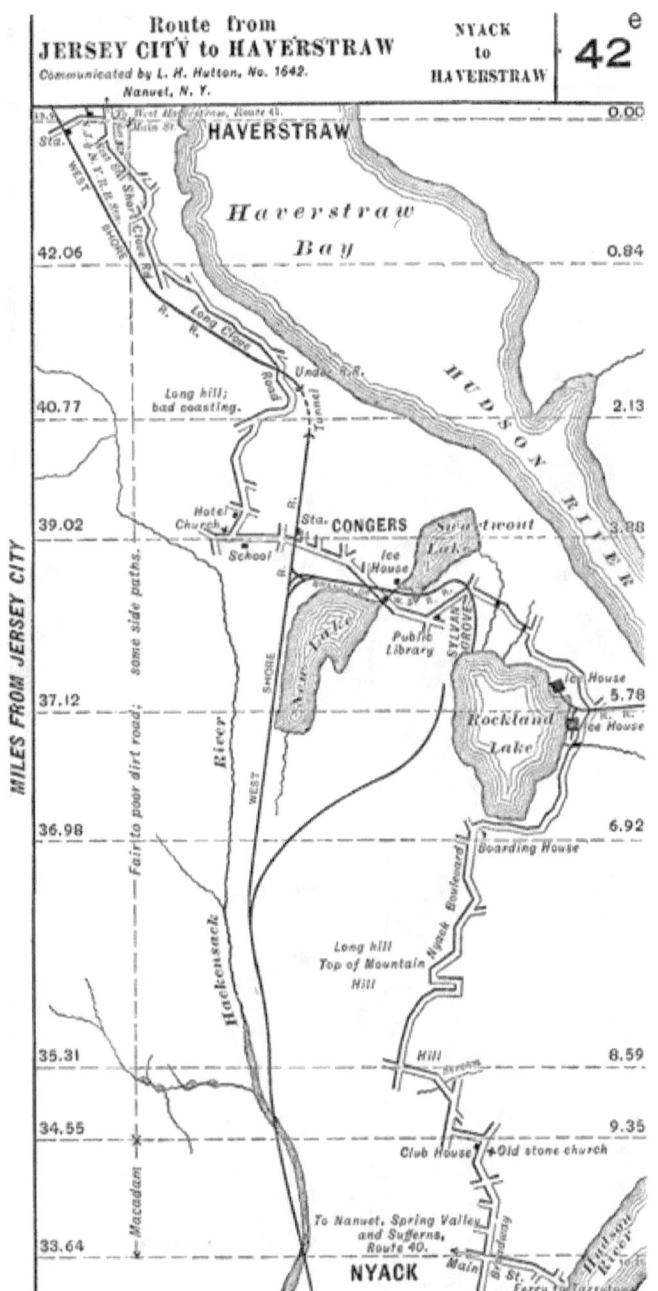

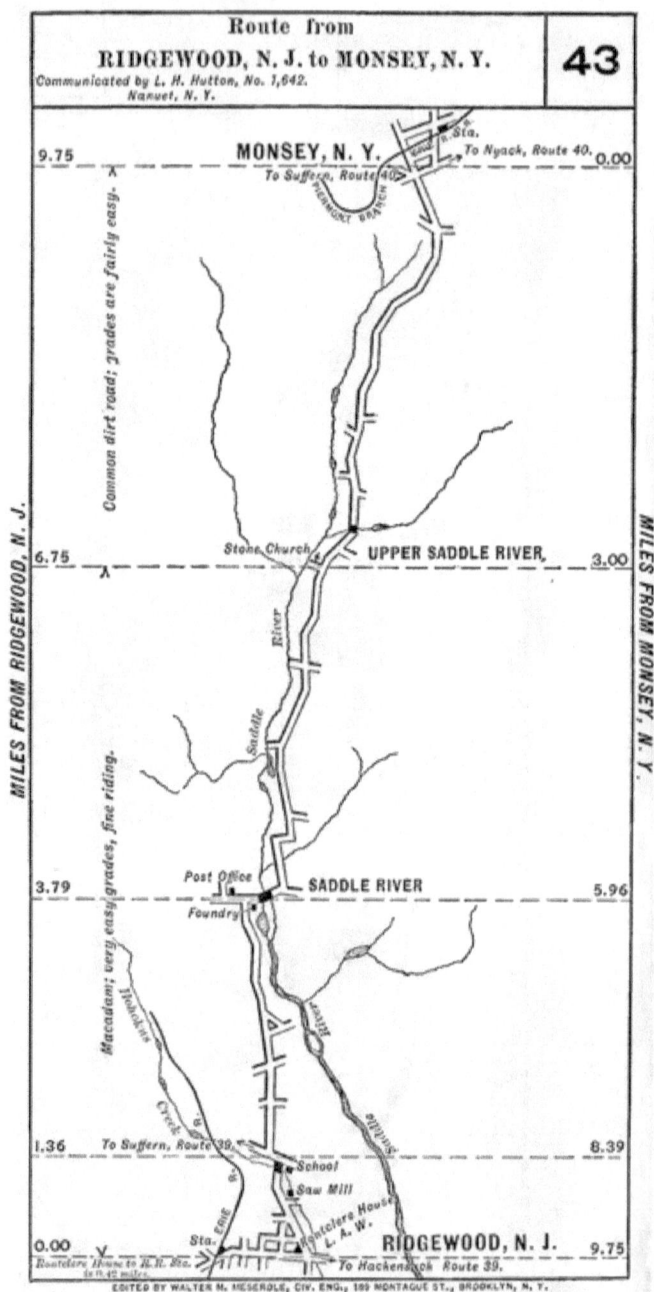

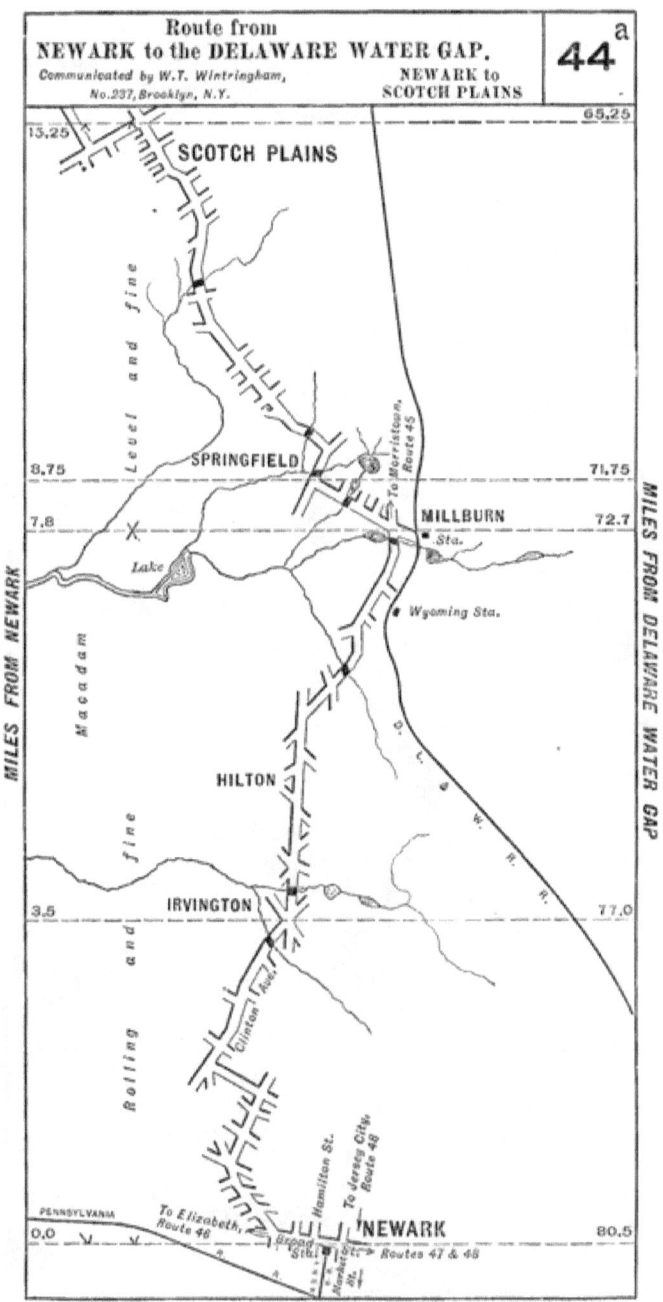

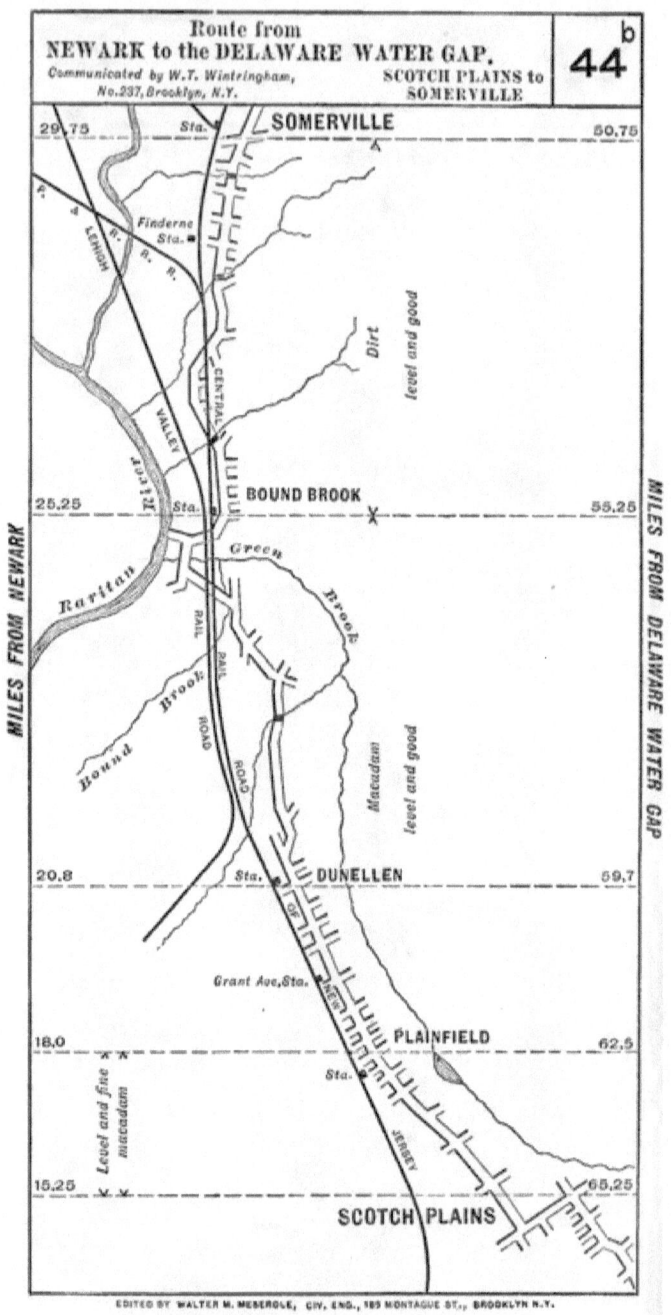

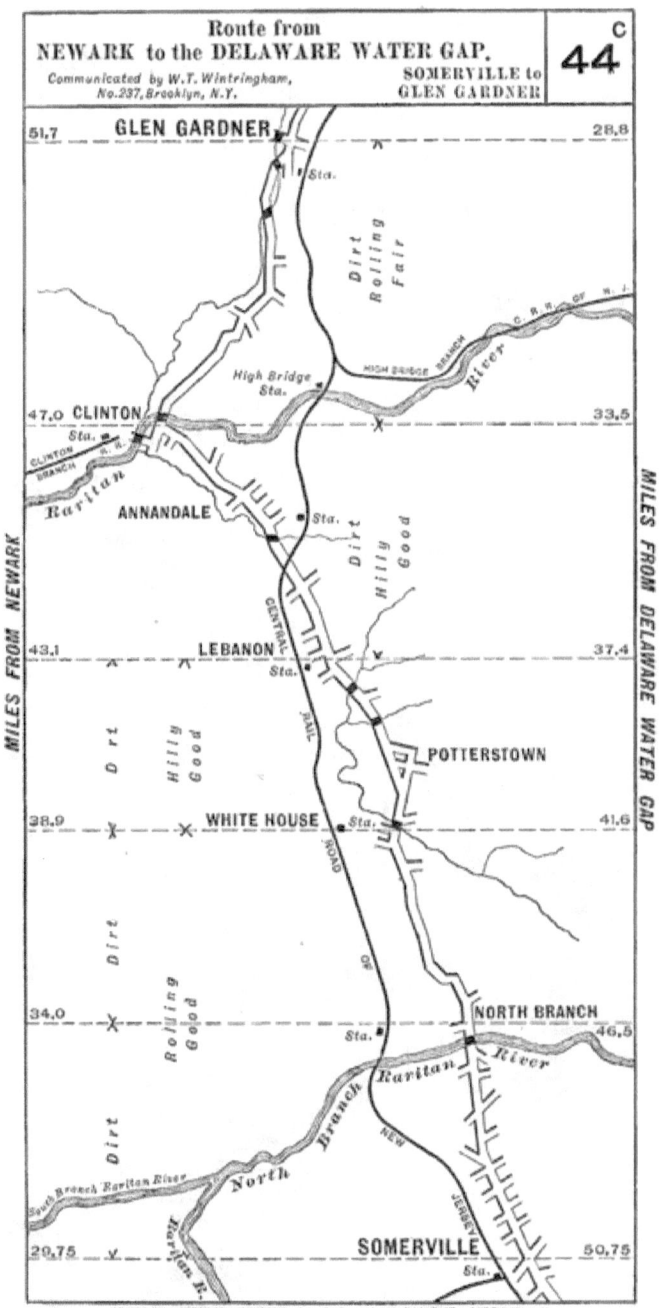

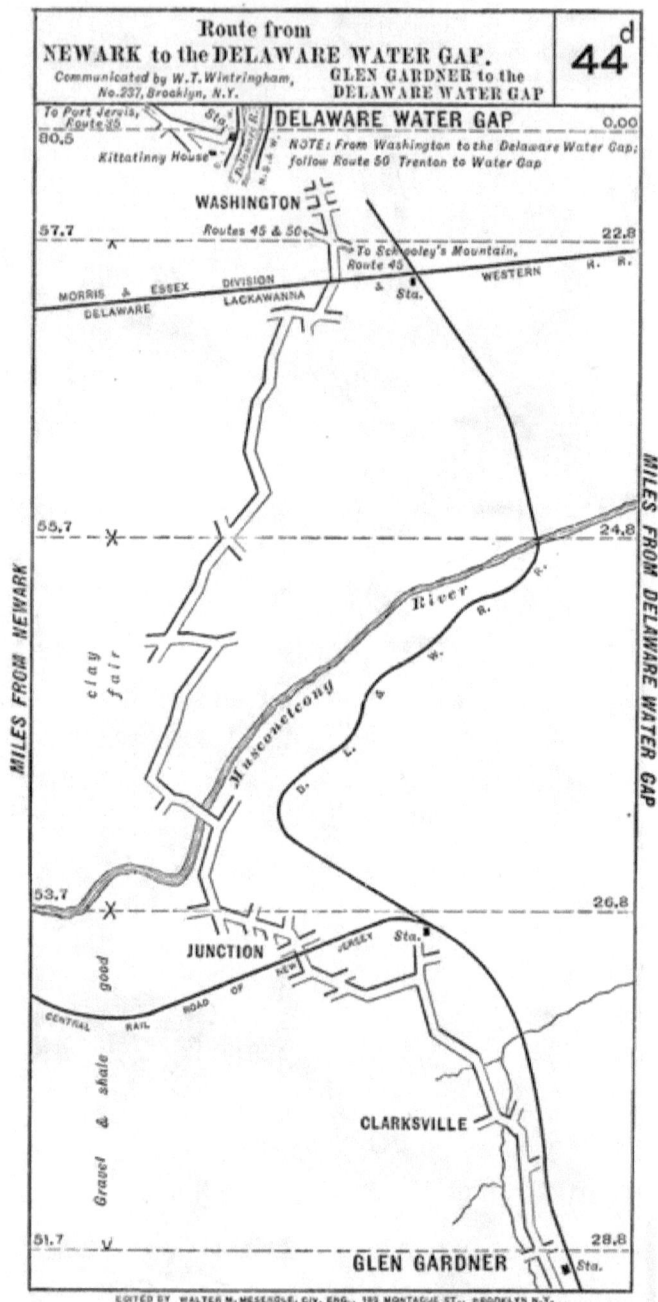

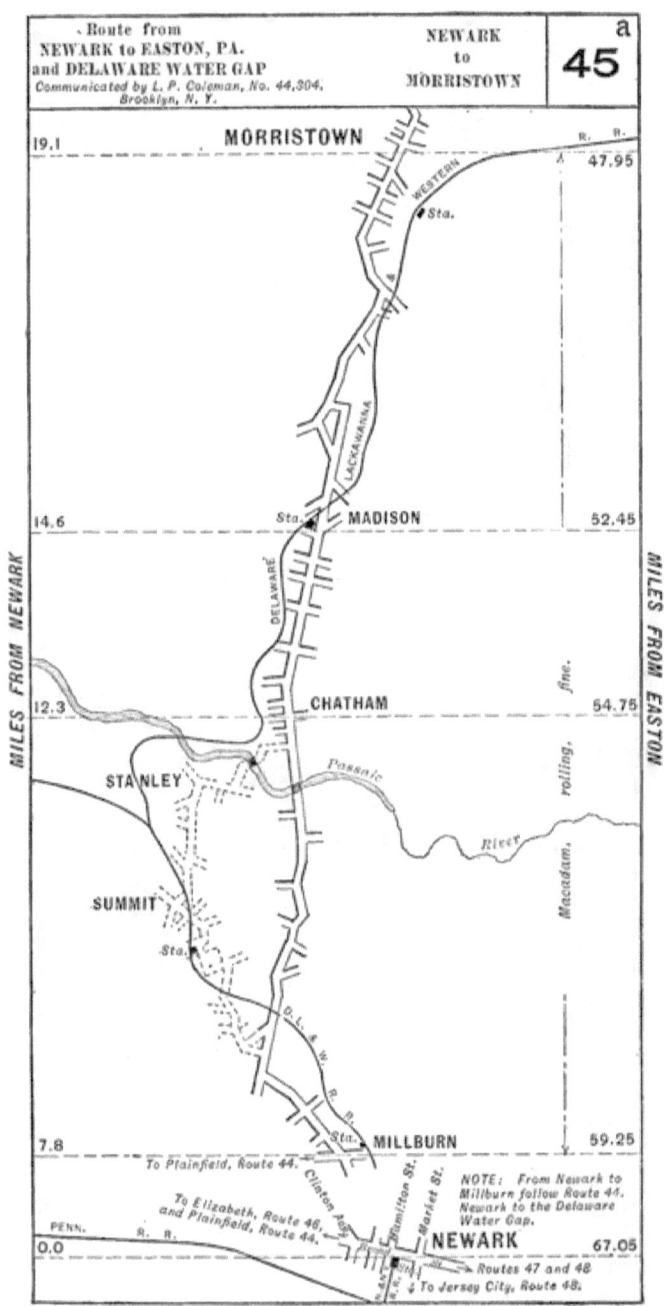

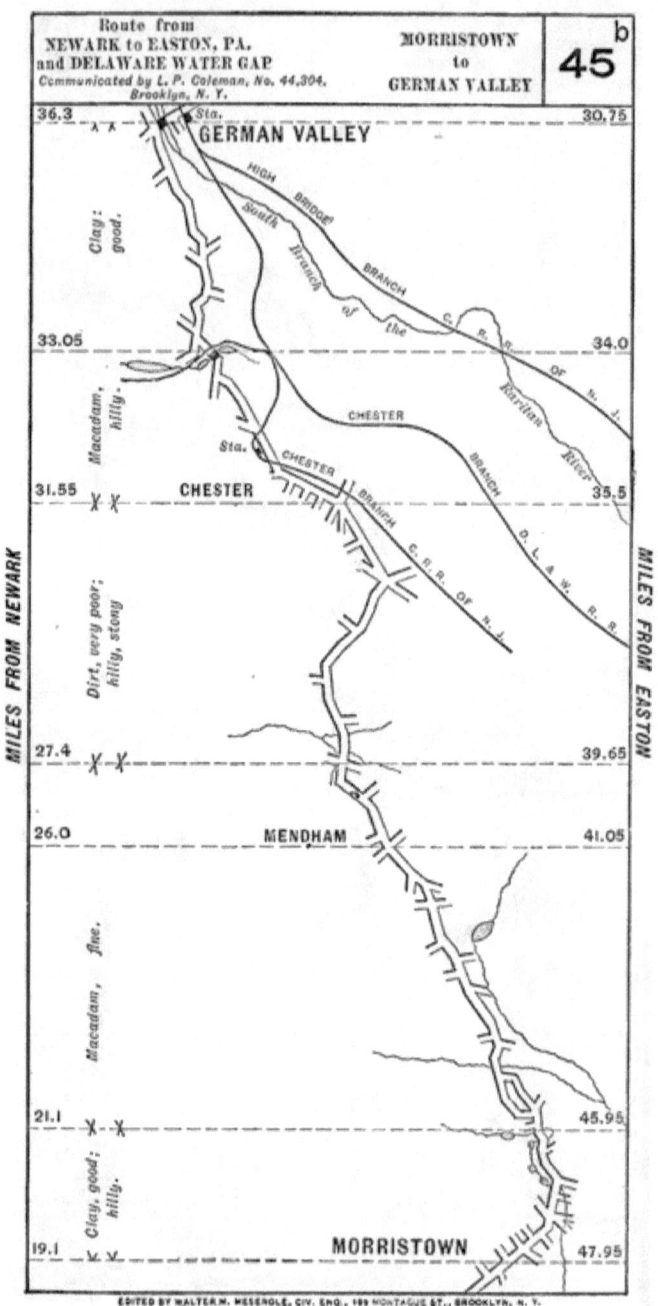

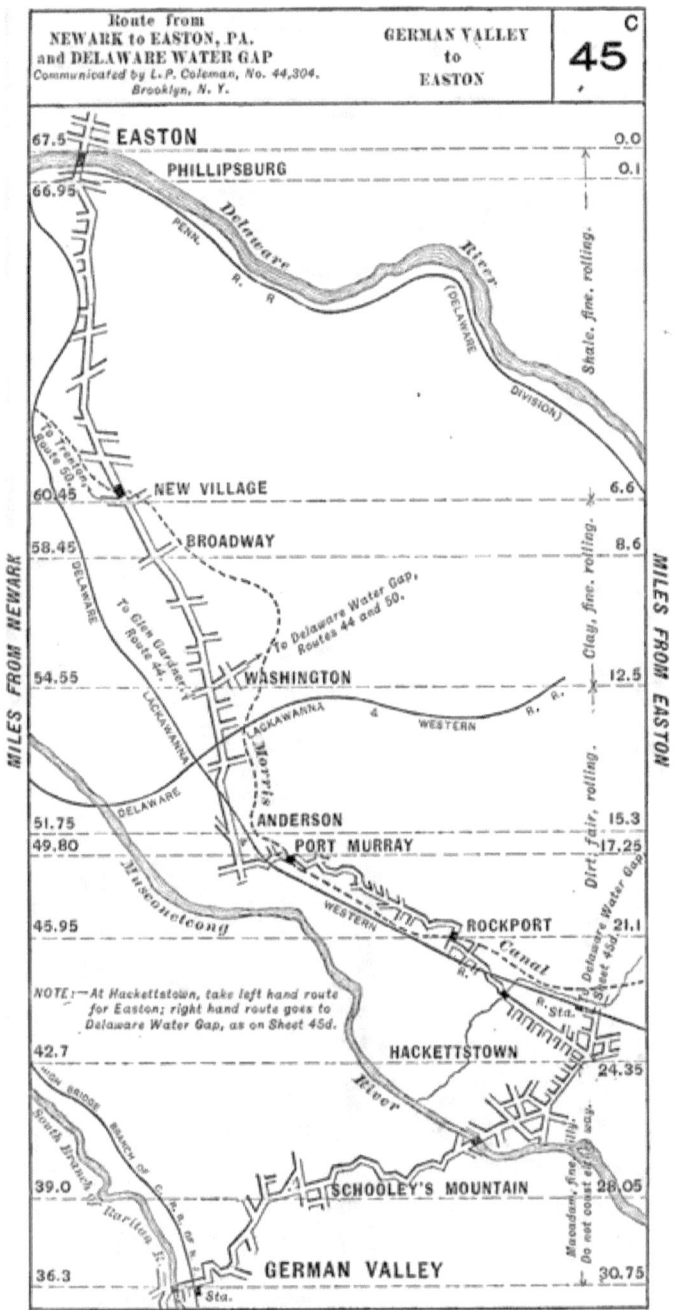

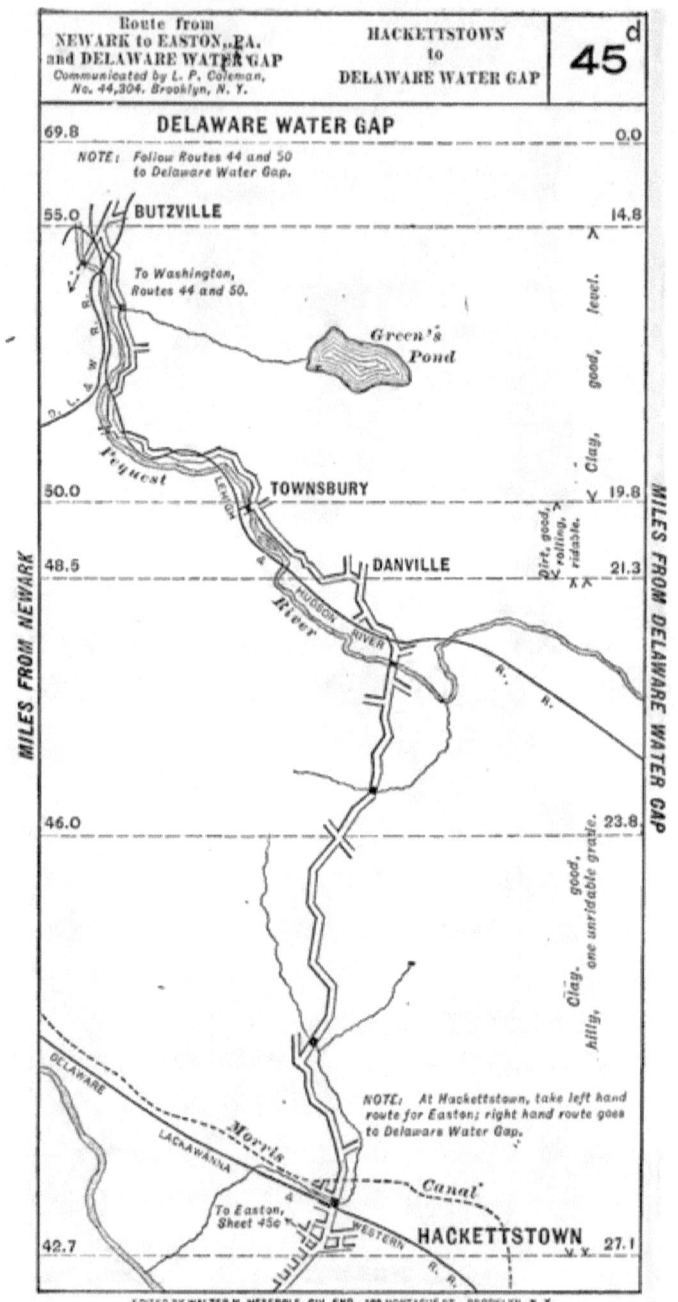

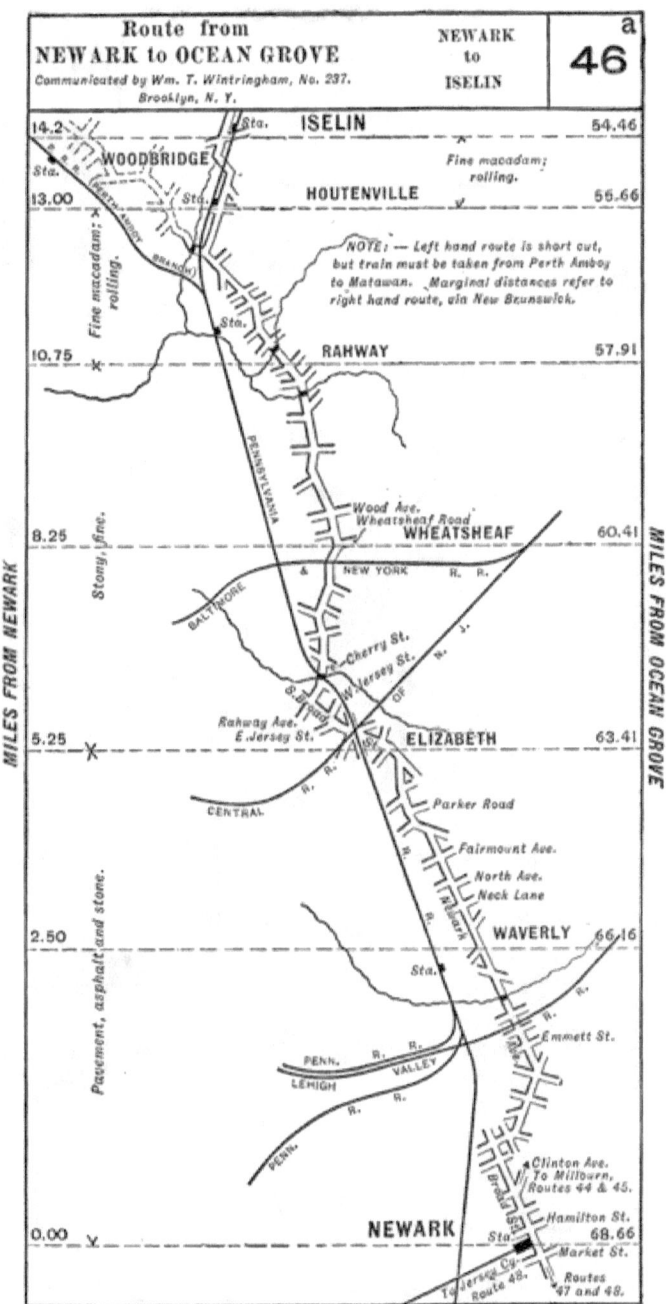

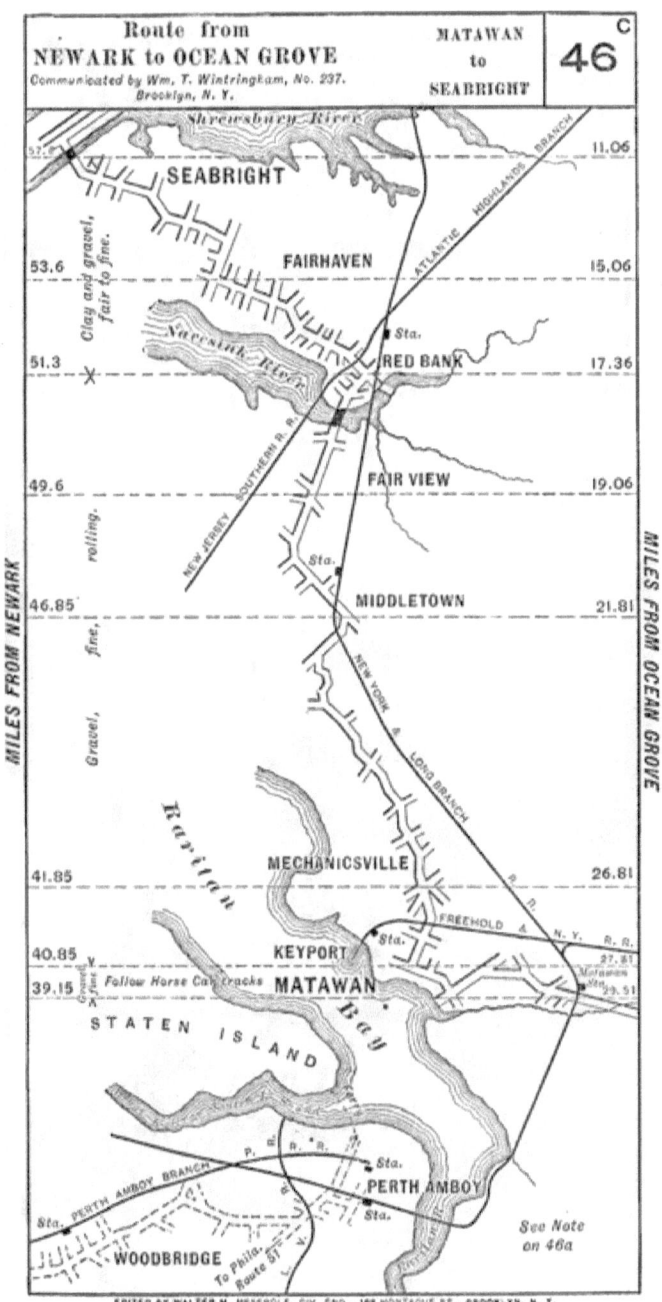

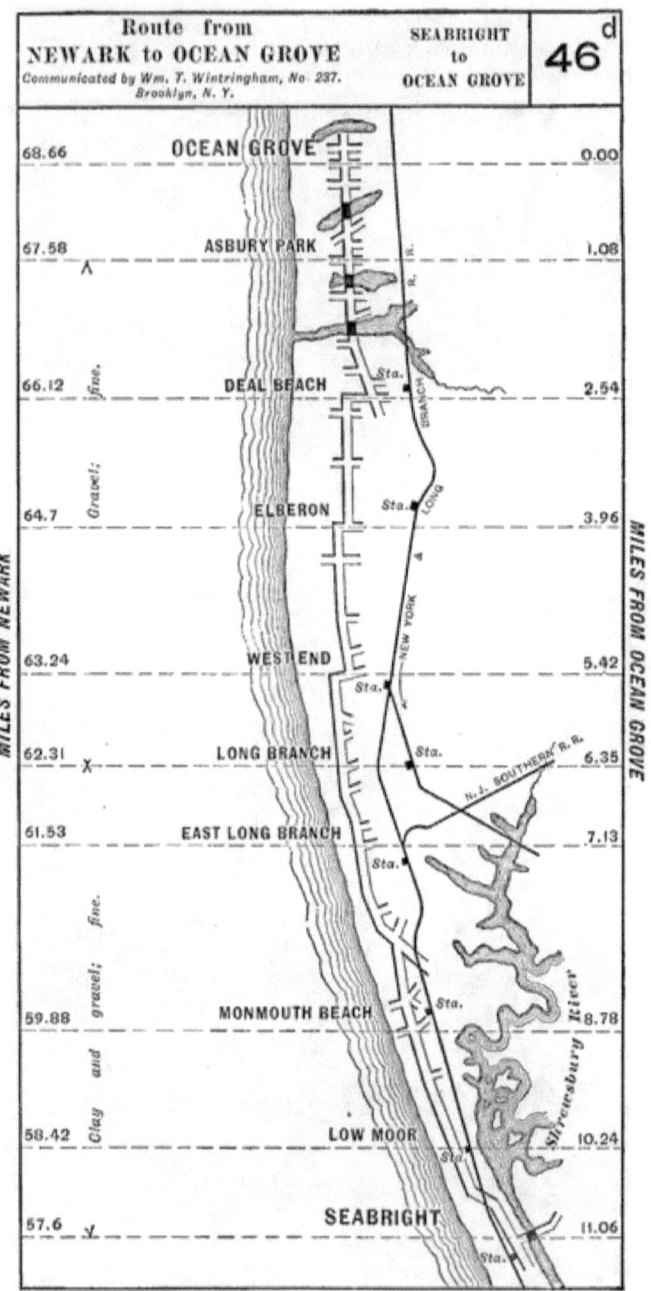

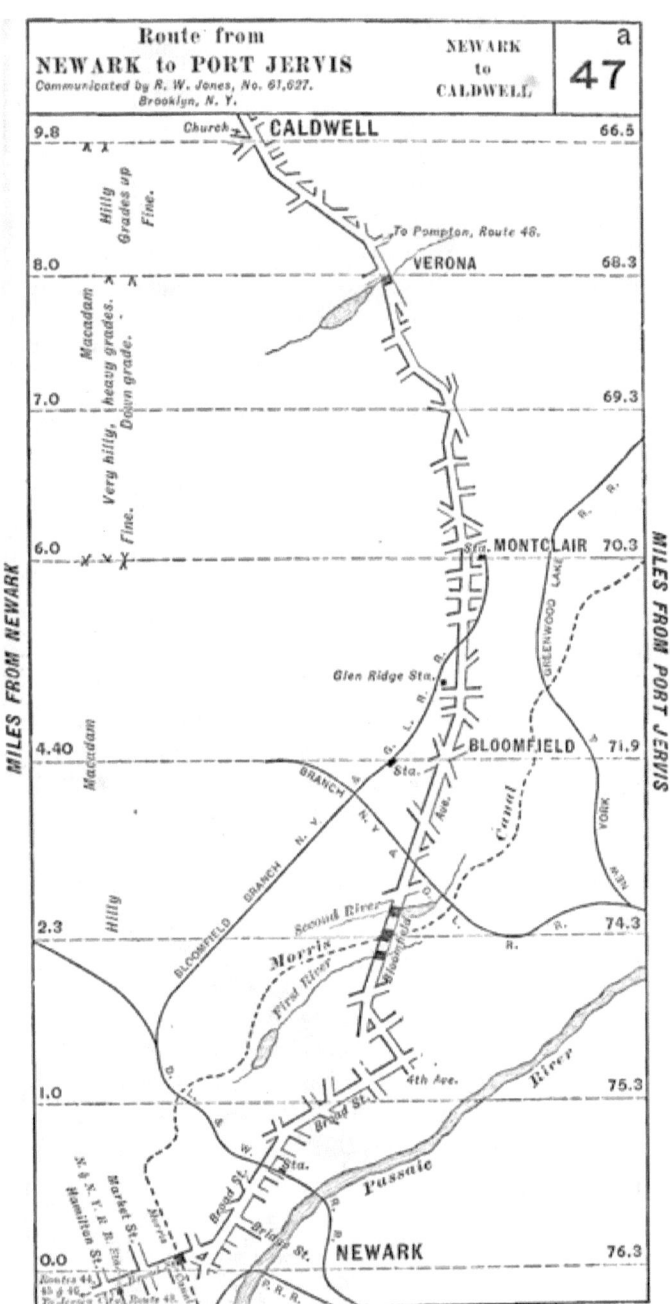

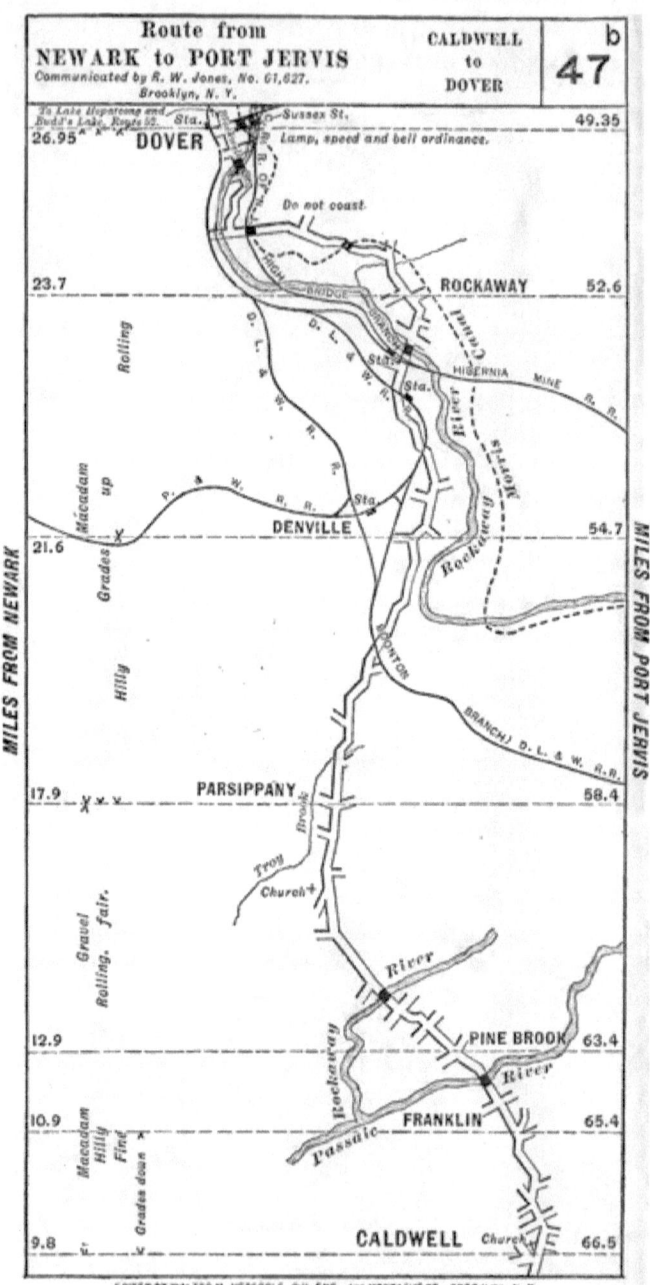

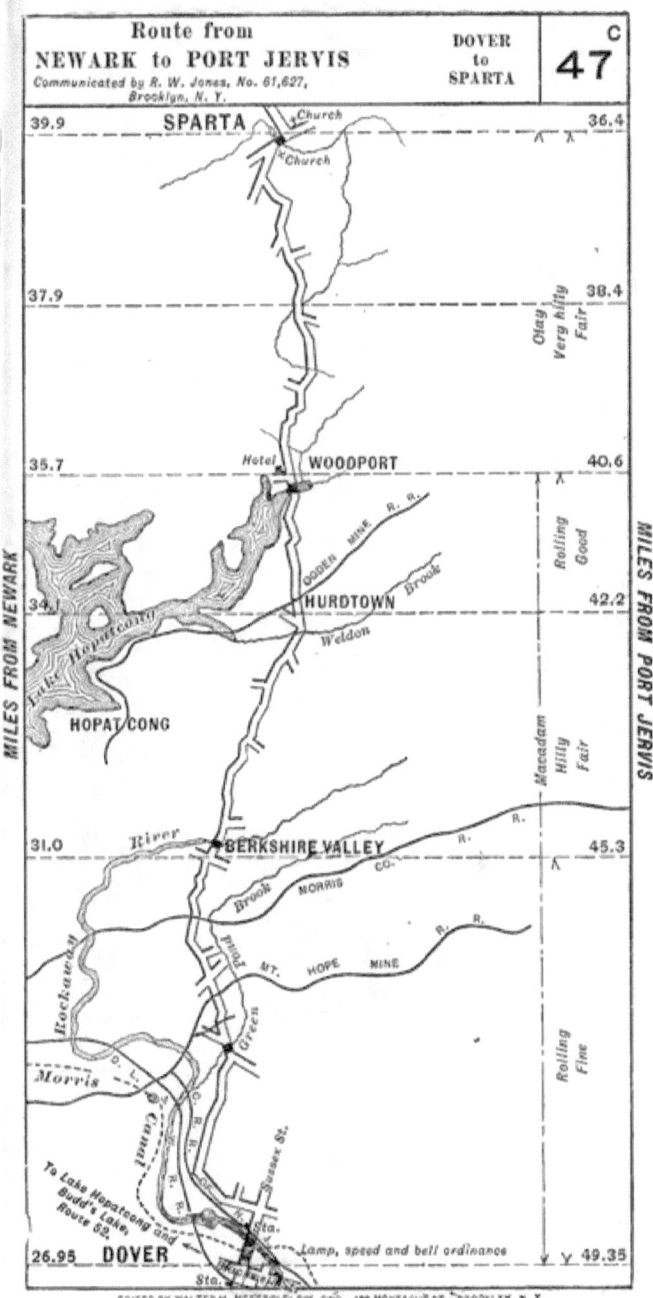

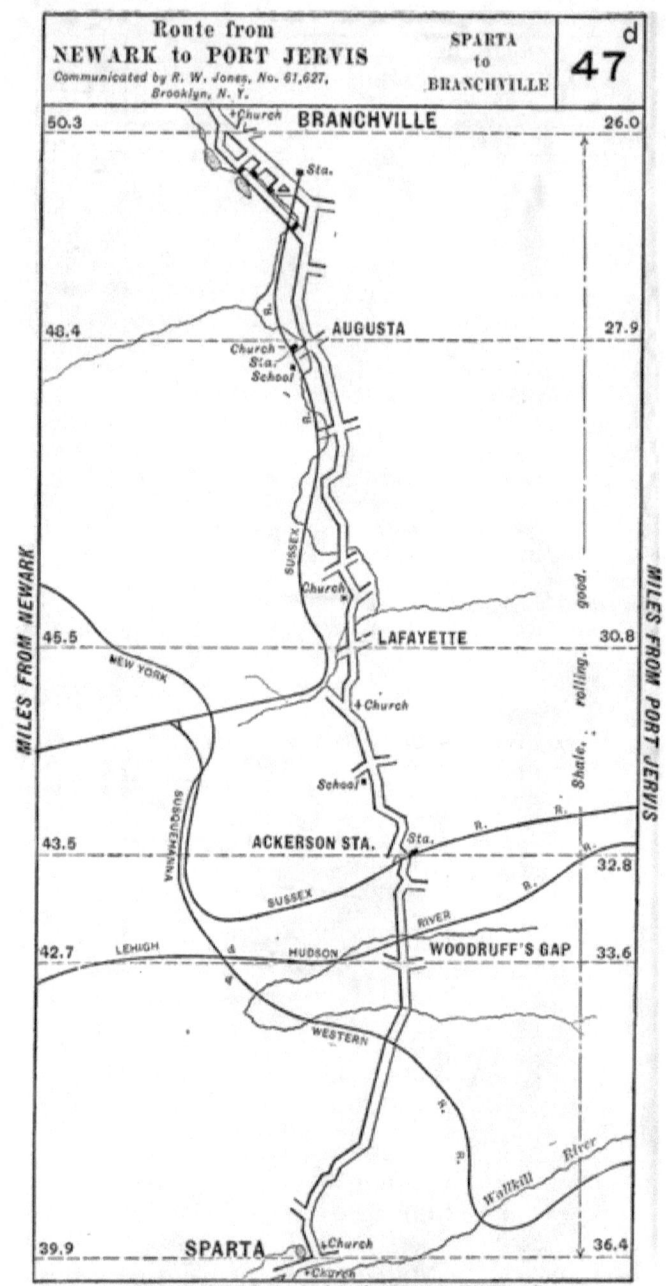

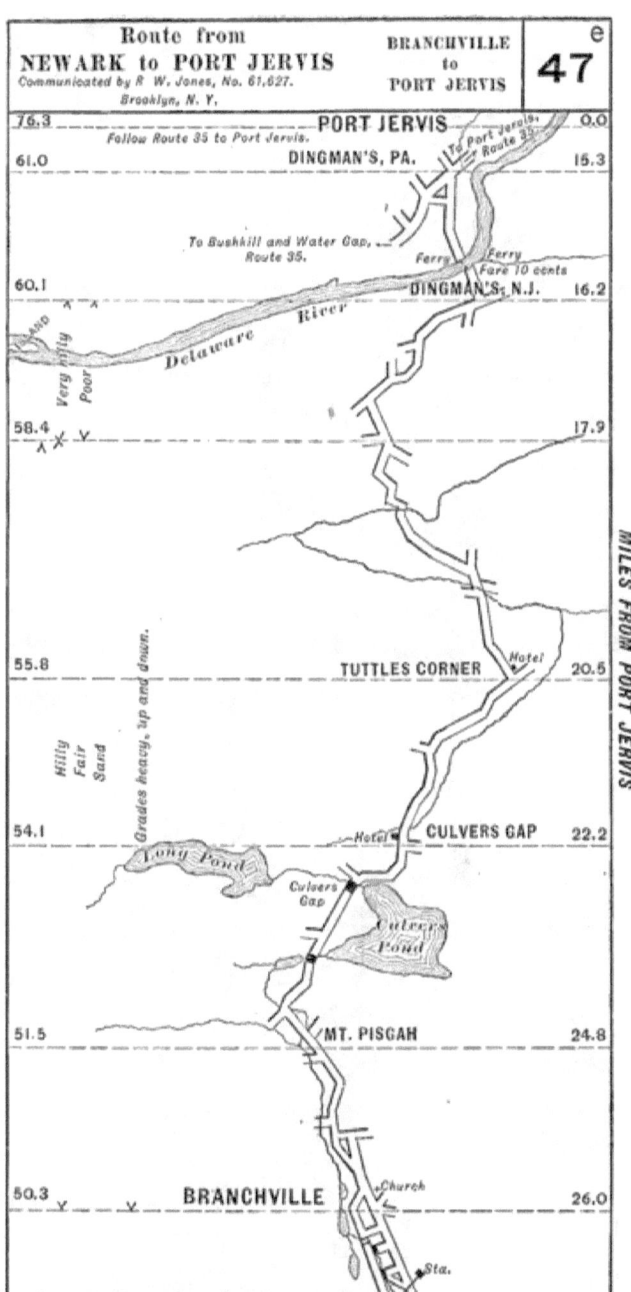

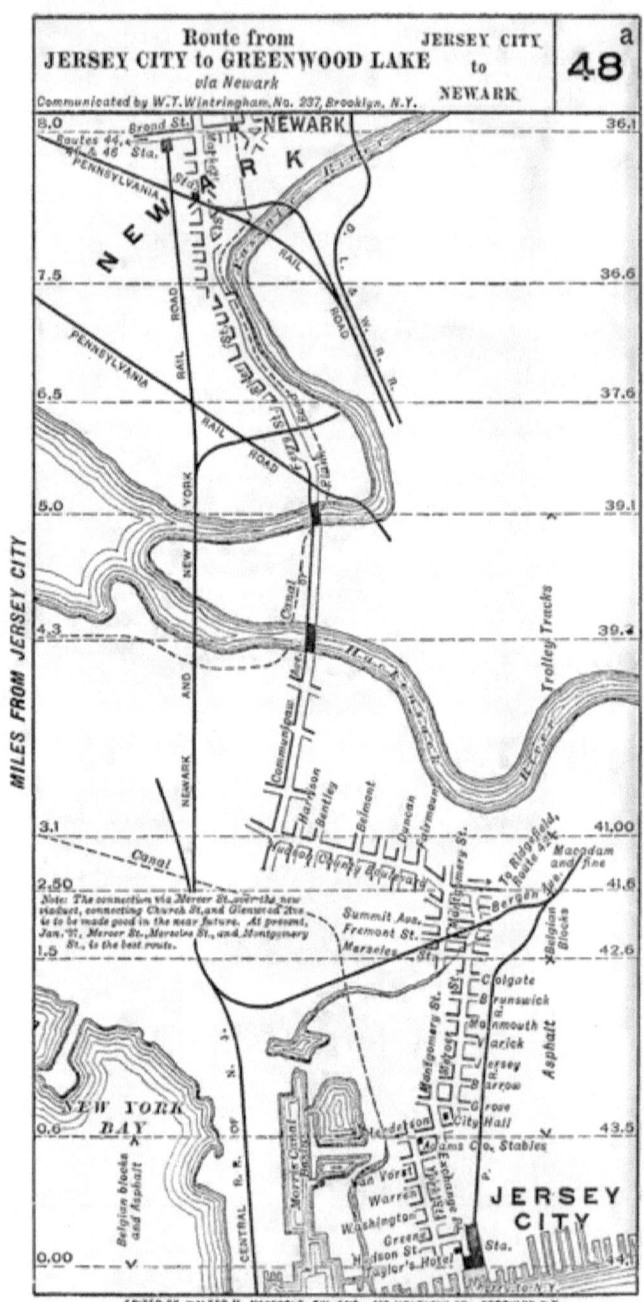

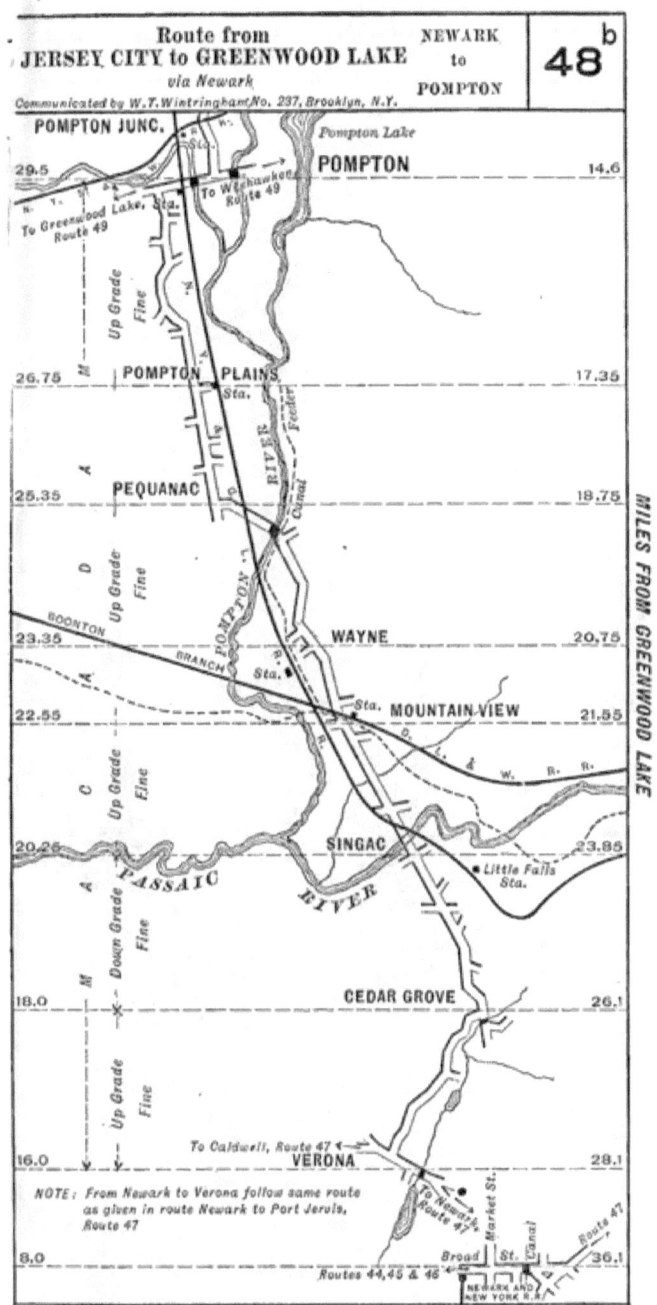

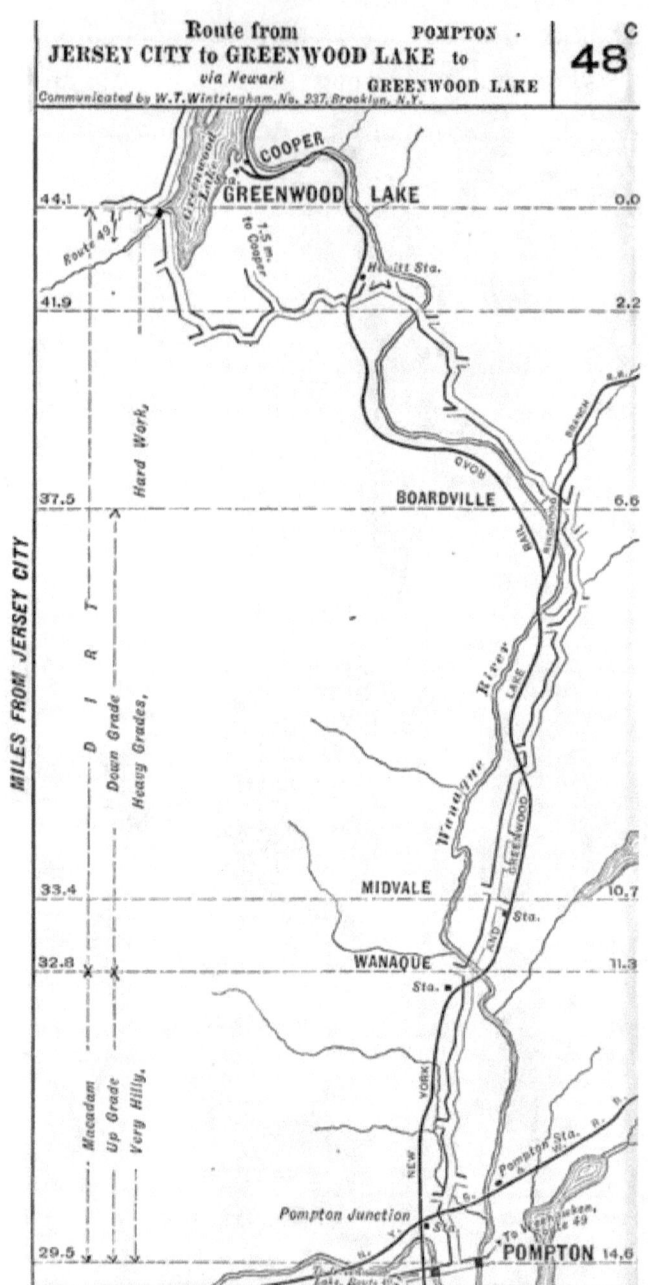

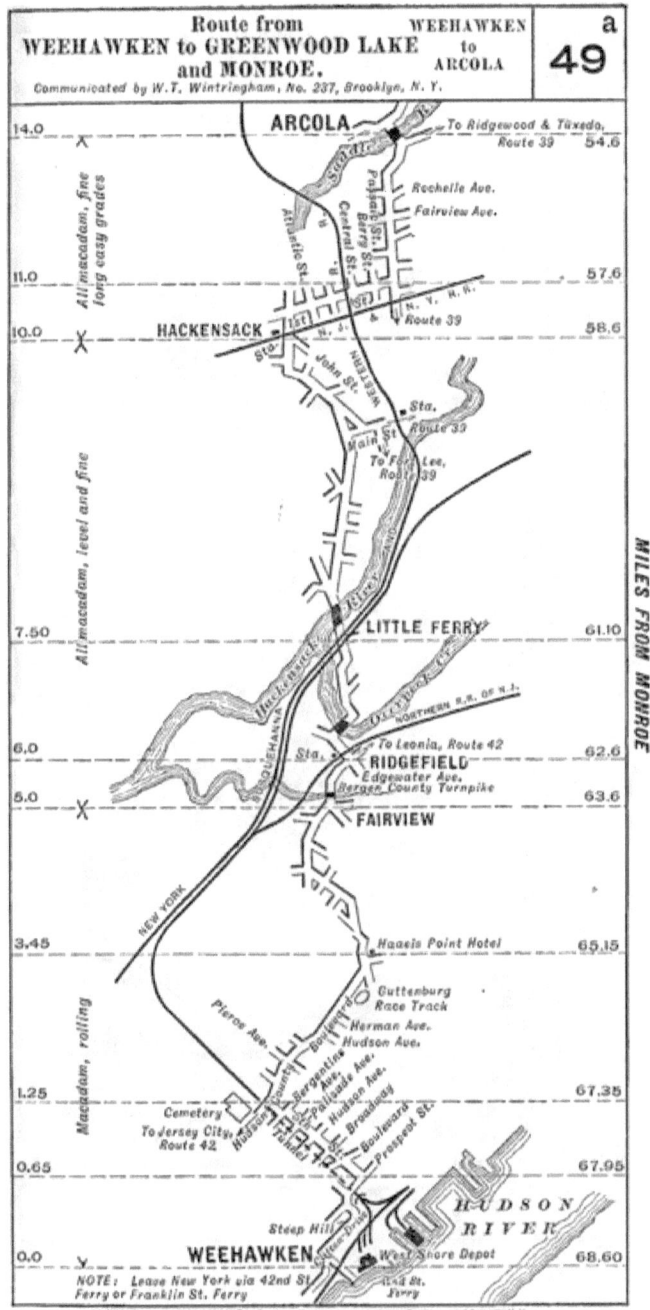

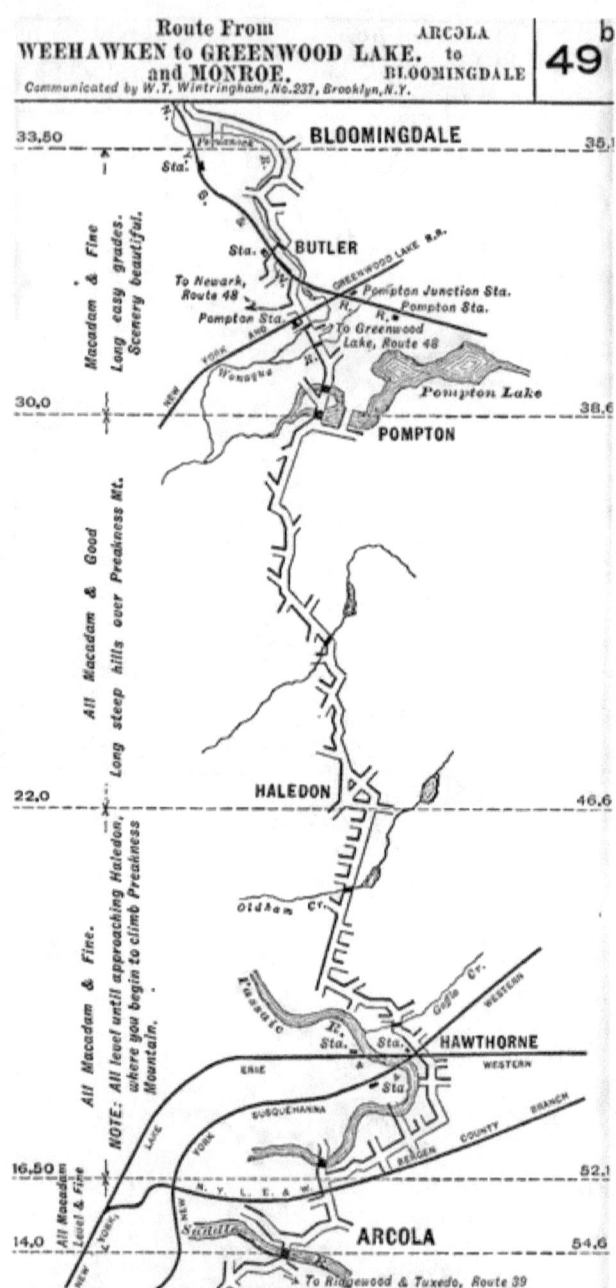

Route From
WEEHAWKEN to GREENWOOD LAKE,
and MONROE.
ARCOLA to BLOOMINGDALE
49 b

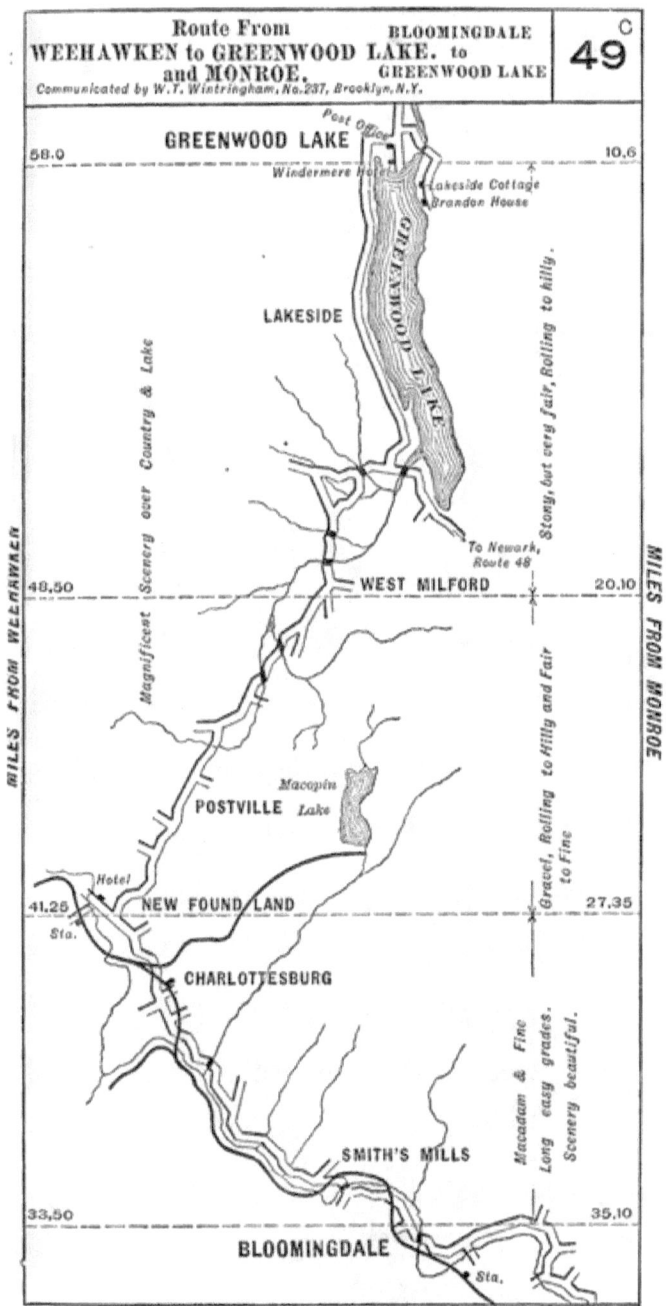

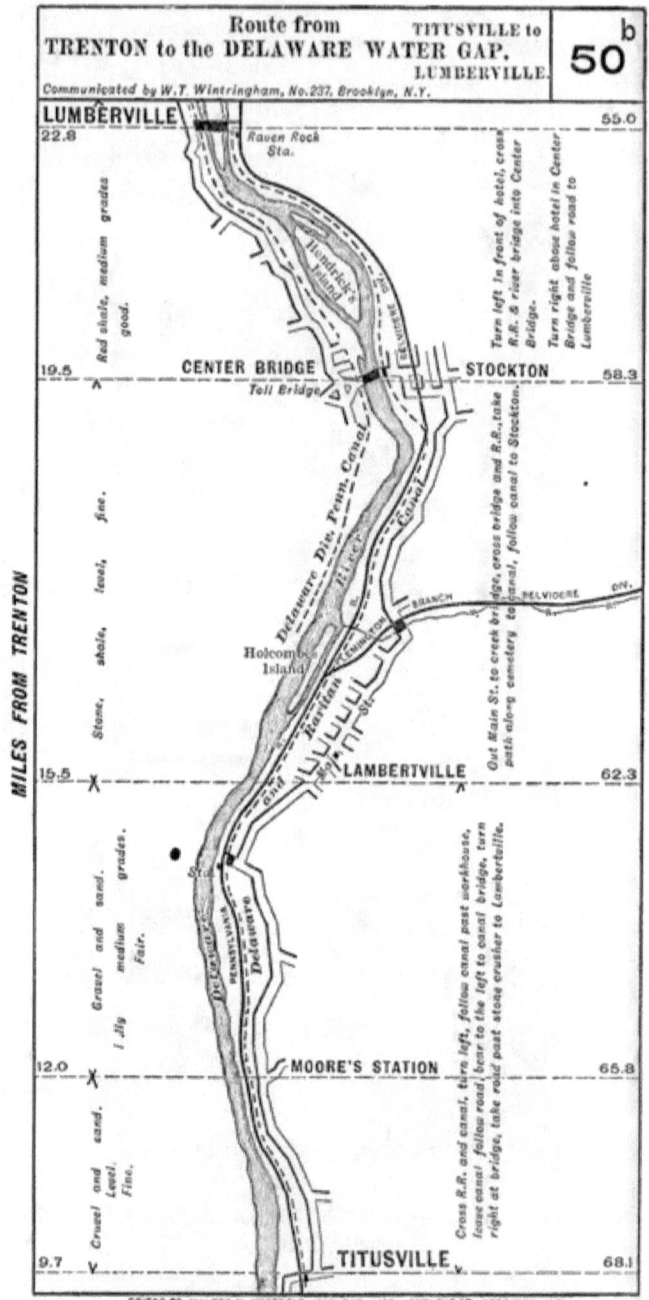

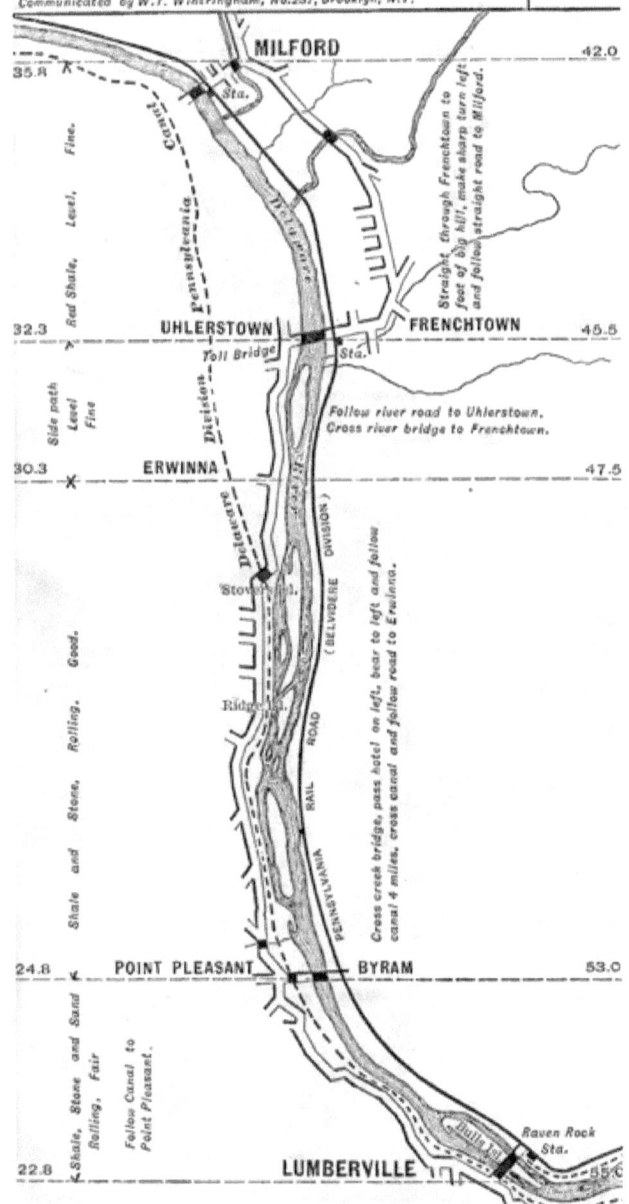

Route from TRENTON to the DELAWARE WATER GAP

MILFORD to OXFORD FURNACE

50 d

Communicated by W. T. Wintringham, No. 237, Brooklyn, N. Y.

Map annotations (miles from Trenton on left, miles to destination on right):

- 60.0 — OXFORD FURNACE — 17.8
- 55.0 — WASHINGTON — 22.8
- 51.0 — BROADWAY — 26.8
- 49.0 — NEW VILLAGE — 28.8
- 46.5 — STEWARTSVILLE — 31.3
- 43.0 — BLOOMSBURY — 34.8
- 38.0 — SPRING MILLS — 39.8
- 35.8 — MILFORD — 42.0

Route notes:

Turn left 1st road past St. Cloud Hotel, cross canal, & at cross roads turn right for about 1¾ miles, turn left at 1st road, follow road over mountain down into Oxford Furnace.

For 4 miles Rolling, Fine. For 2 miles very Hilly, Fair.

Clay, Rolling, Fine.

Clay, Rolling, Fine.

Gravel & Clay Rolling Fine

Clay & Gravel Rolling Fine

Continue on same road past Stewartsville, cross Canal and turn right, cross R.R. and take right, cross creek and turn left and then turn right. Follow telegraph poles through New Village and Broadway to Washington.

Take Easton Pike out of Bloomsbury ¾ mile, turn right, cross creek and follow creek to Stewartsville.

Follow road 2 mile turn right and bear to left to Bloomsbury.

Shale & Gravel Mountainous Generally unridable Dangerous Fine for 4 miles Bad for 1 mile

Shale Hilly Fine

Continue on same road past Milford, bear to the left for 2 miles, turn right at Spring Mills Cross Roads.

EDITED BY WALTER M. MESEROLE, CIV. ENG., 189 MONTAGUE ST., BROOKLYN N.Y.

COPYRIGHT, 1888, BY THE NEW YORK STATE DIVISION, L. A. W.

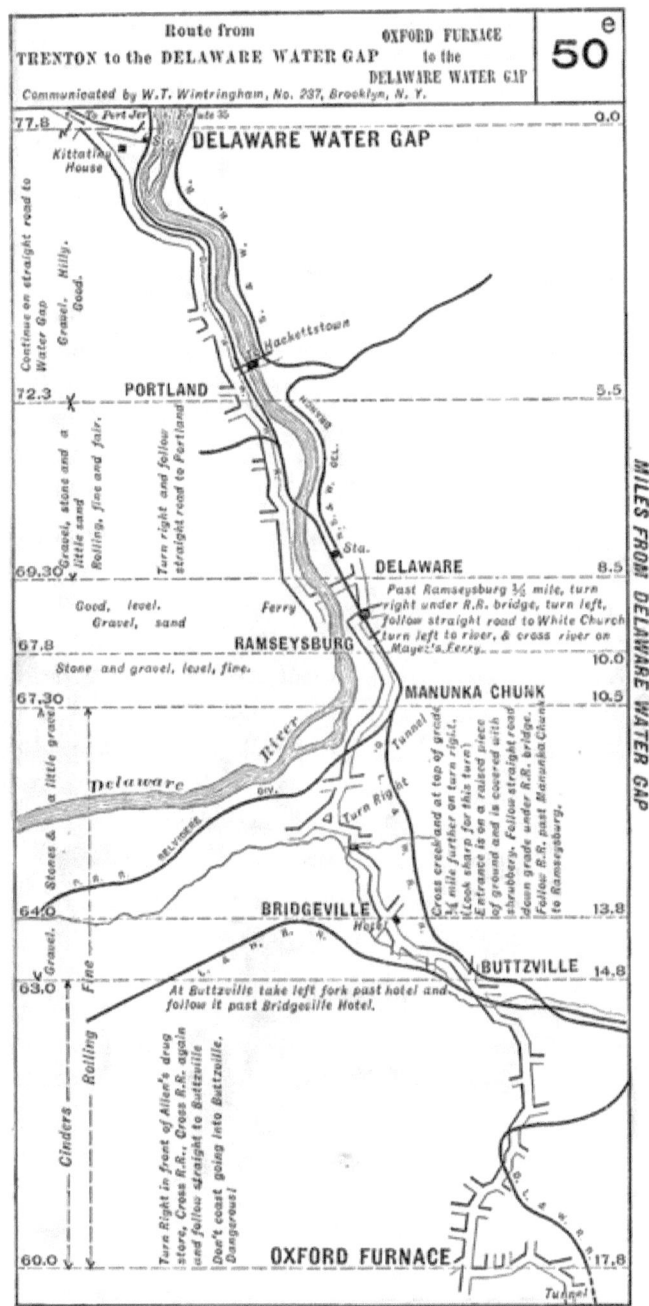

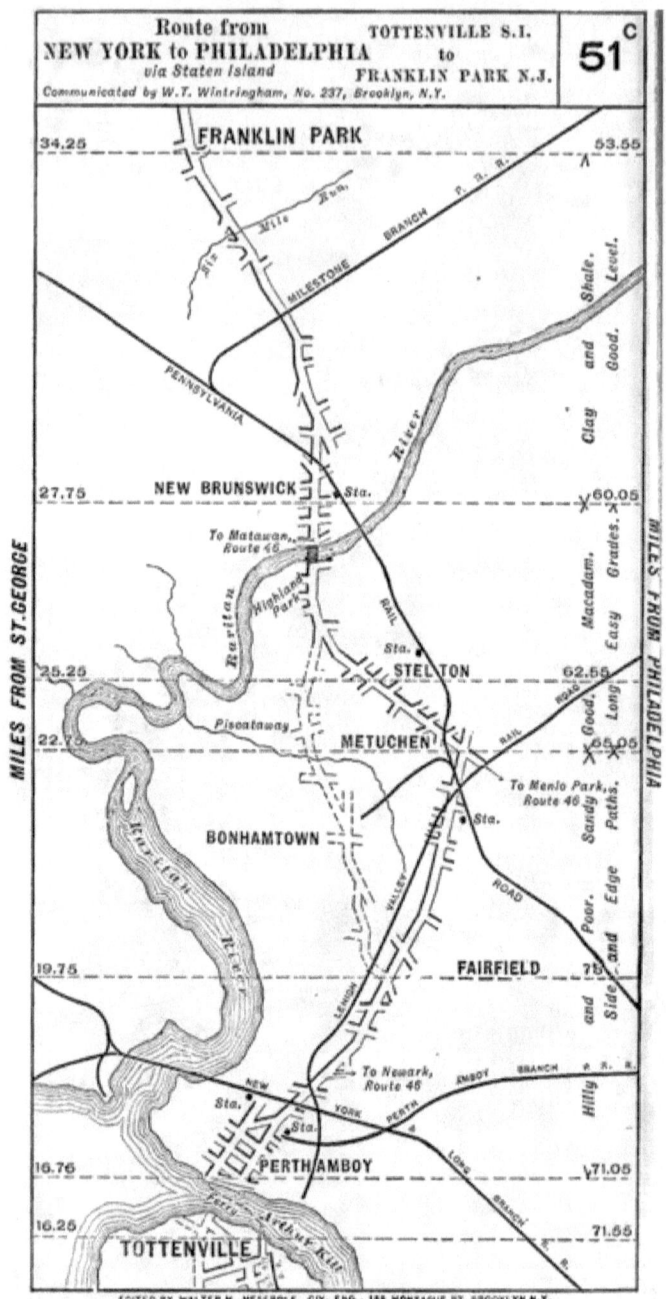

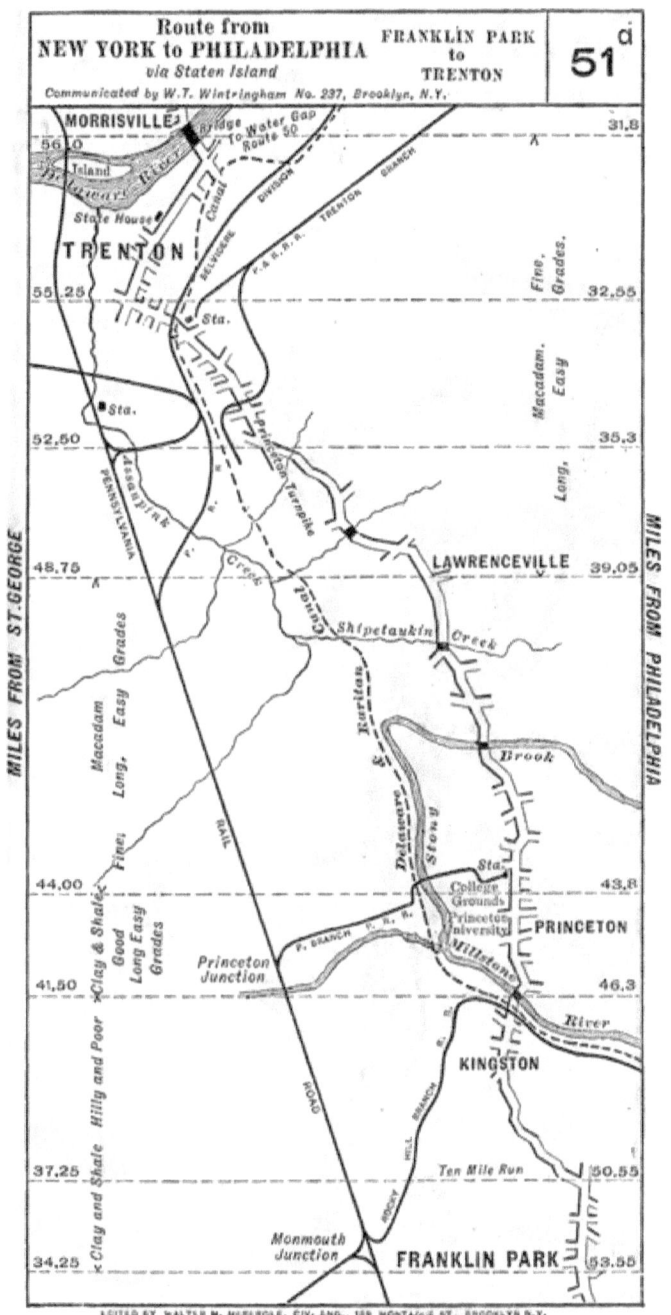

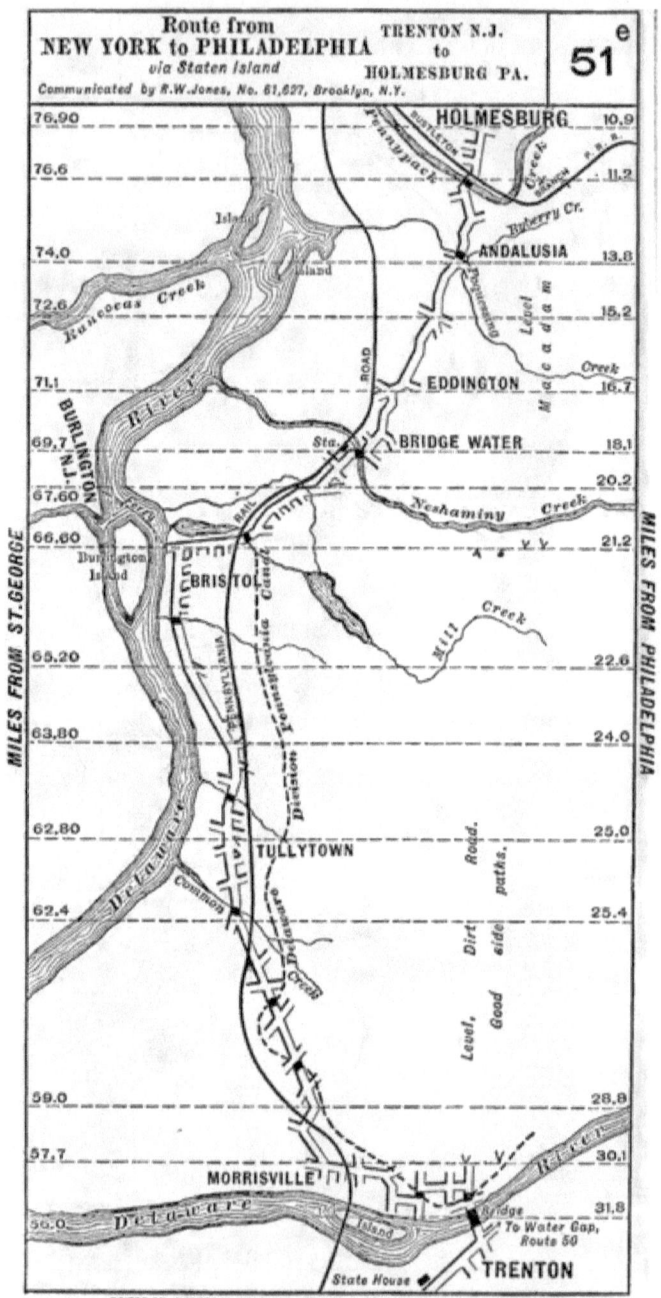

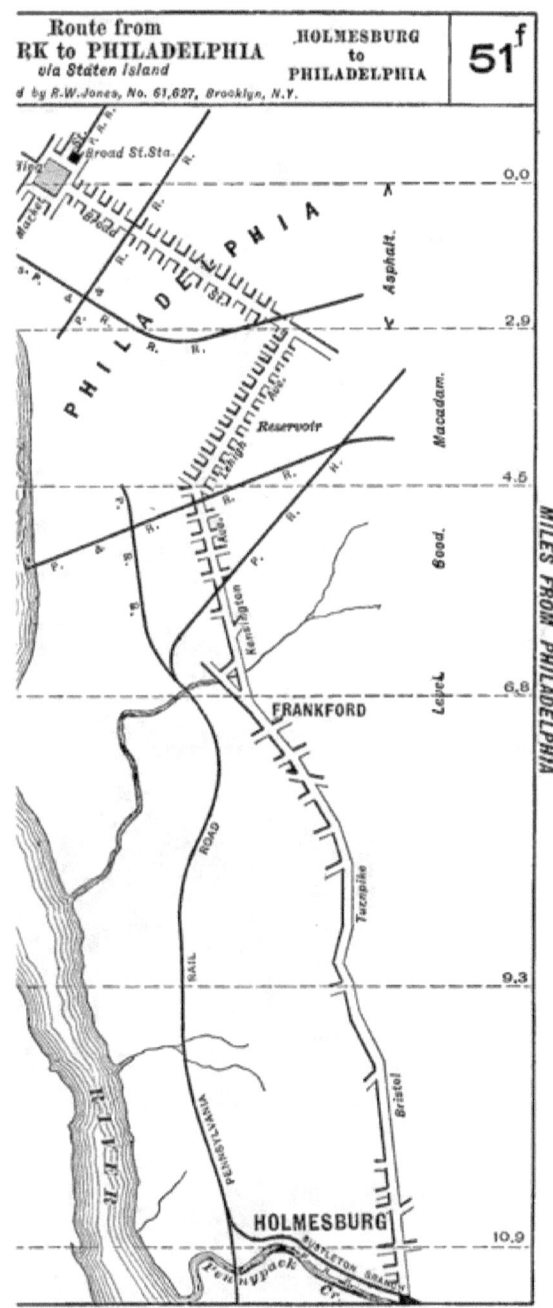

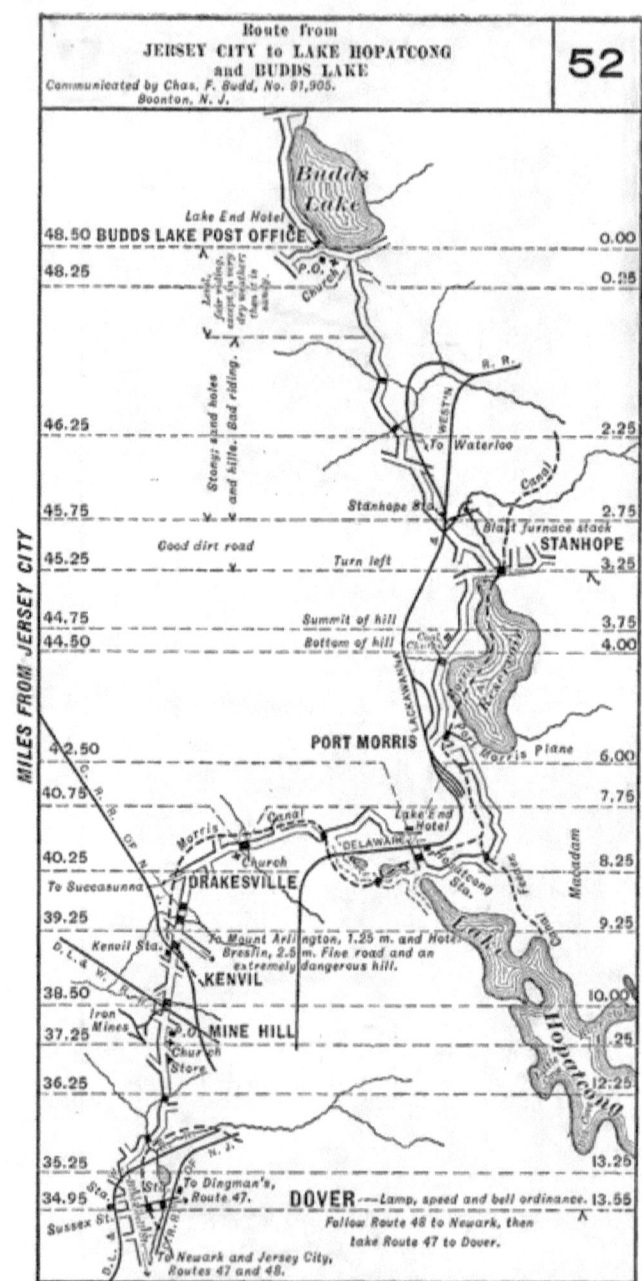

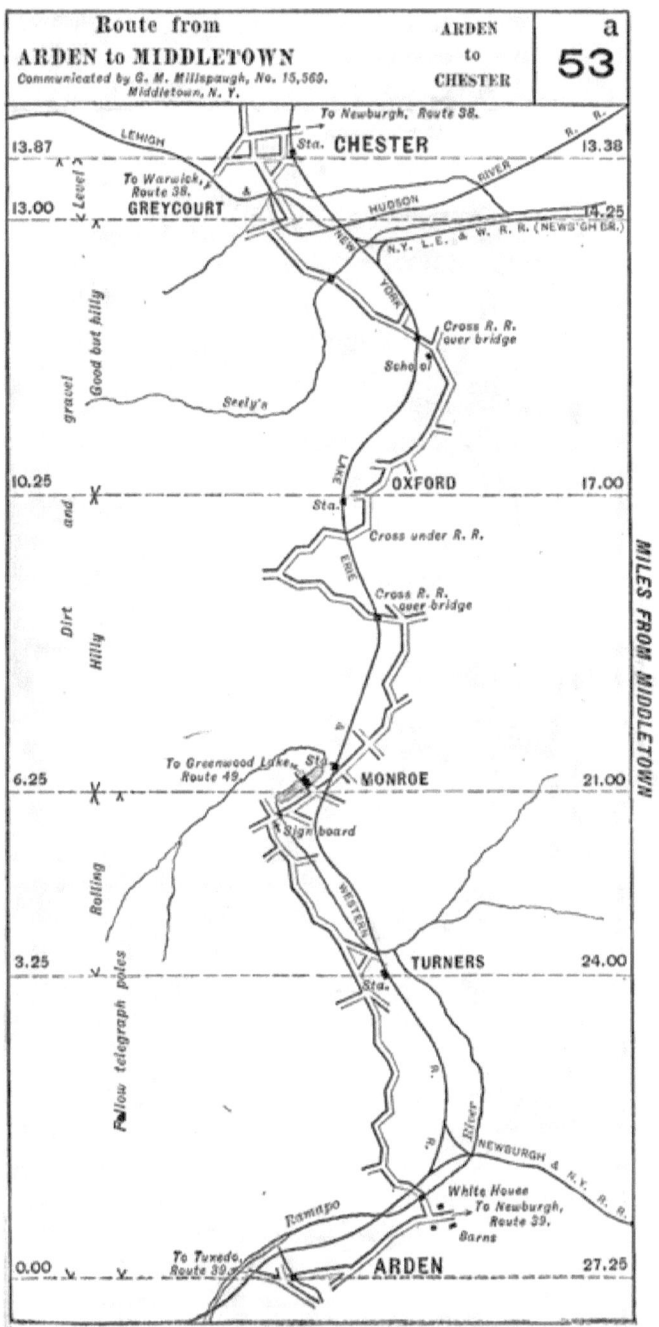

Route from ARDEN to MIDDLETOWN
Communicated by G. W. Millspaugh, No. 15,569, Middletown, N. Y.

CHESTER to MIDDLETOWN

53

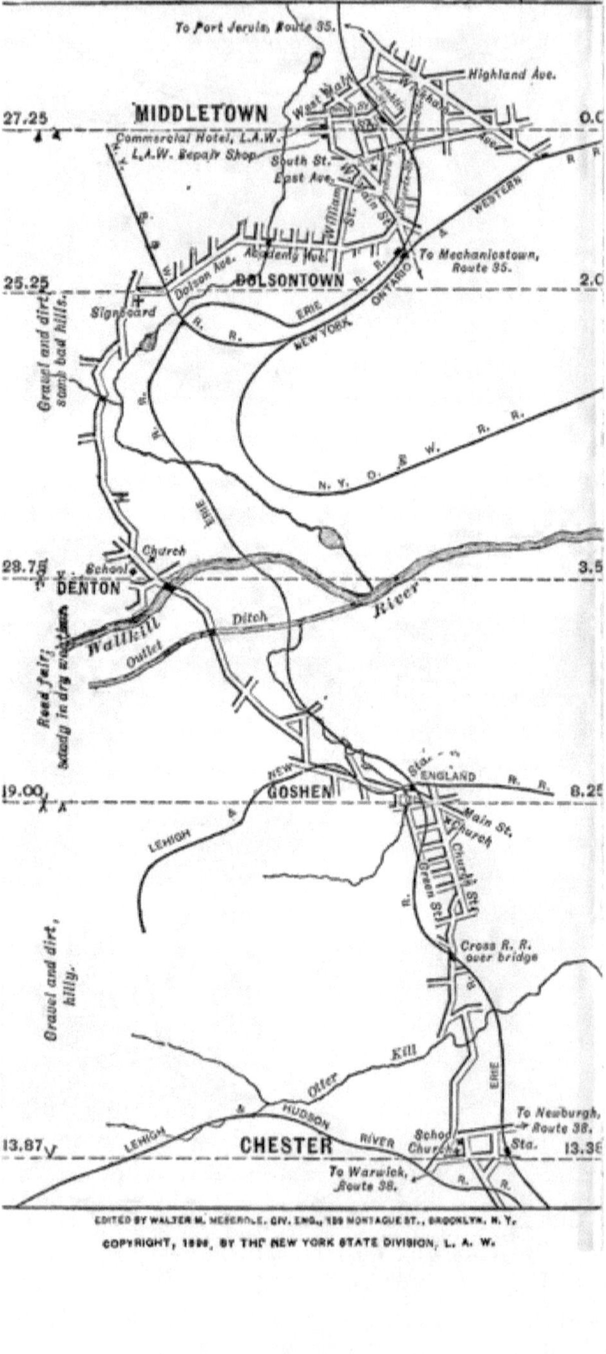

EDITED BY WALTER M. MESEROLE, CIV. ENG., 159 MONTAGUE ST., BROOKLYN, N.Y.
COPYRIGHT, 1896, BY THE NEW YORK STATE DIVISION, L. A. W.

CONSULS, HOTELS AND REPAIR SHOPS.

Important Note.—Every League member is requested to notify the Chief Consul of every violation of official contract by a League hotel proprietor which may come to his notice. Each of these proprietors has made a sealed contract with our State Division, in which he agrees to keep a clean and hospitable house and to supply good meals. He further agrees and represents that the rates mentioned in connection with his hotel in the following list are his regular rates to transient guests and that he will allow a discount or rebate (to League members *only*, and only to League members *on presentation of unexpired membership ticket*), amounting to a certain percentage named in contract. These percentages of discount are mentioned in the following alphabetical list. These hotels have been widely advertised by the L. A. W., and League members are *exclusively* entitled to the benefit of these discounts. Each hotel proprietor agrees to forfeit the sum of $50 in case he allows similar discounts to wheelmen who are not members of the L. A. W., in or case he violates his contract in any other substantial particular. The Chief Consul would be pleased to receive the fullest particulars of any case where the proprietor fails to discriminate in favor of L. A. W. members or violates his contract in any other respect.

In the following alphabetical list the following abbreviations are used: C, Consul; H, Hotel; R, Repair Shop.

Appointment of Consuls, hotels and repair shops will be further extended wherever the League may be benefitted by further appointments.

The figures annexed to the title of each hotel refer to the prices upon which discount is computed. The first sum given is the regular charge per day, next the ordinary charge for breakfast, then the dinner charge, then the supper charge, then the ordinary price charged for lodging, and then the percentage of discount from these prices to which League members will be entitled on presenting their membership tickets. For example, if you read " The Pines, $2.00, .50, .50, .50, .50, 20%" you will understand that the hotel called "The Pines" makes a customary charge of $2.00 per day and a charge of 50 cents each for breakfast, dinner, supper and lodging, and that in settling your bill at that hotel you will be entitled to 20% discount from those prices.

AMAGANSETT.—(C) George E. Jones; (H) The Pines, $2.00, .50, .50, .50, .50, 20%; (R) Thomas H. Bennett. AMENIA.—(C) J. Stuart Chaffee; (H) Amenia House, $2.50, .50, 75, .50, .75, 10%. AMITYVILLE.—(C) Thomas Wardle; (H) Hotel New Point, $2.50 to $4.00, .75, .75, 1.00; $1.00 to $2.00, 15%; Wright's Hotel, $2.00, .50, .50, .50, .50, 10%. ANNANDALE.—(C) Sam'l S. Fontaine; (H) Oetgen's Hotel, $1.50, .35, .50, .35, .50, 20%. ANNANDALE.—(H) Annandale Hotel, $1.50, .40, .50, .40, .50, 10%. ASTORIA.—(C) Herbert D. Halsey; (R) Baab & Co. BABYLON.—

(C) James W. Eaton and Jas. B. Lowerre. BATH BEACH.—(H) The Pines, $2.50, .50, .75, .50, .75, 20%; Avoca Villa, $2.00 a la carte, 20%; (R) E. F. Fisher. BAY RIDGE.—(C) A. D. Constant. BAY SHORE.—(C) Henry W. Rowland; (R) Rowland Bros. and Willey & Oakley. BEDFORD PARK.—(C) Geo. M. Shufeldt. BELLMORE.—(H) Bellmore Hotel, $2.00, .50, .50, .50, .50, 10%. BELLPORT.—(C) Harry V. Watkins; (H) Bell House, $2.50, .75, .75, .75, .75, 10%; (R) Hawkins & Boynton. BENSONHURST.—(C) Frank L. Hubbard. BREWSTER.—(C) Chas. Dahn; (H) South East House, $2.00, .50, .50, .50, .50, 20%. BRIDGEHAMPTON.—(C) Edwin J. Hildreth; (R) Halsey & M'Caslin. BRIGHTON BEACH.—(H) Van Buren's Hotel, $3.00, .60, 1.00, .60, 2.00, 10%.

BROOKLYN Consuls.—Fred Allart, 80 Hanson Place; Alexander Balmanno, 184 14th Street; John Barnett, 157 Garfield Place; H. C. Berry, 708 Dekalb Avenue; G. A. Boettner, 368 13th Street; Mrs. Charlotte L. Bolton, 132 Prospect Place; James R. Brennen, 164 Montague Street; Robert M. Briggs, 548 Lexington Avenue; Joseph Caccavajo, 262 55th Street; E. A. Carleton, 261 Carroll Street; Mrs. J. H. Clarence, 476 1st Street; L. P. Coleman, 216 Carlton Avenue; John L. Cornish, M.D., 92d Street and Third Avenue; R. P. Crandall, Navy Yard; J. E. DeMund, 1740 Cropsey Avenue; A. Denison Woodford, 749 Macon Street; Dr. R. L. Dickinson, 145 Clinton Street; Robert W. Dye, 131 Prospect Place; Charles Ekstrand, 120 Stuyvesant Avenue; Horace S. Flagg, 828 Flatbush Avenue; William A. Force, Jr., 438 Franklin Avenue; A. M. Franklin, 146 Lafayette Avenue; H. B. Fullerton, 842 President Street; Edwin C. Gibson, 984 Butler Street; B. R. Gray, 100 Hicks Street; Charles W. Hadley, 101 Newell Street; Thomas M. Henderson, 22 Irving Place; James W. Hobbs, 46 Brooklyn Avenue; Jos. H. Hobby, 80 Hanson Place; T. Harry Holmes, 290 Vanderbilt Avenue; Mrs. Etta Morse Hudders, 308 Lewis Avenue; F. Adee Hulst, 108 Taylor Street; George K. Jarvie, 159 Joralemon Street; Arthur N. Jervis, 60 Irving Place; Richard W. Jones, 36 Van Siclen Avenue; Victor Juster, Crescent Street and Jamaica Avenue; C. E. King, 92 Pulaski Street; James F. Larby, care of Metropolitan Bicycling Co., Boulevard and 60th Street, New York; C. E. Losee, 350 Jefferson Avenue; William Lowey, 198 Winthrop Street; James T. McElhinney, 36 Seventh Avenue; William Murray, Surrogate's Office; Frank E. Nattrass, 133 St. Marks Avenue; Jacob E. Nielsen, Jr., 80 Conselyea Street; DeFine Olivarius, 12 Coney Island Avenue; Louis People, 1175 Bedford Avenue; Andrew Peters, 437 Washington Avenue; Louis E. Phipps, 14 Macon Street; Eugene B. Reynolds, 1181 Grand Street; J. Addison Robb, 178 Dekalb Avenue; Jos. Rogers, Jr., 76 Buffalo Avenue; Jas. G. G. Ross, 50 Logan Street; Cornelius A. Ryerson, Bedford Avenue and Grant Square; Alex. Schwalbach, 135 Madison Street; Chas. Schwalbach, Flatbush Avenue near Prospect

Park; Frank W. Sheldon, Bedford Avenue and Grant Square; Mrs. R. L. Stillson, 34 E. 5th Street, Windsor Terrace; Norman S. Tongue, 143 Willoughby Street; H. M. Valentine, 26 Maiden Lane, New York City; D. B. Van Vleck, "Eagle" Office; Edward H. Walker, 19 S. Oxford Street; Miss Clara B. Walling, 635 Hancock Street; Maurice Weil, 381 Marcy Avenue; William T. Wintringham, 168 Hicks Street; Duane Wyckoff, 469 Greene Avenue; John C. Young, 1185 Bushwick Avenue.

BROOKLYN (Repair Shops).—Edward W. Holt, 71 Broadway; Dwight A. Foster, Bedford Rest, Eastern Parkway; Henry W. Somerset, Avenue P. and Boulevard; Edward G. Black, cor. Prospect and Washington Streets; William H. Boynton, 1084 Bedford Avenue; W. Barber & Co., Ocean Boulevard, opposite Park Entrance; Bushwick Cycle Co., 1199 Bushwick Avenue; Frank Joyce, 326 Myrtle Avenue; Albert Schock, 69 Montague Street; Holman & Lane, 1144 Bedford Avenue; Frank N. Bruner, 9th Street and Sixth Avenue; Geo. W. Sherman, Glenmore and Grant Avenues; Walter Henry, 1090 Flatbush Avenue; Morse & Eiseman, 1324 Third Avenue; Hilbert B. Ruggles, cor. Schermerhorn Street and Boerum Place; Suits & Burtis, 1144 Bedford Avenue; Chas. A. Carlson, 1039 Bedford Avenue; Frank Fischlein, Eighteenth Avenue and 86th Street, (Bath Beach); Elmwood Park Cycle Co., Ocean Parkway near Twenty-second Avenue; A. M. Franklin, 6 Third Avenue; James S. Longhurst, Jr., 72 Nevins Street; Michaux Cycle Co., Prospect Park West and 9th Street; DeFine Olivarius, Howe's Hotel, Coney Island Cycle Path; Geo. A. Webb, 2543 Atlantic Avenue.

CAMPBELL HALL.—(C) W. H. Rogers; (H) Campbell Hall, $2.00, .50, .50, .50, .50, 25%. CENTRAL ISLIP.—(C) Capt. Wm. H. Phillips. CENTRE MORICHES.—(H) Hotel Griffing, $2.00, .50, .50, .50, .50, 10%. CENTREPORT.—(C) Joseph F. Kentana. CHAPPAQUA.—(C) C. W. Page; (H) Lewis' Chappaqua Hotel $2.00, .50, .50, .50, .50, 25%. CHESTER.—(C) John P. Bull; (H) American House, $2.00, .50, .50, .50, .50, 20%. CLERMONT.— (C) F. P. Rivenburgh; (H) Columbia House, $1.70, .40, .50, .40, .40, 20%. CLIFTON, S. I.—(R) E. Juillerat & Co. COLLEGE POINT.—(C) A. C. M. Reimer; (H) Grand View Hotel, $2.00, .25, .75, .50, .50, 10%. CONEY ISLAND.—(C) Fred B. Henderson; (H) Hunt's Hotel, $2.00, .30, .50, .30, 1.00, 15%; (R) James J. McCullough and DeFine Olivarius. CORNWALL.—(C) Gilbert T. Cocks; (H) Smith House, $2.50, .50, .75, .50, .75, 20%. CORONA.—(C) G. J. Talleur. CROTON-ON-HUDSON.—(C) Harrison A. Cornell. CUTCHOGUE.—(C) Chas. F. Smith. DOBBS FERRY. (C) A. O. Kellogg; (R) Frank I. Lester. DOVER PLAINS.—(R) Frank L. Feeney. EAST HAMPTON.—(C) J. Finley Bell, M.D.; (H) Osborne House, $2.00, .50, .50, .50, .50, 20%; (R) Ernest B. Muchmore. EAST MORICHES.—(R) Geo. H. Baker. EASTPORT.—(C) Wm. H. Pye; (H) Pine Mere Inn, $2.00, .50, .50, .50, .50, 10%; (R) Louis S. Tuttle. EAST QUOGUE.—(C)

Benjamin A. Vail; (H) Carter's Hotel, $2.00, .50, .50, .50, .50, 20%. EAST WILLISTON.—(C) Henry H. Tredwell. ELLENVILLE. —(C) C. D. Divine; (H) Terwilliger House, $2.00, .38 to .50, .38 to .50, .38 to .50, .38 to .50, 10%; (R) C. J. Burhaus. ELTINGVILLE.—(H) Arden Cottage Hotel, $1.50, .35, .50, .35, .50, 20%. FAR ROCKAWAY.—(C) Frank Jennings; (H) Central Avenue Hotel, $2.00, .25, .50, .25, 1.00, 20%; (R) Dalmar L. Starks and Theo. E. Pettit. FISHKILL-ON-HUDSON.—(C) Irving B. Cammack. FLORAL PARK.—(C) Geo. H. McCoun. FLORIDA.— (C) Herbert Roe; (H) Dill House, $2.00, .50, .50, .50, .50, 10%. FLUSHING.—(C) R. D. Bailey; (H) Plaza Hotel, $2.50, .50, .75, .50, .75, 25%; (R) Sam'l N. Petersen, 5 Jagger Avenue, and Chas. S. West, 99 Main Street. FORDHAM.—(C) J. J. Peugnet. FORDHAM HEIGHTS.—(C) Theo. M. Millspaugh. FREEPORT.—(C) Huyler Ellison; (H) Benson House, $2.00, .50, .50, .50, .50, 10%; (R) David Miller and Elvin A. Dorlon. GARDINER.—(C) Philip S. Elting; (H) McKinstry House, $1.60, .40, .40, .40, .40, 10%. GARRISON.—(C) J. W. Garrison; (H) The Highland House, $2.50 to 3.00, .75, 1.00, .75, 1.00 20%; (R) John P. Donohoe. GIFFORDS.—(H) Old Gifford House, $1.50, .25, .50, .25, $1.00, 20% and Carroll's Hotel, $2.00, .40, .75, .40, .75, to $1.00, 20%. GLEN COVE.—(C) R. Frank Bowne; (H) Lake View, $2.00, .50, .50, .50, .50, 10%. GOSHEN.—(C) Frank C. Hock; (H) Occidental Hotel, $2.00, .50, .50, .50, .50, 20%. GRANT CITY.—(H) Atlantic Inn, $3.00, .50, 1.00, .75, 1 00, 10%. GRAVESEND.—(H) Elmwood, $3.00, .75, .75, .75, .75, 10%. HAMDEN.—(H) Cottage Hotel, $1.40, .35, .35, .35, .35, 25%. HASTINGS-ON-HUDSON.—(C) Irving L. Smith. HAUPPAUGE.—(C) Chas. M. Sanford. HAVERSTRAW.—(C) Dr. E. Marquez; (H) United States, $2.00, .50, .50, .50, .50, 10%. HEMPSTEAD.— (C) C. F. Norton; (H) Roth's Hotel, $2.00, .50, .50, .50, .50, 10%, and The Pines, $2.50, .50, .75, .50, 75, 20%; (R) Skidmore & Rhodes, 21 Greenwich St. HEWLETTS.—(C) W. H. E. Jay. HIGH BRIDGE.—(H) Woodbine Hotel, $3.00, .75, $1.00, .75, $1.00, .25%. HIGHLAND.—(C) J. W. Feeter; (H) Upright's Hotel. $2,00, .50, .50, .50, .50, 20%. HIGHLAND FALLS.—(C) Robert Altshimer; (H) Fort Clinton Hotel, $1.50, .25, .50, .25, .50, 10%. HUNTINGTON.—(C) Clifford W. Hendrickson; (H) Huntington House, $2.00, .50, .50, .50, .50, 10%; (R) Herman F. Rogers, Chas. E. Robertson. HYDE PARK.—(C) John O. Varley; (H) Park Hotel, $2.00, .50, .50, .50, 10%; (R) Chas. S. Piersaull. IRELAND CORNERS.—(H) Ireland Corners Hotel, $1.00 .25, .25, .25, .25, 10%. IRVINGTON.—(C) John F. Dinkel. ISLIP.— (C) Geo. P. Lehritter. JAMAICA.—(C) Newton F. Waters; (H) Broadway House, $2.00, .50, .50, .50, .50, 20%; Bennett's Arcanum Hotel, $2.00, .50, .50, .50, .50, 20%. Dunton Hotel, $2.00, .40, .60, .40, .60, 15%. KINGSBRIDGE.—(C) James M. Ames; (H) Kingsbridge Hotel, $2,00, .25, .75, .25, .75, 20%; Marble Hill Hotel, $1.50, .35, .50, .35, .75, 10%; (R) Geo. Donnelly. KINGSTON.—(C) Wm. C. Crosby; (H) Eagle Hotel, $2.50, .65, .65, .65, .65, 20%; Mansion House, $2.50, .50, .50, .50,

$1.00, 10%; (R) Chas. F. Winkler & Son. KREISCHERVILLE.—(C) P. J. Weller; (H) Universal Hotel, $2.00, .50, .50, .50, .50, 20%. LAKE MAHOPAC.—(H) Mahopac House, $2.00, .50, .50, .50, .50, 20%. LAWRENCE.—(C) D. E. Lennox; (H) Mittenberger's Boarding House, $2.00, .50, .50, .50, .50, 20%; (R) D. E. Lennox. LONG ISLAND CITY.—(C) Geo. T. Walker; (R) Dubon & Son, 487 Broadway. MAMARONECK.—(C) Geo. C. Hains; (H) New York, $1.25, .25, 35, .25, 50, 25%; (R) Ruben P. Stillman. MANHATTANVILLE.—(C) John B. Koch. MARINERS HARBOR.—(C) E. L. G. Van Name; (H) Holland Hook, $2.00, .25, .50, .50, .75, 10%. MARLBOROUGH.—(H) Hotel Pleasant View, $2.00, .50, .50, .50, .50, 15%. MASSAPEQUA.—(H) The Massapequa, $3.00, $1.00, $1.25, .50, .75, 20%. MATTEAWAN.—(C) Chas. F. Getler; (H) The Commercial, $2.00, .50, .50, .50, .50, 20%; Hotel Albert, $1.50, .50, .50, .50, .50, 25%; (R) Frank M. Edmond, L. L. Inman, Bate & Getler. MATTITUCK.—(H) Mattituck House, $2.00, .50, .50, .50, .50, 10%. MELROSE.—(C) Chas. A. Weber. MIDDLETOWN.—(C) G. M. Millspaugh; (H) Commercial House, $2.00, .50 .50, .50, .50, 20%; (R) John H. Clearwater. MILLBROOK.—(C) Wm. D. Smith; (R) Taber Sherow. MONTGOMERY.—(C) Dr. E. Ross Elliott; (H) National Hotel, $2.00, .50, .50, .50, .50, 10%. MONTICELLO.—(C) F. H. Cooper. MORICHES.—(C) Chas. H. Hallock; (H) Wilson Cottage, $1.50, .35, .50, .35, .75, 20%; (R) R. E. Albin. MOUNT VERNON.—(C) W. N. G. Clark, Max Parpart; (H) Mt. Vernon Hotel, $2.00, .50, .50, .50, .50, 25%; (R) Conrad Waechter, Geo. E. Taylor, Geo. Harlett, 205 Stevens Ave., S. L. Gottlieb, 128 W. First St. NANUET.—(C) L. H. Hutton. NEWBURGH.—(C) Clarence B. Moss; (H) Newburgh Hotel, $2.00, .50, .50, .50, .50, 15%; European Plan; The Palatine, $3.00, .75, .75, .75, $1.00, 15%; (R) Jas. N. Firth. NEW DORP.—(C) A. Lee McKelvey; (H) Sea View Hotel, $1.50, .25, .50, .25, .50, 20%; (R) A. L. McKelvey. NEW PALTZ.—(H) Tamney House, $2.00, .50, .50, .50, .50, 10%. NEW ROCHELLE.—(C) L. K. Fries; (R) Wm. Weisskopf, Wm. L. Botelle. NEWTOWN.—(C) A. R. Marvin; (H) Winfield Hotel, $2.00, .50, .50, .50, .50, 20%.

NEW YORK CONSULS.—Chas. Ackerman, care of Stover Bicycle Manufacturing Co., 575 Madison Avenue; Mrs. E. C. Allis, 66 W. 46th Street; Raymond Ball, care of American Athlete, 21 Centre Street; Orrin D. Bartlett, 25 Barrow Street; M. M. Belding, Jr., 455 Broadway; Mrs. Ida Trafford Bell, 203 W. 80th Street; E. L. Bentley, 445 W. 22d Street; Max Bernhard, 319 E. 6th Street; A. P. Black, 523 Sixth Avenue; William R. Bleecker, 79 Wall Street; B. W. B. Brown, 18 Wall Street; Herbert S. Brown, University Club; Octavus Cohen, 45 Park Place; Chas. F. Cole, 428 Broome Street; Lloyd Collis, 12 Cortland Street; Harrie M. Crandall, 58 William Street; A. Eugene Crow, 2 W. 53d Street; A. H. Curtis, Bank State of New York, William Street and Exchange Place; Chas. L. De Gaugue, 80 Broadway; William B. De Voe, 59 Bank Street; John T. Donnelly, 2714 Creston Avenue; Paul P. J. Donvan,

308 W. 19th Street; Dr. W. K. Doty, 413 Lexington Avenue; C. M. Dutcher, 248 Sixth Avenue; T. T. Eckert, Jr., 8 Dey Street; Morris Epstein, 1441 First Avenue; Frank Elmendorf, 200 W. 134 Street; Charles R. Flint, 43 E. 36th Street; Frederick M. Frobisher, 346 Broadway; M. Gibb, 45 Rose Street; Alured E. F. Godard, 259 W. 21st Street; Henry Grese, 175 Seventh Avenue; Geo. A. Heaney, Colonial Club; E. Hellbach, 70 Murray Street; Rud. Hepp, 1719 Lexington Avenue; Geo. L. Hermes, 6 Clinton Place; Geo. E. Huether, 3594 Third Avenue; Dixie Hines, 320 Broadway; Arthur P. Stanley Hyde, 32 E. 84th Street; Dr. A. M. Jacobus, 126 W. 48th Street; Mrs. A. M. Jacobus, 126 W. 48th Street; William Travers Jerome, 66 William Street; Richard F. Junker, 845 Union Avenue; Fred. B. King, 209 E. 15th Street; J. A. King, 699 Broadway; Geo. D. Kraemer, 21 Barclay Street; Mme. Adelaide Lagasse, 108 Waverly Place; Ellen K. Lente, 270 W. 93d Street; Dr. L. C. Le Roy, 6 Lexington Avenue; Nathaniel Le Vene, N. Y. P. O. Carriers' Dept., G. P. O.; Al. Liebman, care of N. Y. Cash Sales Book Co., 534 Pearl Street; M. B. MacFarlane, St. Paul Building; W. J. McCormick, "Evening Post" Building; Mrs. E. S. Merry, 249 W. 74th Street; Arthur C. Mills, 5 Warren Street; Erastus D. Moore, 171 Columbus Avenue; Carroll L. R. Mosher, 26 Delancey Street; Dr. F. A. Myrick, 100 Lexington Avenue; Carleton W. Nason, 71 Beekman Street; J. J. O'Donohue, Jr., 262 W. 73d Street; Geo. William Oppenheim, "World" Building; R. Ottolengui, 104 W. 61st Street; Geo. C. Pennell, 70 Beekman Street; Charles G. Peters, 13 E. 76th Street; Richard Peters, Knickerbocker Club; Will R. Pitman, 520 Vanderbilt Building; Jesse E. Potter, 23 Warren Street; T. A. Raisbeck, 62 W. 66th Street; L. Rauschkolb, 146 W. 25th Street; Otto F. Reese, 109 W. 106th Street; Alfred Reeves, 154 Nassau Street; M. L. Rhein, M. D., 38 E. 61st Street; T. A. Ritson, 65 Broadway; Walter S. Rockey, Eighth Avenue and 35th Street; John E. Roosevelt, 44 Wall Street; Louis Rosenfeld, 887 St. Nicholas Avenue; Francis J. Ryan, 269 W. 10th Street; Geo. E. Scheffler, 330 St. Nicholas Avenue; Jefferson Seligman, Mills Building; Julian B. Shope, 11 Pine Street; Geo. E. Stackhouse, American Tract Society Building; Maurice Sternberger, 117 W. 74th Street; Adolph Stahl, 307 Broadway; Gabriel Teschner, 60 Murray Street; Philip S. Tilden, 332 Lexington Avenue; Bert L. Toplitz, 7 Beekman Street; James B. Townsend, 106 E. 30th Street; Fred. A. Trowbridge, 316 Broadway; William E. Trull, 229 Lexington Avenue; C. A. Underhill, 60th Street and Boulevard; J. W. Walters, 101 W. 72d Street; Oscar E. Walter, 469 Broome Street; Mrs. H. Newell Waslee, 30 Horatio Street; Jos. Weil, 2787 Third Avenue; Albert L. Weissman, 2 E. 80th Street; Philip Wendland, 215 Bowery; John Law Wenzel, 113 E. 127th Street; Henry E. Westbay, 55 W. 42d Street; M. T. Wilbur, 221 W. 136th Street; J. H. Wolford, Pier 25 (new)

North River; Thos. W. Wright, 331 W. 14th Street; Geo. B. Yard, 158 W. 81st Street; John B. Yates, 46 Maiden Lane.

(Hotels).—Bridgeview Hotel, N. W. corner 181st Street and Amsterdam Avenue, $3.00, .35, .35, .35, 1.25 and upwards, 25%; Boulevard Hotel, S. E. corner Jerome Avenue and S. Boulevard, $2.00, .50, .50, .50, .50, 25%; Kronemeyer's Hotel, St. Lawrence Avenue and West Farms, $1.80, .25, .30, 25, 1.00, 10%; Vanderbilt Hotel, Lexington Avenue and 42d Street, meals a la carte, lodging, $1.00, 10%; Union Hotel, 176th Street and Boston Avenue, $1.80, .35, .50, .50, .50, 10%; Mount Hope Hotel, N. E. corner Jerome Avenue and 177th Street, $4.00, .75, .75, 1.00, 1.50, 20%; Pelham Park Hotel, City Island (W. of City Island Bridge), $1.80, .40, .50, .40, .50, 10%.

(Repair Shops).—Henry D. Housley, West End Avenue and 107th Street; August Rotholz, 116th Street and Fifth Avenue; Bill Nye Cycle Co., 632 W. Boulevard; The People's Cycle Exchange, 550 W. Boulevard; The Fifth Avenue Cycle Co., 3 E. 58th Street; Progressive Cycle Co., 21 Lexington Avenue; Charles T. Mauder, 109 2d Street; Frederic E. Wright, 803 Boulevard; Champion Cycle Co., 134th Street and Fifth Avenue; John F. Hessen, 263 W. 19th Street; Royal Cycle Exchange, 472 Willis Avenue; Moore Bros., 171 Columbus Avenue; Du Quesne Manufacturing Co., 226 Fulton Street; Berton L. Wright, 3225 Third Avenue; Nagel & Judge, 728 Eighth Avenue; Graphic Cycle Co., 1666 Broadway; Walter K. Northall, corner Kingsbridge and Highbridge Roads; Burkart & Widmayer, 482 W. Boulevard; Alex. L. Brudi, 171 E. 86th Street; Hugo Klemann, 673 E. 156th Street; Charles K. Starr, 132 E. 23d Street; George L. Hermes, 84 Greenwich Avenue.

NORTHFIELD.—(H) Bay Side, $2.50, .50, .50, .50, 1.00, 10%. NORTH HEMPSTEAD.—(H) East Williston Hotel, $2.00, .50, .50, .50, .50, 10%; Hookers Hotel, $1.50, .40, .40, .35, .40, 15%. NORTHPORT.—(C) F. D. Jackson; (H) Commercial Hotel, $2.00, .50, .50, .50, .50, 10%. NYACK.—(C) G. W. Hoffer, P. Chamberlain, C. T. Broadhead; (H) Palmer House, $2.50, .75, .75, .75, .75, 20%; (R) W. H. Baldwin. OAKWOOD.—(H) Oakwood Park Hotel, $1.75, .35, .50, .40, .50, 10%. OYSTER BAY.—(C) Dr. G. W. Faller; (H) Octagon Hotel, $2.00, .50, .50, .50, .50 to 1.00, 10%; (R) Leonard M. Hicks. PARKVILLE.—(H) Hoenlein Hotel, $3.00, .50, .75, .75, 1.00, 25%. PATCHOGUE.—(C) L. B. Green; (R) J. Roe & Sons, S. G. Van Dusen. PAWLING.—(C) Geo. S. Holmes. PEEKSKILL.—(C) Robt. Valentine; (R) Homer Anderson, F. E. Ward. PIERMONT.—(C) Geo. E. DeGroat. PINE PLAINS.—(H) Stissing House, $2.00, .50, .50, .50, .50, 25%. PLEASANT PLAINS.—(H) Stephens House, $1.50, .45, .50, .45, .50, 20%. PORT CHESTER.—(C) Edw. Kapp; (H) Irving Hotel, $2.00, .50, .50, .50, .50, 15%. PORT JEFFERSON.—(C) J. H. Davis; (H) Townsend House, $2.00, .50, .50, .50, .50, 10%; (R) Davis & Pierrepont. PORT JERVIS.—(C) Theo. Shay; (H) Union House, $2.00, .50, .50, .50, .50, 10%; (R) F. C. Bond, C. Van Norris. PORT RICHMOND.—(H) St.

James Hotel, $2.00, .35, .50, .40, .75, 10%. PORT WASHINGTON.
—(H) Central Hotel, $2.00, .50, .50, .50, .50 10%. POUGHKEEPSIE.
(C) Sam'l J. Latham, 359 Main Street; (H) Morgan House,
$2.50, .50, .75, .50, .75, 20%; Nelson House, $3.00, .75, .75, .75,
1.00, 10%; (R) John Van Benschoten, Herman von der
Linden. PRINCES BAY.—(C) J. T. Shay. QUEENS.—(H)
Queens Park Hotel, $2.00, .25, .50, .35, 1.00, 20%. QUOGUE.—
(R) Wm. H. Jessup, A. R. Aldrich. RAMAPO.—(C) H. Hammill,
Jr.; (H) Terrace Hall, $2.00, .50, .50, .50, .50, 10%. RHINE-
BECK.—(C) E V. Marquardt; (R) J. Vonder Linder, F. W.
Styles. RICHMOND HILL.—(C) Wm. F. Bornson; (H) Forest
House, $1.50, .25, .50, .25, .50, 10%. RIVERHEAD.—(C) J. H.
Perkins, Jr.; (H) Long Island House, $2.00, .50, .50, .50, .50,
10%. ROCKAWAY BEACH.—(C) Wm. H. Ward; (H) Cottage
Place, $2.00, .60, .60, .60, 1.00, 10%; (R) M. Gustafson.
ROCKVILLE CENTRE.—(C) Jos. J. Koen; (H) The Iroquois, $2.00,
.50, .50, .50, .50, 20%; (R) Alfred Roberts. RONDOUT.—(C)
Theo. H. Boice. ROSSVILLE.—(H) Rossville House, $1.50, .25,
.50, .25, .50, 20%. RYE.—(C) J. Henry Halstead; (H) Beck's
Summer Resort, $1.00 to 1.50 a la carte, $1.00 to 1.50, 25%.
SAG HARBOR.—(C) Geo. C. Reney; (H) American Hotel, $2.00,
.50, .50, .50, .50, 10%. SAUGERTIES.—(C) H. T. Keeney; (H)
Phoenix Hotel, $2.00, .50, .50, .50, .50, 20%; (R) H. T. Keeney.
SAYVILLE.—(C) A. O. Albin; (H) Foster House, $2.00, .50, .75,
.50, .50, 10%; (R) Stenger & Rohm. SEA CLIFF.—(C) Wm. C.
Smith; (H) Flavells Hotel Sea View, $2.00 up, .50, .50, .50 .75,
20%. SEAFORD.—(C) Chas. H. Lush; (R) Chas. H. Lush.
SEASIDE.—(H) Gerard Hotel, $3.00, .40, .60, .40, 2.00, 10%.
SHELTER ISLAND.—(C) Walter R. Havens. SHERMAN PARK.—
(R) William Van Tine. SING SING.—(C) J. H. Carpenter.
SLOATSBURG.—(C) Miss Edna Allen. SMITHTOWN,—(C) Wm. N.
Spurge. SOMERS.—(C) Jos. Brown. SOUTHAMPTON.—(C) L. D.
Green; (H) Orion Hotel, $2.00, .50, .75, .50, .75. 10%; (R)
Harry Lillywhite & Son. SOUTHOLD.—(R) M. B. Vandusen.
SPEONK.—(C) Louis S. Tuttle. SPRINGFIELD.—(H) Point
Pleasant, $2.00, .50, .50, .50, .50, 10%. STAATSBURG—(C) E. H.
Lasher; (H) Maplewood Hotel, $1.50, .40, .40, .40, .40, 25%;
(R) John G. Bodenstein & Co. STAPLETON.—(C) Chas. Hoyer.
STONY POINT.—(C) Wm. B. Cavel; (R) Daniel Keesler & Son.
STORMVILLE.—(H) Stormville Hotel, $2.00, .50, .50, .50, .50, 10%.
SUFFERN.—(C) W. S. Slavin; (H) Mountain House, $2.00, .50,
.50, .50, .50, 10%. TARRYTOWN.—(C) W. Wright, August Bing;
(H) Mott House, $2.50, .50, .75, .50, 1.00, 20%; (R) Nicolas
Koenig. TIVOLI.—(C) P. R. Peelor; (H) Madalin Hotel, $2.00,
.50, .50, .50, .50, 10%. TOMKINS COVE.—(C) Mrs. Millie L.
Draudt. TOTTENVILLE.—(C) M. C. Ayers; (H) Excelsior
Hotel, $2.00, .50, .50, .50, .50, 10%. TUCKAHOE.—(C) Frank C.
Garmany. TUXEDO PARK.—(C) Miss Amelia Van Schaick.
VAN PELT MANOR.—(C) Andrew B. Cropsey. WADING RIVER.
—(C) A. M. Howell. WAINSCOTT.—(C) Jacob O. Hopping.
WALDEN.—(H) St. Nicholas, $2.00, .50, .50, .50, .50, 10%.

WAPPINGERS FALLS.—(C) C. Russell Andrews; (H) Rush's Hotel, $1.50, .40, .40, .40, .40, 10%; (R) Wm. Britner. WARWICK.—(C) Jas. A. Ogden. WEST AMITYVILLE.—(H) South Bay Beach Hotel, $1.25, .35, .35, .35, .35, 10. WESTCHESTER.—(C) Jos. Connolly; (H) Westchester Hotel, $2.00, .50, .75, .50, $1.00, 20%; (R) John F. Thompson, Main St., near Westchester Bridge; (R) Lenoire Cycle Co. WESTFIELD.—(H) Huguenot Park Hotel, $1.00, .30, .50, .25, .25, 10%; Oriental Park Cottage, $1.25, .35, .50, .35, .50. 10%; WESTHAMPTON BEACH.—(R) Graphic Cycle Co. WEST POINT.—(C) B. F. McManus; (H) West Point Hotel, $3.50, $1.00, $1.50, $1.00, $1.50, 10%. WHITE PLAINS.—(C) Chas. L. Onderdonk, Dr. Wm. E. Dold; (H) Carlyon, Arms, $2.00, .50, .50, .50, .50, 10%; (R) Edmond P. Horton. WHITESTONE.—(H) International Hotel, $2.00, .40, .50, .35, .75, 25%. WILBUR.—(C) Rev. Dan'l P. Ward. WOODBURY FALLS.—(C) Chas. F. Seaman. WOODHAVEN.—(C) Leslie M. Ogden. YAPHANK.—(C) W. J. Weeks. YONKERS.—(C) H. W. Pagan.

ACCIDENTS.—If you suffer personal injuries or damages to your wheel through the careless or negligent act of a driver, or by reason of serious defects in the pavement or surface of a street, roadway or bridge, write full particulars to the Chairman of our Rights and Privileges Committee,

GEO. E. MINER, Attorney,
Potter Building, New York City.

HANG IT ON THE WALL.

or in the front window of your office, store, shop, hotel or place of business. Ask your neighbors, the druggist, the barber, the postmaster, the cycle dealer and all managers of business houses (where cyclists congregate, or call from time to time) to display these neat little hangers and **see that they are supplied**. With each hanger we send a quantity of membership blanks in an envelope.

This is a small Hanger (only 6½ x 7½ inches), and may be hung in any office without detracting from its appearance. We are going to make a determined fight for Good Roads, and we want 50,000 members in the New York Division. Will you, as a loyal member, help us? Many cyclists call at headquarters, and others write us letters making inquiry "How can I join the L. A. W.? **They have never been asked to join.** Please send for a number of these hangers **at once** to

W. S. BULL,
Secretary-Treasurer,
Vanderbilt Building, New York, N. Y.

TOURING.

By A. B. BARKMAN.

There is little doubt that by far the largest number of active cyclers find their pleasure in touring. The pottering cycler, who never ventures far from home, has no idea of the enjoyments to be found in country rambles on the wheel. The touring field is practically open to any rider who has time to devote to it, and the number of cyclers who thus spend their summer holiday is yearly increasing. These holiday tourists, guided by past experience, or by the advice of their more practical fellows, plan their trips with an eye to personal comfort, and after a few days of enjoyable riding, return home invigorated and instructed.

The first step a prospective tourist should take, after he has acquired a sufficient knowledge of his wheel and confidence in himself, is to join the League of American Wheelmen, an association formed to promote the interests of cyclers in general and tourists in particular. The initiation fee is one dollar, and the annual dues a like amount (payable in advance) and the writer, having filled up the necessary application blank, will have to wait a longer or shorter time for his ticket, usually about three weeks.

Selecting Route.—This matter having been duly arranged, the next thing is to plan the tour and select the route, which can best be done with the aid of the various road books and maps issued by the State Divisions or recommended by the Touring Department.

Each Day's Journey.—It then becomes necessary to decide as to the average day's journey, and on this point it is necessary to utter a very emphatic warning against the error into which so many tourists fall, of fixing a ridiculously high standard which they find it practically impossible to carry out. A large number of beginners fancy they can ride with ease from sixty to one hundred miles daily for a week or so at a stretch, and on this basis plan their tours, with the result that they either break down utterly and are compelled to take the train home, or else they spend a miserable "holiday," riding hard against time during the whole trip, thus converting what should have been a pleasant outing into a period of incessant hard labor and discomfort.

The experienced tourist, on the other hand, rather shortens the day's journey, being satisfied with from forty to fifty miles, and generally allows a spare day in the middle of the week, in case of delay by rain or other causes, or a desire to take in some pleasant side trip or object of interest, thus letting himself off as easily as possible with a view to the more complete enjoyment of the tour as a whole.

For a beginner even shorter distances are advisable at first; for a man who can ride his sixty or seventy miles right off, will find forty miles a day for a week quite a different matter, and considerable of a task until he has learned by experience how to economize and save his physical powers.

Companions.—Except in the cases of some peculiarly constituted individuals, a solitary trip is a very slow performance, and the presence of at least one companion brightens things up materially; yet, the rider had better go alone than journey with a disagreeable companion, or one very much slower than himself. Two fairly equal riders greatly assist each other in maintaining a good rate of progression, as when one lags the other brings him along, and when this man tires the other has perhaps recovered his pace. Large parties are scarcely so satisfactory, especially if club rules are rigidly enforced, as this course means that the whole party shall proceed at the pace of the slowest rider, which soon becomes very irksome to the faster men of the party, causing grumbling and discontent. Under such circumstances, loose riding should always be permitted, and, if possible, the slower men should be started somewhat earlier than their more speedy companions. Again, in large parties, in order to be sure of good accommodations, it is necessary that arrangements be made ahead for meals and lodging. This entails a considerable amount of care and labor upon the promotor or manager of the tour, and renders each day's journey inflexible, which oftentimes results in considerable discomfort to the entire party, as circumstances frequently arise which make delays advisable or render progress inconvenient. My personal experience has been that two are a good number, four are better, and six the maximum for comfort and enjoyment.

Preliminary Training.—The intending tourist should not start out without some sort of training and preparation for the work before him, as this course often produces most unfortunate results. The mere task of sitting in the saddle for several hours daily, is painful to one who has not taken the precaution of undergoing previous practice and seasoning, and for this reason, if for no other, it is advisable that for some time before the day of departure a regular course of riding should be followed, at least three times weekly, and this riding should occupy an hour or more, and should include a little practice at hill work as well as some sharp dashes along the level. Nothing like high training is required, but something more than the easy dawdling which so many riders are fond of indulging in is necessary. It is a good plan to fix upon a stated route, say twelve or fifteen miles, and to ride over it three or four times a week, the trip being carefully timed, and the rider trying to do better on each occasion. This will seem to many somewhat of a task, but it will vastly develop the muscles, improve the wind, and increase the rider's powers for average work. If this course be carefully followed out for a fortnight or three weeks before the tour, it will not only increase the rider's capabilities, but as a natural result add decidedly to his personal comfort. It is scarcely necessary to remark that when touring the highest possible pace should not be attempted, but a fair, steady and regular pace adhered to throughout; and this steady and regular pace will be easier to maintain if the rider has learned the knack of going a great deal faster. This is the theory of training, and it applies to the tourist as well as to the racing man.

Luggage.—The rider having developed his powers by careful practice, it will next be for him to consider what are the necessaries to be carried for his comfort, or sent to various places where he may stop en route, and here again great latitude must be allowed, as tastes differ most notably, one rider regarding a tooth-brush and a piece of soap ample equipment for a week's journey, while another will be loaded down with packages and needless impediments, which contain necessaries from his standpoint. The rider of a bicycle will learn with experience how to carry sufficient for comfort, which is a happy medium consisting of not too much, nor yet too little, but just enough for all reasonable requirements; and such an equipment can readily be carried on a bicycle, and renders the tourist independent of the troubles and annoyances

Shown under suit.   Shown over suit.

Gentlemen's Pneumatic Bathing Vest and Ladies'
... Life Preserving Corset ...

are light, neat and comfortable. Contains air enough to support the body in the water without an effort, **thus enabling the wearer to become an expert swimmer.** Should always be carried by those travelling on the water, as they are absolute life preservers. We make **Ladies' Bathing Corsets**, also **Children's Corsets** and **Vests**, which, when worn, prevent all danger of drowning. Stamp for Catalogue.

Pneumatic Vest and Corset Co.
No. 8 West 14th St., New York City

My desire to render a substantial favor to the wheelmen of America, impels me to say a good word for SALVA-CEA. For that lameness of muscles which comes to the moderate rider whenever he attempts a long day's run, I have found nothing to be compared with it, while for sprains and bruises its curative and soothing effects are really magical. I heartilly recommend it.

                    ISAAC B. POTTER
        Chief Consul N. Y. State, L. A. W.
         and Pres. Brooklyn Bicycle Club

Irving Hotel ..   PORTCHESTER, N. Y.
WM. H. FEHR, *Proprietor*

Opposite East Bound R. R. Station, and one block from Main Street.

Arlington Hotel .   BINGHAMTON, N. Y.
THE LEADING HOTEL IN THE CITY.

New and modern in every respect. Convenient to all Depots. Only five minutes' walk from Binghamton Athletic Association Grounds. Headquarters of the L. A. W. Rates to Wheelmen, $2.

    ... KENNEDY & TIERNEY ...

always incident to the sending of clothing by express, owing to frequent mistakes, delays or miscarriage, most vexatious drawbacks which every tourist has experienced.

Some cyclists fly light in the matter of luggage, trusting to chance for such changes as may be necessary, while they have always the option of going to bed if unable to obtain dry garments in which to sit up. But the prudent rider, or one who has once suffered from the inconvenience and discomfort of being without, will take care to provide himself with at least one complete change of undergarments; one of the best and most convenient forms of which will be found in the full jersey suits, of not too thin texture, sold by all dealers in cycling and athletic goods.

A jersey suit will roll up into a very small compass, and when put on it completely clothes the body from neck to feet in dry woolen attire, which may be worn alone if necessary, and is, by all odds, when so worn, the most comfortable and serviceable riding suit—and over which damp outer garments may be put on again without danger from cold, if not without some little discomfort. It can also be used to sleep in at night, instead of using an ordinary night-shirt, always a bulky matter when space is limited, and the fact that woolen underclothing is a protection, in case of damp sheets, is another argument recommending its adoption by the tourist. The kit is thus reduced by making one garment serve the place of two or more and at the same time the weight to be carried is lessened, an important factor to be considered in studying the convenience of the rider, for even the strongest and most sturdy of cyclers will do well not to overweight himself in this direction.

From my experience, the following is ample for a tour of two weeks, or even longer, and can be readily carried on a bicycle: The rider, when in the saddle, should wear a thin or medium weight merino undershirt, without sleeves; a pair of thin cotton socks, which not only keep the feet clean, but also prevent chafing and soreness; a complete jersey suit, consisting of a high-neck, long-sleeve jersey, and a pair of full tights; low shoes with stout soles, and a cap or other suitable headgear, at the option of the wearer. For riding, the jersey suit has many advantages and no equal for comfort, being easy, giving full and unrestricted freedom to all the limbs and muscles, warm in cool weather, cool in hot weather, and drying very quickly if the wearer chances to be caught in the rain. I have seen fellow tourists on a warm summer day plunge into a cooling stream, jersey suit and all, and dry quickly after resuming the saddle. This practice is not to be recommended, for, while it may be extremely convenient and refreshing for the time being, it is conducive to colds and rheumatism. Stout soles to a tourist's shoes are essential to comfort when an occasional bit of walking is necessary, thin soles not only hurting the feet, but occasionally producing such soreness as will temporarily lame the wearer.

In addition to what the tourist has on when clothed as above, he should also carry the following outfit: Uniform of cycling coat and knee breeches, extra jersey suit, two pairs of socks, one undershirt, from three to six handkerchiefs, one neck handkerchief or scarf, comb, tooth-brush, razor, etc., if necessary, a small sponge, and a small chamois or soft leather bag with a stout drawing string, made like a tobacco pouch.

If preferred, the extra jersey suit may be omitted, and a flannel riding shirt and pair of long woolen stockings substituted, in which case attention is called to the new self-supporting stockings now generally sold by dealers, and which are

Long Island

THE CYCLISTS'
...PARADISE

120-Mile "Straightaway" Course. The level "Merrick Road," made famous by many "Century" runs. The rolling "North Shore" road, with its "coasts," shade and smooth surface. Fine hotels at frequent intervals. Beautiful Bays, Lakes and Forests. Hunting, Fishing, Boating, etc. The best route between New England and the West. Stations of the

Long Island Railroad Company

always near at hand. The first railroad company to recognize cyclists by appointing an official to attend to this new class of travel. Maps, Routes and full information sent on request.

SPECIAL RATES TO CLUBS

.. H. B. FULLERTON ..
SPECIAL AGENT, PASSENGER DEPARTMENT
LONG ISLAND CITY

most comfortable, answering the purpose of drawers as well, and doing away with any garter encumbrances.

Having purchased two pieces of rubber cloth, of the quality known as dull finish rubber sheeting, each about one yard square, proceed to roll the things up tightly in two packages, each about twenty inches long and as small in circumference as it is possible to get them, placing the coat and breeches in one and the extra jersey suit and underclothing in the other, the other articles being conveniently divided between the two. Roll as tightly as possible—they cannot be too tight or snug—and wrap up securely, each in a piece of the rubber cloth, commencing at one corner, that the ends may be more firmly tucked in and made water-tight, and two sausage-shaped parcels is the result, which should be fastened with stout rubber bands or straps to prevent unrolling. The tourist, thus equipped, if overtaken by rain, may regard a wetting as a matter of no serious consequence, he being clad in woolen garments and his luggage protected by its rubber covering. But to proceed. One of these packages—and it should be that which contains the coat and pants—is attached in front of the handle-bar by means of a good luggage carrier, care being taken that the action of the brake is not interferred with. Arriving at the noonday resting place, if it is necessary or desirable to appear in full regalia, the coat and breeches are easily got at and slipped on over the jersey riding suit, the neck handkerchief—which should be in the same package—being neatly adjusted, the tourist is presentable to appear in any dining room. The other package, which should contain such things as will not be required until the day's journey is finished, is likewise attached to the handle-bar of the machine, just below the first package, by means of the luggage carrier.

The chamois bag before mentioned is to contain smoking materials, odds and ends, not forgetting a needle and thread, frequently most useful; and such an amount of ready change as the tourist requires for incidentals during the day, the bulk of his finances being securely fastened in the pocket of his coat and wrapped with it in the bundle. This bag is safely fastened at the end of one of the handles of the machine, preferably the left, as most riders dismount and stand on that side; it is handily gotten at and it is most useful in many ways. To the other handle many fasten a handkerchief, but if a loop of twine be fixed to the sponge, just large enough to easily pass over the handle, and the sponge be kept clean and moist by frequent washings at the springs and wells en route, this will be found most refreshing and more satisfactory on a hot day, besides being a great economy in handkerchiefs.

There is considerable knack, if not skill, in doing up the parcels nicely, which can only be acquired by experience or by being taught by the experienced. An old hand will put a great deal into a very small compass, but the novice will generally make a great deal, in the way of a package, out of a very little, and the reason usually is that the articles are not *folded* properly before rolling.

All the luggage may be conveniently carried on the handle-bar, and it is recommended that the luggage be divided in two parcels for convenience en route.

For those who, when touring, will insist upon carrying an immense amount of luggage, there is no excuse, as luggage can be sent to the various points through the usual channels if one will insist in having an elaborate wardrobe. A rider is not supposed, even by the most punctilious host, to carry a wardrobe of this description, and if a host really does expect this the guest had better go himself by train, or forward his portmanteau on before him. On the other hand, it is not necessary for

The New Aladdin

 is what the wheelmen want

Small in Price
Light in Weight
Great in Lighting Power

Can be lit in any wind

Will not jar out

There are many built on Aladdin lines, but only one Aladdin

The Aladdin Lamp Company

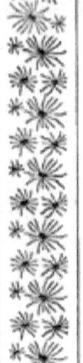

 518 Broad Street
Newark, N. J.

107 Chambers Street, New York

the cycling tourist to be always in *dishabille*; a very small amount of care and forethought will enable him to appear carefully and appropriately dressed, if nothing more.

Examine Machine Before Starting.—The tourist, before he gets away from home, will do well to look over his machine, which should be done a sufficient time before the day of departure to allow for the repair of any break or damage which may be discovered. Every part should be carefully and thoroughly overhauled, the head adjusted, each nut and spoke critically examined, the brake particularly being looked to, and strict search made for any flaw or crack or unexpected wear, as the slightest weakness in this important point may endanger the life or limb of the rider. The bearings should be carefully adjusted if any looseness is apparent, but they should never be screwed up so that there is no side shake at all, as the balls are thus liable to be broken. If the bearings are dirty or gritty they should be dosed with kerosene, which should be put in with an ordinary oil can and the wheels rotated rapidly, when the coagulated oil will be liquefied and the grit be brought out with it. After the exudations from the bearings have been wiped off, they should be carefully oiled up anew with good oil and all the kerosene worked out. The tool bag should be looked over, and contain an adjustable wrench, an oil can carefully filled with good oil, a piece of adhesive tire tape, a yard or two of stout string, and some cloth in which to wrap tools to prevent their rattling. Last, but not least, the tires should be examined all around, and should any portion, no matter how small, be loose, it should be at once attended to and made sound to undergo with safety the work before it. That you will take with you a compact and convenient repair kit is, of course, understood.

PRACTICAL POINTS.

The Fit of a Wheel.—One of the principal things in the choice of a bicycle is a proper fit. There is at present a disposition upon the part of cyclers generally to ride a machine with the highest frame that they can possibly reach. This is as much of an error as riding a machine with a very low frame or a cramped reach. While men generally are prone to go to one extreme women up to the present appear to have gone to the other, and in a majority of cases have been riding wheels with too short a reach.

How awkward a woman appears when riding a wheel that is too low for her. Her knees pump up and down in front of her and make her look as if she were trying to walk up the side of a wall. Besides that, it is harder to propel a wheel that is so low as not to give proper action to the legs, and wears the rider out much sooner.

A good test for the height is this: Have the wheel high enough so that when the rider sits in the saddle he can just reach with his heel the pedal when in the lowest position it can reach in making a revolution. That distance, with the toe instead of the heel on the pedal, gives the proper reach and swing to the leg and enables the muscles to be used to best advantage.

The average man can stretch with comfort and safety the 23 and 24-inch frame, and very few riders should go higher than the 25-inch, the adjusting of the saddle will give any extra stretch beyond what the 25-inch frame gives that may be necessary.—*American Cycling.*

How to Clean a Chain.—Procure a can about an inch wider than the diameter of the chain when coiled up. Get a piece of

Royal Blue Line...

BETWEEN New York, Philadelphia, Baltimore and Washington via

Baltimore and Ohio R. R.

Fastest, Finest and Safest Trains in the World.

The entire equipment is brand-new, and consists of the finest Baggage Cars, Coaches, Parlor, Sleeping and Dining Cars ever built by the Pullman Company.

The trains are vestibuled from end to end and protected by Pullman's improved

ANTI-TELESCOPING DEVICE

ALL THE CARS IN ALL THE TRAINS ARE

Heated by Steam and Lighted by Pintsch Gas

NO EXTRA FARE

Passengers occupying Parlor Car seats or Sleeping Car berths will pay the ordinary charges for same.

This is the only line running trains from New York in

5 Hours to Washington

TICKET OFFICES

NEW YORK—172, 235, 261, 415, 785, 942 and 1140 Broadway, 73 Murray Street, 314 Canal Street, 31 East 14th Street, 325 Columbus Avenue, 53 West 125th Street, 400 Grand Street.

BROOKLYN—333 Washington Street, 344 and 726 Fulton Street, 74 Broadway Williamsburg.

Station foot of Liberty Street, N. R.

galvanized wire cloth, with three-eighths to one-half inch mesh, and have it cut into circular form about one inch wider than the diameter of the can. Make a number of cuts half an inch deep around the edge and bend the wire down, making a continuous shoulder, and set it in the can, thus making a raised false bottom. Coil up the chain on it and pour in benzine till it is covered to the depth of half an inch. In a couple of minutes, agitate the chain by pushing it from side to side of the can. Then let it stand quietly for several minutes till the loosened grit and grease have been led to the bottom, when you can lift your chain perfectly clean out of the clear benzine above the wire. Pinch the edge of the can to form a spout, so you may, if economically minded, pour off the clear benzine to be used again.—*Selected.*

Inflating the Tire.—Generally speaking, a small tire requires more pressure than a large one, if it is to carry the same weight; and a given tire requires more pressure in proportion as the rider is heavy.

A tire should always contain enough air to keep its rim from the ground. If, in riding, you feel the slightest jar as your wheel runs over ordinary obstacles, it is because there is not sufficient air pressure.

There is no danger of bursting a tire, as many riders seem to fear, when the small hand pump is used, and even with the best foot pump, only the very weakest tires could be burst, while any good road tire will hold more than double the pressure which you could get into it with a foot pump.

Don't let the air out of a tire when not in use, " to save it." It is much better off, when standing, to be well inflated.

In considering the comfort of both the rider and the care of the tire, it is important that enough pressure be maintained to prevent the outer and inner parts of the air tube from coming in contact. As this depends upon the diameter of tire and weight of rider, each one must settle it for himself; no rule embodying pounds per square inch would be of general use.

An extensive observation has found a great many tires which were very much too soft, while we have rarely seen one that was too hard.

When the rider is sitting still upon the saddle and the wheels are resting on a smooth surface, the floor should be touched by the tire for a distance of about four inches; this will bring the edge of the rim within seven-eighths of an inch of the ground, allowing for the thickness of tire. This will leave nearly three-fourths of an inch for the extra compression caused by striking stones or other narrow obstacles.—*L. A. W. Bulletin.*

Care of Nickel Plating.—The bright nickel surface on the handle bars, cranks, hubs, etc., of your bicycle, is put on by an electric process, and being evenly "deposited," can only be smooth when the surface of the foundation metal has been made smooth to receive it. All polishing materials and processes involve the use of a very fine gritty or cutting substance which, when rubbed in contact with a metal surface, brightens it by an infinite number of fine scratches, so fine indeed as to be invisible to the naked eye. Even the lustrous surface of the most beautiful watch case is polished in this way. Now the nickeled parts of a bicycle, when subjected to the polishing process, are likely to be rubbed somewhat unevenly; that is, the most accessible and most exposed parts oftentimes receive rather more than a due share of the polisher's attention, and if by the slightest mischance a minute scratch penetrates through the nickel so as to touch the steel beneath, rust is

TAG=A=MAC

Do Your Tires Leak?

An eminent French chemist has solved the problem. The oldest, most porous tires made air tight.

Why Buy New Tires

Sent by mail on receipt of price, $1.50 per tire, with full instructions, or send your tires with amount to

COPELAND, SIMONSEN & SELWYN

Sole Agents

TAG-A-MAC CHEMICAL MFG. CO.

167 Greene Street, New York City

Circulars on Application

An absolute guarantee given with each pair of tires treated.

THE PNEUMATIC ROW BOAT

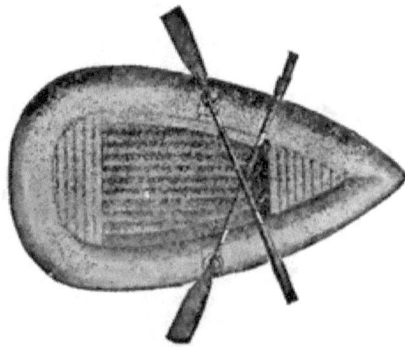

The combination of a pleasure boat, life-preserver, outing and sporting boat are all contained in our Pneumatic Row Boat; absolutely safe, non-capsizable and unsinkable, even if filled with water. They are light, strong and durable; deflate and pack into a small compass. Also Pneumatic Corsets, Bathing Vests, Swimming Jackets, Head Rests, Pneumatic Mattresses, etc.

Stamp for Catalogue.

PNEUMATIC ROW BOAT CO.,
8 West 14th Street, New York.

likely to form as soon as the nickel surface is exposed to dampness. You may have noticed at times that when your handle bar has been rained on and not wiped, in a few hours small spots of rust appear, although the surface of the nickel seems intact and the rust was easily wiped off. The formation of this rust may be prevented by rubbing vaseline thoroughly over all the plated work and immediately wiping off the surplus. By this process the vaseline is made to fill up all the little imperceptible scratches and prevent water and dampness from doing harm. If this precaution is attended to it will not be necessary to use scouring or brightening compounds, which are only required in cases where the nickel has been exposed to the air for a considerable time without the thin film of protecting vaseline. If you do not intend to use your wheel for some time, even in summer, put on "vaseline," "cosmic," "carboline" or "petroleum jelly" (the same thing under different names) and your machine will need only an occasional wiping with a cloth to keep it free from rust.—*L. A. W. Bulletin.*

RIDING.

Begin Slowly.—Any unaccustomed motion will soon tire the muscles. With care and patience you will be surprised to see how fast your power will grow. Hills which at first seem insurmountable will soon be climbed easily.

In learning, select a stretch of level road, and confine your riding to it until you feel perfect confidence in your management of the machine. Get well used to the steering and brake before trying a hill.

Hills.—Let your first hill be a gentle incline, and practice climbing and coasting it until you can do so with perfect ease. But do not coast in any case until you have acquired full control of the bicycle.

It is important that all riders who dispense with the brake should learn to use the sole of the shoe on front wheel tire in place of it, as that is one way to avoid a bad accident. It is perfectly easy and effective to brake in this way; also learn to control the wheel by back-pedaling, both on hills and for quick stops.

Pedaling.—A steady uniform pressure should be the rule. It is a great though common mistake, to strike the pedal a sudden blow as soon as it passes the top of the stroke. It should receive strong, steady pressure from top to bottom of the stroke. Practice ankle motion. Do not work with the ankles stiff. The feet should follow the pedals throughout the stroke. This will add much to the power.

The saddle should be adjusted so that you can comfortably touch the pedal at its farthest point with your *heel*.

Always stop short of fatigue. There is no easier way for a new rider to get discouraged than by riding to excess. Keep within your strength. Remember it is as far back as it is out.

Sit Up Straight.—It is easy to bend over when racing, with handles adjusted to allow an upright position.

Remember the greatest enjoyment and benefit are had by moderate speed. You are not obliged to go fast simply because you can.—*Overman Wheel Co. Handbook.*

OILING AND ADJUSTING.

Oiling.—All bearings should be properly oiled, little and often is the best rule. Machine bearings are sometimes ground to death for want of proper oiling. Spring oilers ar

Knicker Top

IT'S A LITTLE THING, YET

A COMPLETE BICYCLE COSTUME
.... IN ITSELF ....

No More Knickerbockers

No more Long, Heavy Stockings

No More Trouser Guards

The Knicker Top has Superseded them

Patent Applied for.

It Converts your Trousers into Knickerbockers
It Transforms your Socks into Golf Hose

AN IMMENSE ECONOMIZER

A Great Time Saver. For Sale by all leading dealers. Price, 50c. and 75c. a pair.

No more need of changing your Clothes, Shoes and Hose TWICE with each outing.

INVENTED AND MANUFACTURED BY

··· HYMAN STARR ···
48 AND 50 WALKER STREET, NEW YORK

frequently provided at the ends of both axles, and, also, of the pedals. In using, press back the ball which closes the oil hole with the nozzle of the oil can, and inject a small quantity only, of the oil.

Points to Oil:—1. Front and rear wheels, at each end of axle. 2. Crank axle bearings. 3. Pedals, through one of the arms at each end of pedal. 4. Steering head bearings. 5. Brake lever joints. 6. Brake spoon joints. 7. Chain— *Use no Oil.* Use a good Chain Lubricant. For best result clean and lubricate the chain as often as once in every 10 miles. Chain should be hot before it is put into the melted lubricant.

To clean pedal bearings, the pedal may be taken off its axle bodily, and the balls will not drop out.—*Id.*

Adjusting.—All nuts should be kept tight. When you hear a rattle you may be sure something is loose that should be tight. Follow it up till you find it. Bicycles, if properly built, have means of adjustment at every joint, and there is no excuse for rattle.

If you are a novice, do not tinker your machine. Take it to some one who knows how to adjust it. Use wrench carefully. See that the jaws are closed to fit the bolt head, or nut, and use the wrench so as to bring the strain upon it edgewise.

Carry your Tool Bag with you.—Don't think you'll never need tools because you seldom need them.

Bearings.—Let the wheel be ever so fine, if the bearings are imperfect no good results will follow. Again, wheel and bearings may be perfect, but, if out of adjustment, their perfection is of no avail. A bearing, if properly adjusted, will be both tight and loose; tight enough to prevent any side play of the wheel, and loose enough to run with perfect freedom.—*Id.*

Remarks.—Wood rims are not meant to crush stones with, nor to ride curbstones. Bicycles, like everything else, need to be used reasonably.

You cannot expect good service without proper attention. Do not lend your machine. A novice may injure a machine more in an hour than an expert would in a month.

Blame yourself part of the time. The machine usually means well if you will give it a chance.

How to true a wheel—don't.

How to repair a bicycle—send to the makers and get a duplicate part and, if it does not fit without being touched with a file, send it back for one that will fit.

Should your pump become dry and work hard, soften piston with oil or vaseline. Also keep the piston rod lubric Watch your brake spoon. It will cut the tire if worn d a sharp edge.

When bolts or nuts turn hard, a little oil applied to thread will help. This is also true of all shoulders and bearing pa of screws.

If you expect to ride hands off leave your steering head adjusted free. It is difficult to steer with a tight head. I fact, no bearing on the machine should be adjusted tight, as good ball bearing will run under such close adjustment a cause undue wear though the extreme pressure may no apparent.

Storage of Cycles.—Do not store in barn or stable. Ch a dry place. Pneumatic tires should be deflated and mac suspended so it shall not rest on the rims.—*Id.*

The Star Bicycle Lamp

Patented Oct. 13th, 1896

The most reliable Lamp made. Used by all up-to-date Wheelmen. All brass, full nickel finish. Perfect combustion. Powerful magnifying lens. Positively will not jar or blow out.

PRICE, THREE DOLLARS

Patented March 9th, 1897   PRICE, TWO DOLLARS

Excelsior has all the merits of the Star Lamp and is smaller. Sold by all reliable dealers

Light Lamp Company   478-482 Broadway, New York

Factory, Newark, N. J.

ROAD RULES.

1. In meeting riders, pedestrains, and vehicles, keep to the right. In overtaking and passing them, keep to the left.
2. In turning corners to the left, always keep to the outside of the street.
3. In turning corners to the right, keep as far out as possible without trespassing on the left side of the road.
4. Never expect pedestraius to get out of your way; find a way around them.
5. Never ride rapidly by an electric car standing to unload passengers.
6. Never coast down a hill having cross streets along the way.
7. Never ring your bell except to give notice of your approach.
8. In meeting other riders ascending a hill, where there is but one path, always yield the right of way to the up-riders.
9. Bear in mind that a rider meeting an electric car carrying a strong headlight is unable to see beyond the light; keep out of his way.
10. When riding straight ahead, never vary your course suddenly to right or left, without first assuring yourself that no other rider is close in your rear on the side toward which you turn.
11. Always ring your bell in overtaking riders and pedestrians to give warning of your approach. This does not mean that they are to get out of your way.
12. Do not ride too close to a novice, and in meeting a novice give plenty of room.
13. When riding after dark always carry a lantern.

(*O. W. Co. Hand Book.*)

ODDS AND ENDS.

Toe Clips.—Take a friend's advice and use them. They make pedaling easier, and the foot pressure more uniform and more constant; they keep the foot in place, prevent the slipping of pedals at critical times and in difficult places, and save the rider many bad falls and some serious accidents. Riding with toe clips is vastly easier than without, and no rider who ever used toe clips continuously for a week was afterwards satisfied to ride without them.

Brakes.—A wheel and rider having a total weight of one hundred and twenty pounds or upwards, moving at the rate of twelve miles per hour, have acquired a momentum which "back pedaling" will not promptly overcome. Brakes are neither heavy, bulky nor inconvenient. Scorchers who stick to the race-tracks may be excused for riding without brakes, but to other people they are likely to be mightily and suddenly convenient. Like the Texan's revolver the brake is apt to be wanted under conditions where a motion to adjourn would be out of order.

L. A. W. Membership.—The league wants members in large numbers, but it does not want everybody. Help us to increase our membership from good people; people of character who would feel a pride in the good work of the organization and who are willing to aid this work by their voices and influence. One good citizen who respects himself and obeys the law is a better league member than forty hoodlums who are forever shouting "What do I get for my dollar?"

The New York Tribune

A PAPER WHICH NEVER MISLEADS

In American Journalism, THE NEW YORK TRIBUNE ranks among its contemporaries with *The London Times* in England. It is a great, dignified, decent and thoroughly patriotic newspaper, loyal to its country, honest, never stooping to fakes, and admired even by rivals for the variety, accuracy and excellence of its news.

The man who grows up reading THE TRIBUNE will never have anything to unlearn and will be sound, progressive and respected by friends. There are newspapers so absolutely wrong and even malicious in their news, that if a man should read them for a month, he will never get some things straight in his mind if he lives to be a hundred years old, and the longer he reads them the worse off he is.

THE TRIBUNE IS, BEFORE ALL OTHERS, THE TRUE NEWSPAPER FOR A DECENT MAN AND A DECENT FAMILY.

AMPLE REPORTS ARE PRINTED OF ALL NEWS OF INTEREST TO LOVERS OF THE WHEEL.

FOR SALE BY ALL DEALERS.

LAWS OF NEW YORK.

1. **For the Protection of Cycle Paths.** Section 652 of the Penal Code (as Amended by Chapter 267, Laws of 1897), provides as follows: "*Subdivision 1.—A person who willfully and without authority or necessity drives any team or vehicle, except a bicycle upon a side path, or wheelway, constructed by or exclusively for the use of bicyclists, and not constructed in a street of a city, is punishable by a fine of not more than fifty dollars, or imprisonment not exceeding thirty days or both.*"

2. **For the Punishment of Tack and Glass Throwers.** Section 661 of the Penal Code provides as follows: "*Section 661: A person who willfully throws, drops or places, or causes to be thrown, dropped or placed upon any road, highway, street or public place, any glass, nails, pieces of metal, or other substance which might wound, disable or injure any animal, is guilty of a misdemeanor.*"

NOTE.—The penalty for an infraction of this law is a fine of Five Hundred Dollars, or one year's imprisonment in the Penitentiary, or both fine and imprisonment; and there is a special reason why every wheelmen in the State should co-operate in its enforcement. The original purpose of the law was to protect animals from wanton or needless injury, and more particularly horses which traverse the public roads and streets by the hundreds of thousands, and are exposed not only to needless suffering but also to a frightful death from lockjaw by the practices which this law is intended to suppress. It is evident that the throwing upon public places of any substances which might wound or disable an animal, may result in injury to the pneumatic tires now in universal use as a necessary part of the bicycle. Under the *general* law, there is no adequate or certain remedy for injury to the owner of a wheel which may be injured in that way, since it is always necessary for the injured party to prove that the injurious article or substance was placed upon the road or streets with *malicious intent* to injure property, while the court may go so far as to require proof of an intent to injure the particular wheel which has been damaged. The result of this difficulty is that many wheelmen submit in silence to a malicious wrong which interferes with their pleasure and injures their property, rather than undertake the trouble and expense of a doubtful prosecution.

If, however, all wheelmen in the State of New York, would simply assist in carrying out the *original intention of section 661* of the Penal Code, they would not only serve the cause of humanity but secure protection for themselves against a needless and irritating annoyance. In prosecuting offenders against this section, it is not necessary to prove a malicious *intent*, but simply the *fact* that a person has, knowingly, and therefore, "willfully, thrown, dropped or placed, or caused to be thrown dropped or placed upon any road, highway, street, or public place, any glass, nails, pieces of metal, or other substance which *might* wound, disable or injure any animal."

New York City Ordinances.

TRUCKS ON WESTERN BOULEVARD. Except when going or coming directly from or to their place of departure or destination on said Boulevard, and except when actually passing another vehicle or an obstacle, all trucks, express wagons, vans and business vehicles of all sorts shall keep in single line upon their extreme right of the Western Boulevard at all points between 59th Street and Manhattan Street. (R. O. 1896, Sec. 380).

SPEED AT STREET CORNERS. Nor shall it be lawful for any cart, wagon, coach, public cart or any other vehicle to be driven around the corner of any of the streets of said city with the horse or horses thereto traveling at a faster gait than three miles per hour. (R. O. 1896, Sec. 371).

DRIVERS MUST GIVE NAME AND ADDRESS. It shall be the duty of every person driving or having charge of a public cart to give to any person requesting it, his name and place of residence, the number of the cart he is driving or in charge of and the name and place of residence of the owner thereof; and the refusal to do so shall be deemed a violation of this Article. (R. O. 1896, Sec. 400).

LIGHTS. Any person using a bicycle, tricycle, velocipede or other such vehicle of propulsion on the public streets of this city shall be required to carry on such vehicle after sundown and before sunrise a light of sufficient illuminating power to be visible at a distance of 200 feet; also an alarm bell; and a signal shall be given by sounding said bell or otherwise on approaching and crossing the intersection of any street or avenue; and no person using a bicycle, tricycle, velocipede or other such vehicle of propulsion on the public streets of the city shall propel said bicycle, tricycle, velocipede or other such vehicle of propulsion at a rate of speed greater than eight miles an hour, nor shall any greater number than two persons abreast parade the streets of the city at any time on said bicycles, tricycles, velocipedes or other vehicles of propulsion. Any violation of this ordinance shall be punished as a misdemeanor. (R. O. 1896, Sec. 379).

It shall not be lawful for any cart, wagon, coach, public cart or any other vehicle to be driven through any of the streets of the City of New York at a greater speed than five miles an hour; nor shall it be lawful for any such vehicle to be driven around the corner of any of the streets of said city with the horse or horses thereto traveling at a faster gait than three miles per hour. (R. O. 1896, Sec. 371.)

DOGS. If any dog shall attack any person peaceably traveling on any highway, or his horse or team, and complaint thereof be made to a justice of the peace, such justice shall inquire into the complaint, and if satisfied of its truth, and that such dog is dangerous, he shall order the owner or possessor of such dog to kill him immediately. The owner or possessor of any dog, who shall refuse or neglect to kill him within forty-eight hours after having received such order, shall forfeit the sum of $2.50 and the further sum of $1.25 for every forty-eight hours thereafter, until such dog is killed. (County Law, page 765, Sec. 125).

Hereafter it shall not be lawful to permit any dog to go abroad loose or at large in any of the public streets, lanes, alleys, highways, parks or places within the corporate limits of the City of New York under a penalty of $3 for each offense to be recovered against the owner, possessor or person who knowingly harbored such dog, within three days previous to the

Like a Bird...

Run wheels that are lubricated with

3 in One

In a Looking=Glass

You cannot see your face better than in your enamel when it is polished with

3 in One

Ask your dealer for it

No Rust Gathers

when wheels have been rubbed over with

3 in One

The Old Reliable Standard

of Cyclists, Gunners and Typewriters

Send Two-Cent Stamp for Sample

G. W. Cole & Co.

(Room 201) 111 Broadway
New York

Try "Pacemaker" for lubricating chains

time of such dog being found going abroad loose or at large, and the Commissioners of Police are hereby authorized and directed to cause complaint to be made to the Corporation Attorney against the owner or possessor of every dog permitted to go loose or at large within the corporate limits, as aforesaid, for the recovery of the penalties prescribed in this Article, such penalties when collected, to be accounted for semi-monthly and paid to the Comptroller of said city. Nothing in this article shall prevent any dog from going into any such street, lane, alley, highway, park or public place, provided such dog shall be held by such owner or other person securely by cord or chain, to be not more than four feet long, fastened to a collar around the neck of the animal. (R. O. 1896, Sec. 672).

Brooklyn City Ordinances.

"KEEP TO THE RIGHT. Sec. 1. Every bicycle or other vehicle using the public streets in the City of Brooklyn, shall keep as near as practicable, to the curb line on the right of the road and any such bicycle or other vehicle passing any vehicle or vehicles in front thereof and going in the same direction, shall pass to the left of such vehicle or vehicles.

Sec. 2. Any person who shall violate the provisions of this ordinance shall be liable for a penalty in the sum of five dollars for each and every offence. Adopted June 7, 1897)."

If there is a .... **Pathlight** within 1,000 miles of New York which is not giving satisfaction send it to us, and we'll fix it free of charge.

The Pathlight is indisputably the best bicycle lamp ever made. It is made to use — not merely to sell.

Absolutely jolt and cyclone proof.

Important to Wheelmen.

Its Name is "SAFETY"

American Service Union.

GENERAL OFFICES:

256 and 257 Broadway,   =   New York.

OFFICERS AND DIRECTORS.

SAMUEL GREEN, President, New York.
JUSTIN F. PRICE, Vice-President, Brooklyn, N. Y.
A. L. TAYLOR, Sec'y and Treas., New York.

WM. H. McCABE, New York.	JOHN S. WARDWELL, Rome, N. Y.
HERMAN KUEHN, New York.	L. A. MYERS, New York.
ARTHUR C. SALMON, Brooklyn, N. Y.	HOWARD H. MORSE, New York.

TRUSTEE FOR CONTRACTHOLDER:
KNICKERBOCKER TRUST COMPANY OF NEW YORK.

The Union offers facilities for savings and for a reserve which especially interest members of the **Royal Arcanum** and other **Fraternal Orders.**

It secures best results from investments in Building and Loan Associations in the State of New York, where values are most reliable, and the laws governing building associations most rigid.

The interest, instead of accumulating, is employed in the payment of contractholders' dues and assessments in the Fraternal Order, sparing him annoyance and promoting his individual convenience and profit.

It pays your dues and assessments in advance of their call.

It places the contractholder in a few years where his Savings will earn interest enough to thereafter take care of Fraternal Benefit Society membership or the remainder of his life.

It is a mistake to suppose that real estate investments are not profitable as well as safe.

Small sums grow to large if they are placed right.

The art of saving consists in committing one's self to a start that forces one to go on in spite of feasts or fire-works.

Add to this a method of saving that relieves the saver from any care or anxiety as to the investment of his savings and the art of saving is nearly perfect; but it reaches the fine art of perfection when the saver gets a chance to get back a great deal more than he puts in, even with compound interest added at ten per cent.

We'll tell you in a practical way how this saving *small* sums and investing in *right* ways applies to you; or, in other words, what *small* and *right* mean, if you will mail a postal giving name of your Council and rate of your assessment.

PUNISHMENT OF TACK THROWERS. 'That any person who shall throw, drop or place or who shall cause or procure to be thrown, dropped or placed in or upon any road, highway. street, avenue or public place within the City of Brooklyn, any glass, tacks, nails, pieces of metal or other substance which is likely to injure or damage a bicycle, tricycle, or any other vehicle commonly called a 'cycle or wheel,' shall forfeit and pay a penalty of not more than $25 and not less than $5. (Adopted Oct. 21, 1895)."

Saddles.—Everybody is trying to make a saddle to fit everybody else. Give your saddle a chance. Did you ever note the fact that most old saddles are comfortable and most new saddles are not? A new saddle is like a new boot or shoe and sometimes like a new hat. It fits better and seats its rider more comfortably after a few weeks of use. If you have a new saddle that seems to be wrong try to improve it by adjusting it until it "rides" more easily. The best saddle in the world can be made into a clumsy, hateful seat by giving it the w tilt on the saddle post, and a very poor saddle can be made fairly comfortable by giving it the right adjustment. Don't throw away your saddle or exchange it for another until you are very sure it is the fault of the saddle.

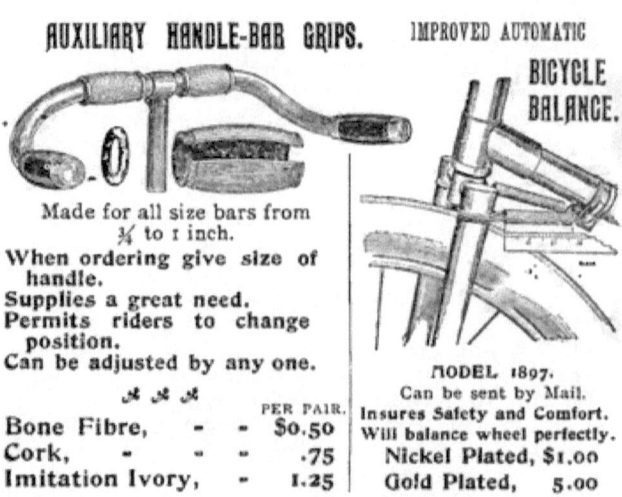

AUXILIARY HANDLE-BAR GRIPS.

Made for all size bars from ¾ to 1 inch.
When ordering give size of handle.
Supplies a great need.
Permits riders to change position.
Can be adjusted by any one.

	PER PAIR.
Bone Fibre,	$0.50
Cork,	.75
Imitation Ivory,	1.25

IMPROVED AUTOMATIC BICYCLE BALANCE.

MODEL 1897.
Can be sent by Mail.
Insures Safety and Comfort.
Will balance wheel perfectly.
Nickel Plated, $1.00
Gold Plated, 5.00

... **LUBRICANTS** ...

For the preservation of chain and bearings you should have our high-grade Sonora Graphite, or Chain Lightning Lubricant. None better. Prices: 5c., 10c., 15c. and 20c. Can be mailed.

THE SPECIALTY SUPPLY CO.,
150 Fifth Avenue, New York.

PETERS & DRAKE
107 Chambers St., New York

Bicycle Pumps
OF EVERY DESCRIPTION

New York Agents . . .
WATERBURY WATCH COMPANY'S
"TRUMP" Cyclometer
and "TRUMP" Bicycle Watches.

WRITE FOR CATALOGUE AND PRICES.

The Neverout
TRADE-MARK

No more greasy lamps. Can be handled with kid gloves. Patented in the United States and principal countries of the world. Send for copy of "Neverout," March, free. Price, $4.00 of your dealer, or delivered free on receipt of price by Rose Manufacturing Co., 511-13 North Third Street, Philadelphia.

CAUTION.—Do not be deceived into taking any other, as the "NEVEROUT" is the only lamp that is guaranteed to positively stay lit (or money refunded), that is free from grease—yet burns kerosene—and that is absolutely non-explosive.

SAY! The NAME of the Best Bicycle money can build is not spelled DU CANE, nor DO CAIN, but plain

DUQUESNE

Call and see what we can do for you before you buy. Our prices are:

$100.00 CASH for DUQUESNE SPECIAL,
$105.00 on time, $25.00 down and $10.00 per month.

$50.00 CASH for DUQUESNE STANDARD,
$55.00 on time, $20.00 down and $10.00 per month.

OFFICIAL L. A. W. BICYCLE REPAIR SHOP.

Duquesne Mfg. Co., 226 FULTON STREET
Cor. of Greenwich Street, N. Y. City.

MAURICE B. ATKINSON, MANAGER.

U.S. CYCLOMETERS (MODEL '96)
DETACHABLE
Odometers and Lamp Brackets
FOR CARRIAGES

10,000 Miles   Weighs 1¼ ounces
One Inch Long

FULL SIZE.
ABOVE READS 4652 9/10 MILES.
U. S. Cyclometers for Bicycles
PRICE, $1.50

U. S. Manufacturing Co.
FOND DU LAC, WIS., U. S. A.

Imperial White Cycle Lubricant.

Will not Soil the Clothing nor Collect Dust

We defy the world to produce a better article. One which will make speed and win more friends than will our Imperial. Used on the chain, it is a wonder; and in the bearings, here's where we make our big claim, and if you will try our stick and use as directed, we will guarantee perfect satisfaction. Send for descriptive circular. 274 Washington Street. Ask your dealer for it. If he cannot supply you send 12 cents in stamps to

H. B. NEWCOMB & CO.
274 Washington Street — — — — NEW YORK CITY

The Little "Hatch Patch"

A Steel Spring with a Rubber Washer can be attached in one minute. Repairs punctured Bicycle Tires automatically.

No Tape, Plugs or Cement required.

PRICE, 25 CENTS

THE "HATCH PATCH" COMPANY
253 Broadway, New York

THE CYCLISTS' FRIEND

Peerless Lubricant — *Purol* TRADE MARK — Preservative and Illuminant

ODDIE MFG. CO.
All Dealers — Brooklyn, N. Y.

Club Buttons
Cap Pins
and Souvenirs

Low Priced but Not Cheap.   Made of best Jewelers' Enamel.
Colors "burned in" same as on chinaware.

O'Hara Waltham Dial Co.,
Waltham, Mass, U. S. A.

WARWICK BICYCLES AND TANDEMS

Strength
Rigidity

Grace
Beauty

WARWICK CYCLE MFG. CO.
34 Union Square, East, New York City

Up-town Branch and Academy
316-320 Western Boulevard

STANDARD AND TANDEM SIZES

The Famous 20th Century Bicycle Headlight.

THE FAMOUS
20th CENTURY BICYCLE HEADLIGHT

Maker of the '97

Enameled Honor Medals

for the New York State Division

Medals, Badges and Prizes of all Kinds

MADE BY

JEWELER   **JOHN FRICK**   **MEDALS**

6 & 8 Liberty Place, (Opp. 21 Maiden Lane) bet. B'way & Nassau Sts., N. Y. C.

L. A. W. Pins, Solid Gold, $2.00 each   Designs and Estimates
Filled Gold, $1.00 each   Furnished, Etc.

The Andrae CYCLES

NEVER DISAPPOINT.

Wilson Brothers' Co.,
119 CHAMBERS STREET,
NEW YORK.

Are only one class and that the highest.

Material and Workmanship of the very best, and nothing is sacrificed to reduce cost.

If a low-priced wheel is wanted, we have them. Call and see us.

L. A. W.
COAT, CAMERA, or
LUGGAGE CARRIER
FOR REAR FORK

IN USE

Does not mar the appearance of the bicycle, or interfere with lamp, handle, brake or bell. The only practical devise for carrying camera. Will carry any size package, protected with mud guard. When not in use, it is scarcely noticeable. Made of good quality of leather — Russet or Black. Weight, 3 ounces. Price, 50 cts. No stamps.

NOT IN USE.

G. ELDER ADAMS, 32 Warren St., N. Y.

✿ THE QUAKER ✿

Its popularity is evidenced by the large number of them seen in the Metropolitan district . . . .

Most popular mount of '97 . . . . .

MADE BY ———————

PENN MFG. COMPANY
ERIE, PA.

All Models in Stock . . . .

METROPOLITAN AGENTS

STARR WHEEL CO.

Lexington Avenue, corner of Twenty-third Street

ON THE leading up-town thoroughfare . . . . .

A. W. OFFICIAL REPAIR SHOP

Discount to League Members

BICYCLE RIDERS

"Cyco" Heals Punctures

Stops All Leaks

EDWARD W. DE BOW, Sole Eastern Agent
62 Reade Street, New Yo[rk]

KIO

..... THE NEW LUBRICAN[T]

FOR

Sprockets, Chains, Bearings

It does not run and so is [?]
Reduces friction 25 per cent.

KIO MANUFACTURING CO.

99 Chambers Str[eet]
New York

ALL DEALERS

SCHRADER UNIVERSAL VALVES

MANUFACTURED BY

A. SCHRADER'S SON

30 AND 32 ROSE STREET

NEW YORK, U. S. A.

ESTABLISHED 1844

Physicians Endorse It....

Physicians have been for years interested in cycling, and they pronounce it beneficial. There has only been one drawback and that has been the saddle. There has been but one perfect saddle on the market which they could recommend, that is the **Christy Anatomical Saddle.** See how it is constructed. The base is made of met that cannot warp or change its shape. It has cushior where cushions are require to receive the pelvis bone and a space so that th be no possibility of pressure on the sensitive parts and positiv vents saddle injury. When ordering your wheel insist that yo **Christy Saddle.** Once a Christy rider; Always a Christy advo Booklet: "Bicycle Saddles from a Physicians Standpoint," free.

HIGH GRADE MAKER are offering as a regul equipment, without add tional cost to their buyer **Christy Anatomical Saddles** and agents will not sale on account of preference. They co than inferior leather dles, and are worth n

REAR VIEW, SHOWING COIL SPRINGS.

A. G. SPALDING & BROS.
126, 128 and 130 Nassau Street
Up-town Depot: SPALDING-BIDWELL CO., 29, 31 and 33 West 42d
.... NEW YORK ....

THE ORIENT

Here's Another F

that our competitors ca down—the **FRICTION-SAVIN** qualities of the **PITCH LINE** gearing is a mechanical truth of which we can furnish mathematical proof—and **FIGURES DON'T LIE**. saves 45 per cent. chain friction, and riders a finding it out. If you ride for pleasure—if yo race—if you like coasting—**then this 45 per cent.** will mean a big advantage to you. **TRY IT.**

Yours very truly,

Waltham Mfg. Co. . . . Waltham, Mass.

Gordon

SOFT...
POMMEL

WHEELER
REFORM

AND ..

...RY KNOWN MAKE OF HIGH GRADE

SADDLES

We Sell all
SADDLES ON
... DAYS'
TRIAL

Money refunded
after trial if
wanted.

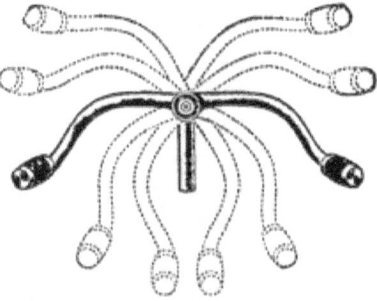

YANKEE ADJUSTABLE HANDLE-BAR.
Sent prepaid anywhere for
Price, $4.00.

... UNSATISFACTORY ...

Saddles Taken in Payment

FOR OTHERS WANTED ...

Largest assortment of Saddles in United States. Send stamp for list

Agency
SMITH ROLLER SPRING
SEAT-POST.
Sent anywhere prepaid on
receipt of price, $2.50 each

Bicycle Saddle Exchange

26 West Broadway, New York

THE PRICE OF THIS BOOK.

The first edition of these Road Books has been prepared at great expense and at the end of much labor, and published for the special use of the members of the New York State Division of the League of American Wheelmen. Every amateur cyclist (of either sex) of the age of eighteen years or upwards, is eligible to membership (initiation fee $1.00, yearly dues $1.00, payable in advance). Each member of our Division resident within the district covered by this book is entitled to receive one copy free until further notice. Members residing in other parts of the State will be entitled to receive one copy each, on payment of the sum of fifty cents to the Secretary-Treasurer. Other purchasers will be charged as stated below:

To persons not Members of the L. A. W., per copy, . . . $2.00
To Members of the New York Division who have already received a Free Copy, per copy, ... 2.00
To Members of other State Divisions of the L. A. W., one copy, 1.00
To Members of other State Divisions of the L. A. W., each subsequent copy, ... 2.00
Every Cyclist should join the L. A. W. and Retain his (or her) membership.

Loaning League Membership Tickets. A person who gains an advantage by the use of a membership ticket of an organization of which he is not a member, commits fraud, and a member who aids in this fraud by loaning his membership ticket, is unworthy of his position. Such an act is sufficient ground for expulsion, and should be reported by every member whose notice it may be brought.

Road Improvement. Send a two-cent stamp to Secretary-Treasurer Bull, if you are interested in the work of improved roads, and get a copy of "Country Roads" and "Macadam Roads," two illustrated practical hand-books on the improvement of country roads. See that your Senator and Member of Assembly are Good Roads' men, and watch their votes on the Good Roads measures in the Legislature at Albany.

Accidents to Wheelmen. *If you sustain an injury to your person or property through the reckless driving of another, or by reason of a serious defect of the street pavement, road surfaces or bridge, write full particulars to the Chairman of our Committee on Rights and Privileges, George E. Miner, Attorney, Potter Building, New York.*

Stolen Wheels. Always keep a written memorandum of the number of your wheel, its make, size, pattern, color and other facts making up a complete and careful description. If your wheel is stolen, send your name and League number, with full description of wheel and particulars of theft to W. S. Bull, Secretary-Treasurer, Vanderbilt Building, New York. Our Division offers a reward of $25.00 for the apprehension of bicycle thieves. One of these thieves was recently sent to Sing Sing for a term of nine years by Judge Aspinwall of the Kings County Court. This thief is lonesome and wants company.

Hotels. Read carefully the important note at the head of the list of consuls, hotels and repair shops on another page. Help us to enforce our contract and to prevent fraudulent "L. A. W. Hotels." The Chief Consul will be glad to have your co-operation in these matters at all times.

New Members. Have you seen the beautiful Honor Badge of 1892 shown on the first page of this book? It will be easy for you to get new members now, since the Road Book is in your possession. Tell your cycling friends that a copy of the Road Book will be sent promptly to each new member. Write postal card to Secretary-Treasurer Bull and get a little pocket of membership blanks, and carry it with you at all times. When you get an application for membership send it direct to Mr. Bull, and he will give you credit for all you send. In due time you will receive an Honor Certificate and Honor Badge, and they will be valuable souvenirs in years to come.

Road Maps and Tour Books. The free distribution of the old edition of the Road Maps and Tour Books discontinued among the members of the New York and Brooklyn district. Members residing within this district and desiring copies of the Tour Book or Road Maps will be supplied on receipt of fifty cents by the Secretary-Treasurer, with a written request stating whether a set of Maps or the Tour Book is required.

The New York Journal

A MAGNIFICENT SUCCESS!

Positively Unique in All Departments.

Circulation Guaranteed Over 510,000 Copies Per Day for the Morning and Evening Editions.

The Sporting Pages of the New York Journal Stand Unequalled!

THEY cover the entire field of Cycling, Baseball, Football, Trotting, Racing, Boxing, Yachting, Shooting, Rowing, and all forms of Athletic Sports.

EVERYBODY READS THEM.

The Journal's Bicycle Page is conducted by A. G. Batchelder, Official Handicapper of the L. A. W. for the New York Division.

In the quality of News, Literary Features, Illustrations—in everything that goes to make up the Great Modern Newspaper, THE JOURNAL keeps ahead.

TELL YOUR NEWSDEALER TO LEAVE THE JOURNAL AT YOUR HOME EVERY DAY.

www.ingramcontent.com/pod-product-compliance
Lightning Source LLC
Chambersburg PA
CBHW031814220426

43662CB00007B/647